POLITICAL PHILOSOPHY NOW

POLITICAL PHILOSOPHY NOW

Hegel on Freedom and Authority

Renato Cristi

UNIVERSITY OF WALES PRESS • CARDIFF • 2005

British Library Cataloguing-in-Publication Data
A catalogue record for this book is available from the British Library.

ISBN 0-7083-1873-8 hardback
     0-7083-1872-X paperback

Printed in Great Britain by Cromwell Press Ltd, Trowbridge, Wiltshire.

To Dallas, Cristi, Stephanie, Tess
and Ashley

Contents

Acknowledgements

My deepest debt of gratitude is to Howard Williams, who generously encouraged me to write this book many years ago. Howard took time to read the entire typescript twice and always gave me excellent advice which proved critical to the clarification of my ideas.

Looking back, I wish to acknowledge James Collins, Frank Cunningham and Brough Macpherson at St Louis University and the University of Toronto for introducing me, as a graduate student, to Hegel and modern political philosophy. I am indebted to many colleagues and friends who have given me the benefit of their enlightened comments: Leo Groarke, Carlos Ruiz Schneider, Pablo Ruiz-Tagle, Doug Moggach, John Burbidge, Gary Foster, Rockney Jacobsen, Barry Allen and Jay Lampert. An anonymous reader selected by the University of Wales Press gave me very good comments.

I thank Wilfrid Laurier University, Philipps Universität Marburg and the Viesmann Foundation for allowing me to complete the bibliographical research for this book at Marburg where, as a bonus, I enjoyed the enlightened conversation of Burkhardt Tuschling and Dieter Hüning. I also thank Fondecyt for a research grant that gave me the opportunity to discuss sections of this book with Pablo Ruiz-Tagle, Angélica Figueroa and doctoral students at the Law School, University of Chile.

Early versions of chapters of this book have appeared in *Political Theory*, *Canadian Journal of Political Science*, *Constellations*, *The European Legacy*, *Canadian Journal of Social and Political Philosophy*, *History of Political Thought* and *Laval théologique et philosophique*.

It is a pleasure to thank Sarah Lewis, Nia Peris and Elin Lewis at the University of Wales Press for their kind support during the preparation of this book. My very special thanks to Robert Campbell, Dean of Arts at Laurier, who broke the rules to allow me to enjoy some extra research time when I needed it most.

My most personal and greatest debt is to my wife and colleague Marcela, who was my most enthusiastic reader and critic.

Author's note

Paragraph numbers in brackets (§) refer solely to paragraphs in
G.W. F. Hegel's *Elements of the Philosophy of Right*, edited by Allen
Wood and translated by H. B. Nisbet (Hegel, 1991a). References to its
preface include the page number of that same edition and are given in
the following style (Preface, 22).

Introduction

I

. . . beset with those that contend on one side for too great Liberty, and on the other side for too much Authority, 'tis hard to passe between the points of both unwounded.

(Hobbes, 1968: 75)

. . . liberty is the perfection of civil society; but still authority must be acknowledged essential to its very existence.

(Hume, 1894)

As a contribution to Harvard's Tercentenary, John Dewey delivered an address on 4 September 1936, which he gave the title 'Authority and social change' (Dewey, 1936). This examined the rise of modern freedom, the mounting revolt against authority and the development of a social philosophy that was 'critical of the very idea of any authoritative control' (ibid.: 130). This philosophy, which 'claimed for itself the comprehensive title of liberalism' (ibid.: 136), postulated the strict separation of the spheres of freedom and authority, and decried the tendency of authority to encroach on freedom. Oppression and tyranny would be avoided only if authority was denounced as the enemy of freedom. But Dewey thought this was a mistake. The real issue concerned the relation, not the separation, of these notions.[1] Freedom and authority, like stability and change, formed an 'intimate and organic union' (ibid.: 131).[2] Liberalism was right to point out that authority had become, as a matter of historical fact, a purely external constraint that had grown unyielding and hostile to initiative and innovation. But, at the same time, liberalism created confusion by denying 'the organic importance of *any* embodiment of authority and social control' (ibid.: 132). This state of affairs defined for him the contemporary crisis in liberalism. The solution proposed by Dewey called for an 'interpenetration' of freedom and authority (ibid.: 137). Authority should not stifle, but direct and utilize change. Freedom ought to be shared by all and not just a few individuals.

Earlier, in *German Philosophy and Politics*, Dewey coincided with other left-Hegelians like E. F. Carritt and L. T. Hobhouse, and opposed Hegel's conservatism, his preference for authoritarian figures like Alexander, Caesar and Napoleon, and his 'depreciation of the individual as an individual' (Dewey, 1915: 193–4: see Ottmann, 1977: 194). But he found an explanation for Hegel's emphasis on authority. Dewey credited Kant, and his notion of duty, with the harmonization of freedom and authority. 'The Kantian principle of duty is a striking case of the reconciliation of the seemingly conflicting ideas of freedom and authority' (1915: 163). But after Kant, the political climate experienced a change in Germany and the 'necessity of emphasizing individual self-assertion had given way to the need of subordinating the individual to the established state in order to check the disintegrating tendencies of liberalism' (ibid.: 192). If Dewey was troubled by Hegel's conservatism, he seemed to accept his stance by interpreting it as an attempt to restore the balance disrupted by more radical versions of liberalism. Extreme assertions of freedom evoked, by way of reaction, extreme exertions of authority. In any case, the influence of German idealism, and of Hegel in particular, in the formation of Dewey's ideas cannot be denied. In 1929, looking back at his own philosophical development, he recognized his debt to Hegel.[3]

Dewey thought that Hegel aimed at the harmonization of freedom and authority,[4] but that he did so by de-emphasizing individual freedom and enhancing authoritative structures. Nowadays, a line of interpretation has gained ascendancy which presents Hegel as a liberal for whom individual freedom is the highest concern. As Alan Patten puts it: 'The key to understanding Hegel's social philosophy, it can confidently be said, is coming to terms with his idea of freedom' (Patten, 1999: 4; see Franco, 1999: p. x; Westphal, 1993: 244). This is the legacy of a line of liberal interpreters who have unilaterally characterized Hegel as a progressive liberal, a champion for the principles of individual autonomy, the rule of law and the modern constitutional state. A corollary of this view has attributed to Hegel the thesis 'that there is a basic opposition between freedom and authority' (Patten, 1999: 65). My contention in this book is that Hegel contrasted the notions of freedom and authority, was prepared to strengthen both to the fullest extent, but cannot at all be considered as a progressive or advanced liberal. He was aware of their opposition and thought that he could bring forth their reconciliation. But his conception of what freedom and authority meant, and how they ought to be reconciled, was vastly different from Dewey's. According to Alan Ryan, liberalism, for Dewey, was detached 'from any connection with private property or with laissez-faire', and it was this feature that made it possible for him to think of the authority of the state 'as an aid to liberty under appropriate conditions' (Ryan, 1995: 316).

Hegel's liberalism was not advanced or revolutionary, but conservative and classical; more in tune with Hobbes or Hume than with Mill or Dewey. By contrast, liberal interpreters have emphasized Hegel's revolutionary stance. According to Joachim Ritter, his philosophy has to be read as a 'philosophy of the Revolution, even in its inner most impulses' (Ritter, 1977: 192). But the same could be said of Fichte's political philosophy, and there is perhaps no other philosopher that Hegel opposed more vehemently in that respect. The Revolution in France had brought to the fore the incompatibility between liberalism and conservativism. Freedom and equality gained absolute precedence over authority and institutional order, and Fichte followed suit. To ensure equal liberty, Fichte relativized property, which Hegel, in the *Philosophy of Right*, conceived of as the immediate existence of freedom (§40), detached from any requirement imposed by equality. Hegel wrote: 'What and how much I possess is therefore purely contingent as far as right is concerned' (§49). And because Fichte followed Rousseau in adopting his views on the social contract, Hegel thought that he also relativized the authority of the state.

Hegel was keen to defend both an absolutist conception of property and a corresponding absolutist conception of public authority (see Schmitt, 1926: 98–9). He looked past the Revolution and focused on the revival of Roman private law during the *ancien régime*. Roman law clearly upheld a classical Quiritarian conception of property which defined it as absolute and unconditional. At the same time, modern absolute monarchies introduced Roman public law which consecrated unconditional royal sovereignty. The lineaments of a pre-eminently capitalist economy stood on these two pillars. Conditional property and the corresponding parcellized sovereignty, both typical of feudalism, had to be superseded. As Anderson suggests, within the modern absolute state 'the enhancement of private property from below was matched by the increase of public authority from above, embodied in the discretionary power of the absolute ruler' (Anderson, 1974: 28). Hegel's admiration for Napoleon has been interpreted as his agreement with a figure whom he saw as advancing revolutionary goals. But what he really admired was the restoration of *ancien régime* policies running parallel to a steady process of economic reforms. A strong state supported by social hierarchy appeared as the best guarantor of property and market institutions.[5]

The balance Hegel intended to strike between the demands of freedom and the strictures of authority are similar to the pre-revolutionary political reflections of Hume. A comparison with Hume serves to illuminate the distance that lies between Hegel's conservative liberalism and advanced versions of liberalism that some interpreters wish to ascribe to him. The comparison strengthens my case because Hume explicitly postulated a host of liberal ideas while simultaneously endorsing ingrained conservative values. David Miller has argued that Hume 'believed that those things which liberals characteristically value are indeed valuable, *provided* that those things which conservatives characteristically value can be securely enjoyed at the same time' (Miller, 1981: 195; see Forbes, 1975: 190–2). Liberal and conservative values may be appropriately represented as stretching along the full length of the continuum that runs between freedom and authority. Hume saw the need to combine those values in a balanced way. In the essay *Of the Origin of Government*, he wrote:

> In all governments, there is a perpetual intestine struggle, open or secret, between AUTHORITY and LIBERTY; and neither of them can ever absolutely prevail in the contest. A great sacrifice of liberty must necessarily be made in every government, yet even the authority, which confines liberty, can never, and perhaps ought never, in any constitution, to become quite entire and uncontroulable. (Hume, 1894: 28)

Hume acknowledged the tension that separates and yet brings authority and liberty closer together. If a balance between them is to be struck, neither should be allowed to overtake its opposite. The sacrifice of a measure of freedom runs parallel to his recommendation that authority be kept within bounds. Though Hume had a slight preference for a republican form of government, he recognized that the ideal circumstances required for republicanism to subsist were nowhere available. He opted for 'civilized monarchies' and by these he meant preferably constitutional monarchies operating under the rule of law. But he had only a few reservations about absolute monarchies where there was no delegation of powers to subordinate officials.

But though all kinds of government be improved in modern times, yet monarchical government seems to have made the greatest advances towards perfection. It may now be affirmed of civilized monarchies, what was formerly said in praise of republics alone, *that they are a government of Law, not of Men.* (ibid.: 53)

British constitutional monarchy, which Hume considered superior to French absolutism, came closer to the ideal he embraced. In his *History of England*, he affirmed the 'maxim of adhering strictly to law' and praised the English for having established this 'noble though dangerous principle' (Hume, 1803: 360; see Hayek, 1960: 172–3). But he was aware that in the course of history no government had been able to subsist without prerogative. Commenting on Parliament's abolition in 1640 of the Court of High Commission and the Star Chamber, both of which exerted high discretionary powers, he observed:

It must, however, be confessed, that the experiment here made by the parliament, was not a little rash and adventurous. No government at that time appeared in the world, nor is perhaps to be found in the records of any history, which subsisted without a mixture of some arbitrary authority committed to some magistrate. (Hume, 1803: 360; see Miller, 1981: 159–60)

This was particularly true for systems of government which allowed excessive liberty. If this was to be the destiny of the British system, becoming a French-style absolute monarchy would be the 'easiest death, the true *Euthanasia* of the British constitution' (Hume, 1894: 35). He thought that in France, as a civilized absolute monarchy, only the prince was allowed the exercise of prerogative. This was not a tyrannical arrangement which jeopardized individual freedom. Existing civilized absolute monarchies did not constitute a danger to private property. 'Private property seems to me almost ["almost" added in 1753] as secure in a civilized European monarchy as in a republic' (ibid.: 53; see Forbes, 1975: 157, n. 2).

Hume valued regular government and the rule of law when the circumstances approximated the relatively sedate Hannoverian period. But his sanguine optimism and trusting nature would have been perhaps thoroughly shaken had he lived in revolutionary France. Because he was spared that experience, he could not notice the extraordinary surge gained by affirmations of popular sovereignty and its counterpart, the monarchical principle, in the aftermath of the

Revolution. Had he witnessed the disruption that affected civil life during this period, he would have possibly allowed for the magnification of monarchical sovereignty, and consequently condoned sacrifices on liberty and on the maxim of strict adherence to the rule of law.[6]

In *The English Reform Bill* (1831), his last political essay, Hegel compares the situation of contemporary England to that of Germany. Hegel worries about England's unpreparedness to deal with the principle of true freedom embraced by the Reform Bill. This is so because 'in England, the contrast between prodigious wealth and utterly embarrassed poverty is enormous' (Hegel, 1964b: 325). An extended franchise will allow access to Parliament to the *novi homines* who support the principles of equality and popular sovereignty. If those who are advocating those principles were allowed to have their say, they would 'inevitably come on the scene only as an opposition to the government and the existing order of things' and this would inevitably lead to a revolution and not mere reform (ibid.: 325). In Avineri's view, 'the crux of Hegel's argument is that mere reform of the franchise cannot by itself cure the social problems of English society . . . English conditions could not be changed unless Britain underwent a social, as well as political transformation' (Avineri, 1972: 208–9). In this way Avineri wishes to dispel the common view that this is one of Hegel's 'most conservative, if not outright reactionary, pieces of writing' (ibid.: 208). This typical *Hegelsche Mitte* defence of Hegel simply doesn't work. Hegel fears the *novi homines* that will arrive at Parliament because they admit the true principle of freedom with French democratic and egalitarian abstractions. Instead, Hegel advocates German monarchical liberalism. Revolutionary upheavals will be averted only if the principle of freedom is tempered by the monarchical principle.

Hegel, very much aware of what the monarchical principle implies, sadly notes that 'the monarchical principle has little more to lose in England' (Hegel, 1964b: 326; modified translation). The Reform Bill has popular appeal in England because it appears further to weaken the influence of the Crown. 'Jealousy of the power of the throne [is] that most stubborn of English prejudices' (ibid.: 300; see Mill, 1972: 71–2). Proof of this is the resignation of the Wellington ministry when it found itself in the minority on a motion concerning the Crown's Civil List, which Hegel considers to be 'one of the few things left to the monarchical principle in England' (1964b: 326). When even this 'relic of regal control' (ibid.: 327) is nullified, when every 'appearance of monarchical influence' is jealously apostatized, when the publicity given by the Ministry to some private remarks made by the King concerning the Reform Bill is seen as an improper demonstration of monarchical omnipotence (or worse a coup d'état), there is no hope for the principle of real freedom to take root in England. According to Hegel,

> in England the monarchical element lacks the power which in other states has earned gratitude to the Crown for the transition from a legal system based on purely positive rights to one based on the principles of real freedom, a transition wholly exempt from shock, violence and robbery. The people would be a power of a different kind; and an opposition which . . . might feel itself no match for the opposite party in Parliament, could be led to look for its strength to the people, and then introduce not reform but revolution. (ibid.: 330)[7]

In Germany the principle of freedom has been able to confront the egalitarian abstractions peddled by democrats by the assertion of the monarchical principle. England should follow the German example.[8]

Allen Wood rightly notes that 'Hegel's political thought needs to be understood in relation to the institutions and issues of its own time' (Hegel, 1991a: p. ix; see Fleischmann, 1986: 70). This statement applies particularly to the singular evolution of constitutionalism in Germany. The French Revolution and the Napoleonic Wars provided the indispensable external stimulus for its development, but it was German monarchical absolutism itself that 'set in train its own gradual removal and the transition to constitutional forms' (Böckenförde, 1991: 92). This alone should suffice to make German constitutionalism a distinctive phenomenon. If one adds the institutional strictures defined by article 57 of Congress of Vienna's *Schlußakte*, which re-affirmed the hegemony of the monarchical principle in German affairs, the picture gains in clarity. The monarchical principle determined that the seat of governmental authority was 'neither the sovereign nation, nor the king and people together, but the king alone' (Böckenförde, 1991: 91). German monarchs, and not the people, continued to be the subjects of *pouvoir constituant* and personal representatives of the unity of the state. One should note that, in practical terms, the monarchical principle did not hinder the operation of a key feature of constitutionalism – the separation of governmental powers (compare with Korioth, 1998). But in terms of theory, Ernst

Rudolf Huber is right when he affirms that 'the monarchical principle was the antithesis of the principle of the separation of power' (Huber, 1975: 653). He also rightly characterizes the early constitutional movement in Germany as aiming at a 'monarchical liberal compromise' (ibid.: 318).

Hegel embraced the liberalizing reforms advanced by Hardenberg and explicitly advocated constitutional monarchy in his *Philosophy of Right*. But, as Treitschke notes, while Hardenberg's reform policies intended the liberalization of Prussia, they were to be implemented under the auspices of the monarchical principle (compare Treitschke, 1917: 256). This determines the idiosyncratic nature of German constitutional monarchy, which would be better categorized as pseudo-constitutionalism. To defend Hegel as a political liberal simply because his constitutional theory espouses constitutional monarchy is misguided. My argument in this book seeks to mark the difference between Hegel and Constant. Constant, a genuine political liberal, first delineated the notion of constitutional monarchy in 1814, only to see it distorted and misrepresented in Louis XVIII's *Charte constitutionelle*. I will argue that Hegel, by abrogating popular sovereignty, cancelling the separation of powers and highlighting the same crypto-absolutist tendencies that nourished the monarchical principle, similarly altered the original meaning Constant ascribed to constitutional monarchy.

II

On 9 June 1820, Hegel sent a 'half the total or somewhat more' of the typescript of his *Philosophy of Right* to his publisher, and promised to send the remainder in a few days when it had cleared the censors (Hegel, 1984: 451). When the censors conferred their *imprimatur* on the second half of the typescript on 25 June, Hegel dispatched the completed work and the book would appear that autumn. Censorship in Prussia? Wasn't this supposed to be the leading reformist state in Germany, under the enlightened guidance of Chancellor Hardenberg? Had not King Frederick William III formally promised a constitution in 1815?

Censorship in Prussia had been imposed by the government during the summer of 1819. On 23 March of that year, Carl Ludwig Sand, a 23-year-old deranged theology student and member of the *Burschenschaft*, assassinated August von Kotzebue, a leading feudalist literary figure. The press in France reported that Frederick William was facing the same situation Louis XVI confronted on the eve of the Revolution. In July, the King signed a cabinet order to begin a police investigation into this affair. The so-called 'Persecution against Demagogues' had begun. A month later, the Conference of the German Confederation meeting at Carlsbad issued decrees which provided for rigid censorship on university publications and press control. They also empowered university authorities to supervise faculty in order to eliminate subversives. The Frankfurt Assembly approved the Carlsbad decrees on 20 September. All of this had taken place in absolute secrecy so that when the announcement came everybody was taken by surprise.

These events marked the end of the reform era in Prussia. The absolute authority of the monarch was reaffirmed and the hopes of his sharing supreme authority with a representative assembly were dashed. Prussia would not follow the constitutional route initiated in Germany by Prussia's southern neighbours. Hegel, who had celebrated the constitutional advances of Wurtemberg, his southern homeland, and thought that Prussia would follow this path, must have felt deeply disappointed and anxious. This state of mind became manifest in the letter he wrote on 30 October to his friend Georg Creuzer, when the fate of the 'demagogues', and his own, was still unclear:

> I am about to be fifty years old, and I have spent thirty of these fifty years in these ever-unrestful times of hope and fear. I had hoped that for once we might be done with it. Now I must confess that things continue as ever. Indeed, in one's darker hours it seems they are getting ever worse. I allowed my reply to be delayed partly in order to respond with a few sheets of my *Philosophy of Right* . . . I was just about to have the printing begin when the Diet's decisions on censorship arrived. Now that we know what freedom we have under the censors I shall give the material over to the printer. (1984: 451)

Hegel had accepted an invitation to teach at the University of Berlin in 1818. He had come to Berlin 'to be in the center of things instead of a province' (ibid.: 470). Prussia had become a great power under Frederick II (1740–86), but defeat by the French at the beginning of the nineteenth century meant political decline and an economic catastrophe. This debacle brought discredit to the old aristocratic elites and sparked a reform movement that espoused liberal economic policies combined with a strong monarchical government. In 1807, Chancellor

Karl vom und zum Stein signed the edict that emancipated the Prussian peasantry, giving a blow to the nobility by taking away their rights over the person of the peasant. In his *Denkschrift* of 11 September 1807, Stein pointed out that only a power similar to revolutionary France could unleash the energy necessary to overthrow Napoleon. Varnhagen von Ense reveals how Stein admired 'the prodigious force and unparalleled power with which the Committee for Public Safety ruled France internally, and victoriously defied all external foes' (see Pinson, 1966: 34). His successor, Prince Hardenberg, stated in his *Rigaer Denkschrift*, the noblest exposé of the aims of the German reform movement, written for Frederick William in the summer of 1807: 'Your Majesty! We must do from above what the French have done from below' (ibid.: 33). In his view, the purpose of reform was

> a revolution in the good sense, one leading to the ennoblement of human-kind, to be made through the wisdom of government not through violent impulses from below . . . Democratic principles in a monarchical govern-ment: this seems to me to be the appropriate form of the contemporary *Zeitgeist*. (Thiele, 1967: 207)

Hardenberg's democratic principles did not refer to pure participatory democracy but to economic and social freedoms. Pure democracy, he cautioned, 'we must leave for the year 2440' (ibid.: 207). As Sheehan rightly points out, the Riga memorandum espoused 'freedom for individuals in the economic and social realm – and virtually unlimited power for the state in the conduct of public affairs' (Sheehan, 1989: 305). Under the leadership of Hardenberg and other statesmen and military leaders, Prussia consolidated economic and social reforms that made it able to defeat Napoleon in 1813 and regain the prestige it had obtained under Frederick II. In October 1810, Hardenberg issued three decrees which aimed at dismantling the feudal system in Prussia, cancelling the authority of local and regional bodies and shifting it to the central state (see Pinkard, 2000: 421–5). This is the Prussia which had become the 'center of things' for Hegel.

Hegel sent a copy of the *Philosophy of Right* to Chancellor Hardenberg as soon as it was published in October 1820, indicating that his book's scientific endeavour aimed at demonstrating 'the harmony of philosophy with those principles generally required by the nature of the state'. In return, Hegel requested for philosophy a warranty for 'the protection and favour alloted to it by the state' (1984:

459). With Hardenberg at the helm of government and the demagogues on the run, Hegel regained his confidence. He would write to his friend Niethammer on 9 June 1821 that he felt that his situation was 'very satisfying and even reassuring with respect to both [his] official efficacy and to the appreciative sentiments shown to [him] in high places'. He had weathered the storm without personal risk and could now fully realize 'the wretchedness and well-deserved fate of the demagogues' (ibid.: 470).

In his anguished letter to Creuzer of 30 October 1819, Hegel had reached thirty years back to 1789. Then, as a young theology student, he had celebrated the Revolution in France. Together with his friends Hölderlin and Schelling, he interpreted it as a victory for the cause of political freedom and the new morality of self-governance espoused by Kant. On 16 April 1795, he wrote to Schelling in tune with the same revolutionary spirit:

> From the Kantian system and its highest completion I expect a revolution in Germany . . . The philosophers are proving the dignity of man. The peoples will learn to feel it. Not only will they demand their rights, which have been trampled in the dust, they will take them back themselves . . . (ibid.: 35)

But those hopes were soon to be disappointed. The French invasion accelerated the internal decomposition of the German Reich. This came to light during the Congress of Rastatt, which began in November 1797 and continued until April 1799. Hegel received news about the developments at Rastatt from his friend Hölderlin, who attended its sessions for a couple of weeks in November 1798. Showing his disappointment at the results attained at the Congress, Hegel wrote that he had reluctantly 'abandoned his hope to see the German state leave behind its insignificance' (Hegel, 1971: 452). He noted that Germany had suffered painful territorial losses and that millions of its citizens had been seized (ibid.: 457). In December 1798, Hegel began writing the first draft of what eventually would become the introductory section on the essay on the German constitution.

In the *Constitution of Germany*, Hegel observed the failure of the Holy Roman Empire to defend the interests of Germany in the face of the challenge presented by the French Revolution. Its opening sentence reflected the pessimism that engulfed Hegel after the Rastatt debacle. 'Germany is no longer a state' (Hegel, 1964b: 143). Germany had lost a war and the causes lay in an age-old constitutional configuration

which reflected an ingrained instinct for freedom. Upholding traditional freedoms was to blame for the German stubborn incapacity to
constitute a central state authority strong enough to demand the
sacrifice of particular social interests. The old Germanic arbitrary
freedom modelled individuals incapable of yielding to the whole. 'Out
of this arbitrary activity, which alone was called freedom, spheres of
power over others were built by chance and character, without regard
to a universal and with little control by what is called public authority'
(ibid.: 148). This is why Germany could no longer be seen as a 'unified
political whole but only as a mass of independent and essentially
sovereign states' (ibid.: 152). Hegel observed that a people could
constitute a unified state only when pressed to defend itself by actual
arms. Political unity presupposed military unity. 'If a multitude is to
form a state, then it must form a common military and public
authority' (ibid.: 154). In no case could this lead to the annihilation of
individual freedom. Hegel distinguished between the necessary
minimum required for the centralization of state authority and the
sphere of action that could be left for individuals to pursue their own
initiative.

> If the general public authority demands from the individual only what is
> necessary for itself, and if it restricts accordingly the arrangements for
> ensuring the performance of this minimum, then beyond this point it can
> permit the living freedom and the individual will of the citizens, and even
> leave considerable scope to the latter. (ibid.: 154–5)

Leaving free scope to individual citizens did not entail the democratization of the state. Only strong monarchical government ensured
economic and social freedom.

> The public authority must be concentrated in one centre . . . If this centre is
> secure on its own account in virtue of the awe of the masses, and
> immutably sacrosanct in the person of a monarch appointed in accordance
> with a natural law and by birth, then a public authority may without fear or
> jealousy hand over to subordinate systems and bodies a great part of the
> relationship arising in society and their maintenance in accordance to law.
> (ibid.: 160)

Hegel concluded this essay with an appeal to 'making Germany into
one state' (ibid.: 241). He recognized that the common people did not

regard unity as a their primordial aim. If unity were to be attained, this would have to be the result, not of deliberation, but of collecting the people together 'by the power of a conqueror' (ibid.). Such unity would certainly not be the result of democratic participation. Whether or not Hegel had Napoleon in mind at this point is difficult to say (ibid.: 241, n. 2). What is certain is that, after Napoleon's triumph at the battle of Jena in 1806, Hegel most definitely set his eyes on this French Theseus.

In his essay *The Scientific Ways of Treating Natural Law* (1802–3), Hegel explored the philosophical prerequisites underlying the process of state creation. He had rejected the idea that the state may be the 'fruit of deliberation' (1964b: 241). He now traced this idea to the contractualist approach of modern natural law in its empirical (Hobbes) and formal (Kant) versions. He rejected modern individualism and instead affirmed the superiority of the classical ideal of the state. At the same time, he acknowledged that the principle of individual freedom made it impossible to restore the classical state without mediation (see Horstmann, 2004: 212). In this essay and subsequent elaborations of the Jena period, Hegel developed the idea of a contractualist sphere of needs, property, and labour in contrast to the living organic unity of the ethical state. Both these spheres constituted the ethical totality, in spite of the fact that the sphere of need and labour, in its negativity, represented a distorted ethical configuration. For the concrete embodiment of these two spheres Hegel appealed to the class division enacted in Plato's *Republic*.[9] In German, the term *Bürger* refers both to *bourgeois* and *citoyen*. Hegel distinguished these two senses when he defined the 'political nullity' of the *Bürger* in the sense *bourgeois*, and 'spared [this class] the necessity (laid on the first class) of exposing itself to the danger of violent death' (Hegel, 1975a: 103; see Schmitt, 1928: 253). The first class flourishes within the bounds of civil society; the second will constitute the ethical state. The crucial distinction between civil society and the state would be drawn later during his stay at Heidelberg (1816–18), but it was already implied in his Jena writings.

After losing a teaching position at the University of Jena in 1806, Hegel secured a job as editor of a Bamberg newspaper, and 'almost every issue of the newspaper from the end of 1807 through 1808 contained some report of the constitutional developments in the kingdom of Westphalia' (Pinkard, 2000: 245). Napoleon proclaimed a constitution for the kingdom of Westphalia, which was to be 'the first constitution in German history, issued by decree in November 1807' (Sheehan, 1989: 260). A letter of 29 August 1807 indicates how eager he was to see this form of non-democratic constitutionalism introduced in Germany by 'the great professor of constitutional law [who] sits in Paris' (Hegel, 1984: 141). Until the very end of Napoleon's career, Hegel manifested enthusiastic and unabated admiration for the man. In 1814, while still occupying the rectorship of the Nuremberg Gymnasium, he wrote to Niethammer, on 29 April, about 'the frightful spectacle [of seeing] a great genius destroy himself'. He blamed that fall on the mediocrity and levelling power of the mass, a power that 'the great individual himself must give the mass . . . thus precipitating his own fall' (ibid.: 307). Hegel's total agreement with Napoleon prefigured his total agreement with Hardenberg (see Kervégan, 2003: 8).

The abdication of Napoleon took effect on 6 April and the French Senate promptly called for the restoration of Louis-Stanislas-Xavier, the brother of Louis XVI. The Senate thought that his long exile in England would have impressed on him a liberal disposition and made him ready to rule under the strictures of a constitution. But as soon as he disembarked in Calais, Louis-Stanislas-Xavier reclaimed his legitimate title as Louis XVIII. Not willing to repeat the tragic destiny that the 1791 constitution inflicted on his brother, he made it clear that only a constitution gratuitously granted by the King would be acceptable. On 4 June, the Charte was communicated by the King to the deputies without a vote being taken. This was the genesis of the so-called 'monarchical principle'. In this respect, the Charte was a reactionary document which intended, as stated in its preamble, to 'renouer la chaîne des temps que de funestes écarts avaient inter-rompue' (see Prélot, 1984: 388). At the same time, it was a progressive document that enshrined individual liberty, freedom of the press and inviolable property rights. Hegel saw in the Charte a 'beacon' built upon the form of permanence (Hegel, 1995: 241), and was at the same time well aware of what was implied by the monarchical principle as a constitutional doctrine.[10] His admiration for the Charte included his endorsement of that principle.[11]

In 1817, Hegel published in the *Heidelbergischer Jahrbücher* a long essay entitled *Proceedings of the Assembly of Estates of the Kingdom of Wurtemberg in the Years 1815 and 1816*. He celebrated William I, King of Wurtemberg, for his expressed intention to give a constitution to his subjects in accordance with the monarchical principle. 'There surely cannot be a greater secular spectacle on earth than that of a monarch's adding to the public authority, which *ab initio* is entirely in his hands, another foundation, indeed *the* foundation, by bringing his people into an essentially effective ingredient' (Hegel 1964b: 251). He also sharply criticized King William's subjects for clinging to their old privileges and rejecting the proposal. Criticized in turn for appearing to side with monarchical reactionaries like Haller, Hegel made explicit the distinction between state and civil society developed earlier in Jena. This distinction allowed him to harmonize his simultaneous defence of a liberal market society and a conservative state defined by the monarchical principle. This crucial intellectual achievement he brought with him when he arrived at the capital of the Prussian state in 1818. When he sent a published copy of the *Philosophy of Right* to Hardenberg he wrote that his aim had been to agree 'with the principle which the Prussian state . . . had the good fortune of having upheld and of still upholding under the enlightened Government of His Majesty the King and Your Highness's wise leadership' (ibid.: 459).

But Hardenberg's role as the leader of the constitutionalist movement in Prussia was on the wane. On hearing the news of Kotzebue's murder he had presciently exclaimed: 'A constitution for Prussia has now become impossible!' (Treitschke, 1917: 254). Still, on 11 August 1819 he laid a final constitutional project before the King, which contained a system of representation strikingly similar to the one proposed by Hegel in the *Philosophy of Right* (Treitschke, 1917: 643–7). This project aimed not at weakening the hand of the sovereign monarch, but at strengthening it. Hardenberg concluded his constitutional plan by insisting on the maintenance of the monarchical principle and the need to harmonize authority and freedom:

> All necessary steps must be taken to ensure that the monarchical principle shall be firmly established, that the true freedom and security of person and property shall harmonize with that principle, and that in this way freedom and security may best and most enduringly persist in conjunction with order and energy. Thus the principle will be maintained: *Salus publica suprema lex esto*! (ibid.: 646–7)

This should not be read as a concession to the opposition Austrian party and its feudalist leaders Ancillon and Haller. It coincided with what Hardenberg and Hegel had maintained all along. But for all practical purposes, constitutionalism had come to a halt in Prussia. When Hardenberg died in 1822, 'detested by the reactionaries, an object of suspicion to the conservatives, he had lost the respect even of the liberals through the pusillanimity of his closing years' (ibid.: 598).

A similar fate would await Hegel on his own death in 1831. Attacked on the left by republican democrats, and on the right by feudalist reactionaries, his apologists defended him as a liberal reformer, as a moderate who sought to theorize about the development of a free-market society within the bounds of a modern constitutional state. Nowadays, this centrist view has gained ascendancy, successfully enshrining Hegel within the liberal tradition, defined as embracing 'the exhaustive polarity of "liberalism" and "conservatism" as those terms are commonly used in contemporary politics' (Wood, 1990: 257). I will argue that Hegel's liberalism was not advanced, but more in tune with Hobbes or Hume than with Mill or Dewey. According to Wood, for example, 'the constitutional monarchy described in the *Philosophy of Right* is quite liberal by the standards of the time in which it was written', standards that encompassed, in Wood's view, Hardenberg's liberalizing project (ibid.). What this centrist interpretation of Hegel does not take into account is that Hardenberg's endorsement of the monarchical principle makes a mockery of constitutionalism, as the term is now commonly used, in that it wrests constituent power away form the people and places it in the hands of dictatorially sovereign monarch. Espousal of Hardenberg's politics situates Hegel at a vast distance from what contemporary progressive liberalism stands for.

III

Liberal interpreters appear most at ease when expounding Hegel's notion of civil society. They rightly see in it the lineaments of a modern market society, a network of contractual relations that tie individuals able to affirm their subjective rights. These rights allow persons to articulate their freedom and stake their own private domain. In his *Philosophy of Right*, Hegel writes: 'Personality contains in general the capacity for rights' (§36). Implicit here is the view that assigns priority to subjective rights and grounds the justification for obligations in consent. According to the *Hegelsche Mitte*, a line of interpretation that has become prevalent since the 1950s,[12] the political expression of this liberal stance is Hegel's conception of constitutional monarchy. This implies a 'replacement of power politics by the rule of law'

(Pelczynski, 1971: 3), and the neutralization of the role assigned to the monarch. In Eric Weil's view, 'le prince n'est pas le centre ni le rouage principal de l'État' (1950: 62). By contrast, Hegel's conservative readers emphasize the priority of duties over rights, and the subservience of individuals to the autonomous and more universal goals of the state. They see that the Hegelian state does not come into existence as a result of a contract. It is not based on the consented transfer or renunciation of rights by individuals, but exists prior to them and has an elevation and dignity that surpasses any claims they may have. Members of civil society do not find in it an instrument pliable to their interests or a servant to their needs. Conservative interpretations accentuate monarchical authority and the 'stabilizing effect of a hereditary establishment' (Scruton, 1986: 49). In a similar vein, Bobbio writes: 'Hegel is not a reactionary, but neither is he a liberal when he writes the *Philosophy of Right*. He is purely and simply a conservative in as much as he ranks the state above individuals, authority above freedom, . . . the apex of the pyramid (the monarch) above its base (the people)' (Bobbio, 1981: 189–90).

Just as liberal interpreters relativize the role of the state, and ignore the special attributes that characterize Hegel's monarch as the subject of constituent power, conservative interpreters ignore Hegel's endorsement of individual rights and his revolutionary recognition of bourgeois freedom and initiative. Hegelian scholarship is thus rent between opposing interpretations of his political philosophy. As Charles Taylor sees it, either–or approaches, particularly when applied to Hegel, are unilluminating (Taylor, 1975: 452). Disagreement among Hegel's interpreters stems from the fact that his system contains both liberal and conservative strands of thought, frustrating the attempts to interpret it in one-sided fashion. Authoritarian liberalism, I submit, rightly describes Hegel's posture.[13] He envisions a strong authoritative state that holds a monopoly on political authority placed in the hands of an hereditary monarch. The authority of this state preserves the freedom individuals exercise in the context of an unalloyed market economy.[14] This rapprochement of freedom and authority should not be understood as an eclectic blend of liberal and conservative strands of thought. A dialectical argument allows Hegel systematically to derive a conservative state from the liberal principles embodied in civil society.[15] According to Taylor, this is precisely the Hegelian tour de force: 'to deduce from reason and freedom a new articulation' (1975: 452).

I examine, in Chapter 1, the position defended by the *Hegelsche Mitte*. This tradition of interpretation seeks to present Hegel as a philosopher of freedom[16] whose conception of civil society is thoroughly liberal and matched by a state presided by a constitutional monarch. One line of argument challenges the perception of Hegel as an ideologue of the Prussian feudalist reaction. He is said to have stood firmly on the side of Hardenberg and supported the aims of the Prussian reform movement. I agree that Hegel's sincere attachment to liberal principles eliminates the possibility of aligning his thought to the Prussian feudalist reaction. But, as shown above, Hardenberg's proposed reforms were to be implemented under the patronage of a sovereign monarch. As Treitschke acknowledges, Hardenberg 'insisted upon the firm maintenance of the monarchical principle' (Treitschke, 1917: 256). My argument seeks to draw the theoretical implications of Hegel's acceptance of that principle. Another line of argument is pursued by Karl-Heinz Ilting, for whom Hegel's political position prior to the publication of the *Philosophy of Right* coincides tactically with that of the *doctrinaires*, but in matters of principle is closer to the 'radically liberal' views of Benjamin Constant.[17] Though Ilting recognizes that Hegel endorsed the monarchical principle, he fails to see how that principle is understood by both Hegel and the *doctrinaires*. Constant interprets the monarch as a *pouvoir neutre*, a neutral third, and not as a higher sovereign third. In contrast, Hegel and the *doctrinaires* maintain that the monarch transcends the limits defined by the constitution and is the subject of constituent power. Proof of this is that while Constant consistently defended the principle of popular sovereignty, Hegel and the *doctrinaires* unambiguously rejected it.

In no case do Hegel's authoritarian propensities rescind his commitment to economic liberalism. Civil society is the locus where he allows those principles to flourish. But I challenge the *Hegelsche Mitte*'s view of civil society as a stable and unified sphere, and conceive it instead as criss-crossed by contradictions similar to those that make survival difficult in a Hobbesian state of nature. The inner structure of civil society, the locus of freedom, leads to fragmentation and instability at an accelerated pace. Hegel's state, the guarantor of unity and stability, is the locus of authority. In this respect, Hegel's *Philosophy of Right* stands in line with Grotius, whose *De Iure Belli* 'is Janus-faced, and its two mouths speak the language of both absolutism and liberty' (Tuck, 1979: 79).

To understand fully the assumptions made by those who defend Hegel as a pre-eminent philosopher of freedom, I examine his conception of freedom as expounded by two recent interpreters. This is the topic of Chapter 2. Allen Patten, in his book *Hegel's Idea of Freedom*, postulates that 'freedom is the value that Hegel most greatly admires and the central organizing concept of his social philosophy' (1999: 4). Similarly, Frederick Neuhouser thinks that the rationality of the institutions recognized in Hegel's social philosophy rests on the 'essential roles' they play 'in realizing the central value of freedom' (2000: 4).[18] My aim in this chapter is to probe the arguments presented by these authors. This should set the stage for my attempt to determine that Hegel's social philosophy acknowledges authority as a companion normative standard. I preface these comments with discussion of Terry Pinkard's recently published Hegel biography. Pinkard detects a dualism in Hegel's personality. He openly supported and celebrated the storming of the Bastille *and* condoned the political persecution suffered by his Berlin colleagues in 1819. 'He led a cozy, Biedermeier life, *and* he went to the Faschings balls decked out in a Venetian cape and mask' (Pinkard, 2000: 453). If his biographical personality successfully combined contradictory elements, it seems plausible that his political thought could embrace both liberalism *and* authoritarianism.

Hegel never ceases to vindicate the philosophical value of his exposition. This could only mean that he intends to derive the entire content of the *Philosophy of Right* from a single concept – the concept of the will. In Chapter 3, I explore this philosophical derivation. First, I examine the epistemology of freedom and authority, the two moments that guide Hegel's dialectic of the will. Though freedom and authority are eminently practical notions, Hegel extends their employment to the theoretical realm. Within the theoretical realm, the highest expression of freedom is universal thought. Universality is manifested by self-identity, maximal expression of freedom and reason. Thought seeks what is fixed and persisting, and thus Hegel assigns to it an authoritative role. The abstraction of thought and the self run parallel. Hegel postulates the need to advance towards concrete thought or concept (*Begriff*), because abstraction by itself is a defective condition. The passage from abstract to concrete thought coincides with the passage from abstract to concrete freedom. Accordingly, both concrete thought and concrete freedom are defined by Hegel as being with oneself in one's other (*in seinem Anderen bei sich selbst zu sein*). Second, I proceed to lay out his critique of both empiricism and idealism, and the dialectical method that supersedes their opposition. Combining a 'development according to historical grounds' and a 'development according to concepts', the dialectical method allows the derivation of authoritative institutions from the categories of abstract free will. The spontaneous authoritative order that springs naturally from the self-seeking behaviour of free individuals is meant to safeguard their freedom.

Freedom is internally tied to the notions of property and contract. Liberal interpreters downplay Hegel's individualist conception of property and claim that a social premise lies at the root of his conception. This relativization of property assumes that it is not constituted by individuals acting autonomously, but by individuals who recognize each other inter-subjectively. In Chapter 4, I argue that Hegel, in the *Philosophy of Right*, bases his conception of property on the notion of subjective rights conceived as logically and temporally prior to objective law and the constitution of a legal system. I refer to Hans Kelsen's forswearing of subjective rights to clarify the Hegelian conception. What Kelsen repudiates is a modern individualist conception of subjective rights and property which coincides point for point with Hegel's own individualist notion of abstract right. Property, defined initially as an abstract right, is constituted prior to inter-subjective recognition. Hegel describes it as a *ius in rem*, and not as a personal right. Accordingly, he acknowledges that the 'more precise determinations of property are to be found in the will's relation to the thing' (§53). As Hegel's argument advances, abstract property is superseded by an embryonic social conception. But this relativization of property is not meant to weaken individual appropriation. Property is duly safeguarded only when social property re-emerges within civil society where a legal system is put in place for its proper protection. Hegel does not subscribe to Hobbes's conception of property as the right to exclude all other individuals *except the sovereign*. Hobbes favours a strong state capable of securing the formation of primary capital accumulation in a society still encumbered by the remnants of feudal institutions. In contrast, Hegel's espouses a strong monarchical state to protect private property from democratic redistribution.[19]

Hegel demarcates his liberal outlook within the confines of civil society. This is the topic of Chapter 5. The dissolution of family liberates individuals from the tutelary authority of parents. Individuals in civil society exercise their subjective rights and seek their own welfare. By applying the principles of political economy, Hegel derives a form of

universality from the self-regarding agency of those individuals.[20]
'Subjective selfishness turns into a contribution towards the satisfaction
of the needs of everyone else' (§199). But since this is conditional upon
one's unequal capital, skills and other contingencies, the end result
only magnifies initial inequalities and yields the 'remnants of the state
of nature' (§200). In order to tame the potential disruption generated
by free-wheeling civil society, Hegel introduces two etatist formations
to help stabilize the market. A judicial state provides guidelines
necessary for the entrenchment of property and the whole slew of rights
it defines. Then, an administrative state attends to those who have
been deprived of effective access to property and suffer iniquitous
poverty. This is not a welfare state as we understand it today but an
institution whose ultimate concerns are the contingencies that impede
the smooth operation of the market order and discipline. These two
etatist formations are purely instrumental and do not depend on
personal allegiance and other internal dispositions. Only corporations
and the spirit of solidarity they inject in their membership assume
those dispositions and prefigure the virtues demanded of citizens
within the ethical state. The futility of this proto-republican
mediation is highlighted by Hegel's affirmation of the monarchical
principle. With this principle in hand he can disregard the need to
form citizens and lower his sights to deal effectively with civil society's
unruly possessive individuals.

Interpretations of Hegel that approximate his political argument to
Hobbes's derivation of political authority present civil society as the
point of departure of a regress argument that demonstrates the
necessity of the state (Ilting, 1971: 91; Riedel, 1971: 143; Horstmann,
2004: 208–11).[21] Once Hegel has established that the revolutionary
tendencies generated within civil society cannot be contained by the
instrumentalist etatist and corporate structures put forward therein,
the next step in his argument requires the institution of an absolutist
state, in accordance with what M. M. Goldsmith has defined as the
'logic of the concept of sovereignty' (1980: 38). The standard objection
to this interpretation is that Hegel defines his sovereign as a constitutional figure, setting it clearly apart from Hobbesian absolutism. In
Chapter 6, I examine Hegel's espousal of constitutional monarchy.
One should note that Hegel takes this step in 1820, when Hardenberg's
efforts to enact a constitution had succumbed to Metternich's opposition. This meant the utter defeat of constitutionalism in Prussia,
so much so that use of the term 'constitutional monarchy' was now

deemed treasonous by the government. In spite of this, Hegel continues to support this notion, because he conceives it as inextricably conjoined to the monarchical principle. The prince, not the people, properly embodies the will of the state. Louis XVIII's Charte is Hegel's model. Like the French *doctrinaires*, Hegel thinks that by embracing constitutional monarchy he is affirming monarchical sovereignty, and thereby is making the polity impregnable to democracy and revolution. From the perspective of a liberal like Constant, the role assigned to the monarch by the Charte was that of a *pouvoir neutre et intermédiaire* who served merely as the protector of the constitution. From Hegel's perspective, the prince is not to be understood as neutral power. Constant could place the monarch within the constitution because he accepted the sovereignty of the people. Hegel postulates the monarchical principle in order to reject popular sovereignty[22] and contractualist interpretations of the constitution, the Achilles heel of Hobbes's leviathan (see Hampton, 1986: 189–207). The Hegelian prince must be seen not as a neutral, but as a higher third.

The authoritarian potential of liberalism, brought to light by Hegel in his Roman argument, is the topic of Chapter 7. Hegel is aware of the weight that Rome assigned to absolutist property and normativism. At the same time he sees that a form of life based entirely on abstract rights could only lead to the erosion of the Roman *populus* and the formation of a *vulgus* or *multitudo*. At one point, republican self-government was no longer sustainable and Rome threw itself into the hands of strong authoritarian rulers. Hegel is fascinated with Caesar's imperial character, with his readiness to forgo legal formalities, assert his personal authority and arrive at utterly final decisions. The figure of Caesar accredits the limits of liberalism. The rule of law cannot sustain itself abstractly and normatively bracket off the contradictions proper to civil society.

The last chapter explores Marx's critique of Hegel's political philosophy. My interest in Marx stems from what I see as his Hobbesian reading of Hegel's civil society, concurrent with an inability to discern Hegel's royalism. This may be explained partly by the historical circumstances that encircle Marx at the time he writes his *Critique* in 1843, while honeymooning in Bad Kreuznach. By then France is no longer a constitutional monarchy, and has in effect evolved to become a parliamentary monarchy. History has enshrined parliamentary rule and seems to move speedily away from decisive assertions of monarchical rule. An alternative explanation is advanced by Ilting. He points out that, in his excitement about Feuerbach's transformative method, Marx leaves unexamined that politically decisive issue. In this respect, my criticism of Marx coincides with the one I direct at the *Hegelsche Mitte*, namely failure fully to grasp the Hobbesian disposition of Hegel's argument in the *Philosophy of Right*.

In order to save Hegel's contemporary political and philosophical relevance, the *Hegelsche Mitte* deflates the authoritative role played by the monarch and presents constitutional monarchy as the enthronement of the liberal rule of law and democracy. To further strengthen this defence, it displaces the exoteric Hegel of the *Philosophy of Right* and favours his Heidelberg and Berlin lectures notes on *Rechtsphilosophie* which were not intended for publication. But it cannot be denied that Hegel's monarchical disposition is long-standing, stretching back to his youthful Jena writings. It is no mystery that Napoleon exercises immense fascination over his mind and that, after his fall, Hegel advocates constitutional monarchy as defined in Louis XVIII's Charte. What motivates the tendency that seeks to underrate Hegel's royalism is his determination to postulate freedom as the true foundation of his philosophical deduction. Not subjective freedom though, but absolute or concrete freedom which he identifies with the state. 'The state is the actuality of concrete freedom' (§260). The state is what ought to be considered the 'primary factor' (§256), the true foundation of his philosophical deduction. Concrete freedom *is* authority. Without the authority of the state, the winds of subjective freedom that swell the sails of civil society reach gale force. Only a strongly unified state, and not the weak state espoused by political liberalism, is immune to the Hobbesian undercurrents that destabilize civil society, the locus of modern subjective freedom.

The value of Hegel's philosophical tour de force derives from this attempt to reconcile the freedom individuals display in civil society with the authority wielded by the state. Like Dewey, Hegel believes it is a mistake to denounce authority as the enemy of freedom. The real issue concerns the interpenetration, not the separation, of these notions. But unlike Dewey, Hegel allows for the development of an unregulated market order which contains the remnants of a state of nature. To avoid the wholesale destruction of civil society implied by this conception, Hegel conceives of a Hobbesian monarch whose role is to restrain the revolutionary forces unleashed therein (see Haym, 1857: 372 and 380). In contrast, Dewey believes the authority of a democratic state demands the development of a democratic social order:

> We need an authority that is capable of directing and utilizing change, and we need a kind of individual freedom unlike that which the unconstrained economic liberty of individuals has produced and justified; we need, that is, a kind of individual freedom that is general and shared and that has the backing and guidance of socially organized authoritative control. (Dewey, 1936: 137)

Hegel is not prepared to acknowledge this democratic conception of freedom and authority, which confirms the appropriateness of Hobbesian readings of his political philosophy.

Hobbesian readings of Hegel encounter significant problems. First, Hegel appeals, at one point, to the republican ideals scorned by Hobbes (see Williams, 2003: 79; Pettit, 1997: 38–9), and demands that the authoritative constitution of the state take into account the patriotism of its members. Patriotism is the subjective disposition that allows citizens to know 'that the community is the substantial basis and end' (§268). The authority of the state ought therefore not to be seen as stifling, but directing and utilizing the energies unleashed within civil society. Second, Hegel is aware of the difficulties affecting Hobbes's derivation of state authority and develops a view that thwarts contractualist justifications based on state of nature arguments. In his view, actual social agreements and conventions presuppose the already existing social disposition to agree and convene. By rejecting the position that all social relations are contractual, he appears to distance himself from Hobbesian contractarianism. But however much Hegel extols the value of patriotism and rejects Hobbesian individualism, this does not deflect the main drift of his argument. I concur with David Gauthier that 'the discussion of property and contract in the first part of the *Philosophy of Right* is a fundamental source for any articulation of contractarian ideology' (Gauthier, 1977: 164). The same can be said of his conception of civil society which Hegel defines as 'the field of conflict in which the private interest of each individual comes up against that of everyone else' (§289). A concern for the development of republican virtues is absent from this sphere. In Gauthier's stark assessment, one that I believe is shared by Hegel, 'the triumph of radical contractarianism leads to the destruction of our society' (1977: 163). Gauthier thinks this is inevitable because the

Hobbesian sovereign that can protect us from the war of all against all is unavailable to us. Hegel's reliance on the monarchical principle is proof that he did not share that view.

1 • The *Hegelsche Mitte* and Hegel's monarch

Établissez l'autorité d'abord, puis crées les libertés comme contrepois.
(Pierre-Paul Royer-Collard[1])

During the twentieth century, the greatest challenge faced by Hegelian scholarship, 'the skeleton in its closet', according to Topitsch, was posed by interpretations accommodating Hegel's political philosophy to the totalitarian worldview and policies of fascism. Authors proposing such views followed the path of those who, in the nineteenth century, sought to assimilate Hegel to the authoritarianism of Bismarck and of the Prussian regime generally. The challenge was advanced not only by those who actually acclaimed Hegel for having developed a political philosophy compatible with fascism (see Ottmann, 1977: 124–82), but also by those who accepted this interpretation and condemned Hegel for his opposition to the individualism of traditional liberal theories (ibid.: 182–203). Nowadays, there is consensus in rejecting this interpretation. 'The picture of Hegel as some kind of authoritarian or proto-totalitarian thinker that is often associated with his claims about freedom and the state is now widely rejected' (Patten, 1999: 164). Nobody denies that Hegel adhered firmly to a liberal conception. The consensus stops, though, when it is further asked whether Hegel consistently maintained a liberal conception throughout his different expositions on political philosophy, particularly in his *Philosophy of Right*. Two opposite standpoints emerged at the very inception of the polemic against those who assimilated Hegel's views to fascism.

The most influential of these standpoints, which has been accurately described as the *Hegelsche Mitte*, seeks generally to 'integrate Hegel again in line with the fathers of Western democracy' (Ottmann, 1977: 226). Characteristically, this position privileges Hegel's definition of the monarchy in his Heidelberg and Berlin lectures on *Rechtsphilosophie* (Hegel, 1973, 1995, 1983b), which introduce a constitutional monarch, divested of a decisive authoritative role and retained, in the words of Avineri, 'as a mere symbol of the unity of the state' (1972: 188; see Franco, 1999: 314–15; Hocevar, 1973: 98). The *Hegelsche*

Mitte locates the monarch within an institutional framework, where he 'remains bound by the laws and the constitution and by the objective advice of his ministers' (Franco, 1999: 317). A commitment to liberalism is said effectively to limit the authority of Hegel's monarch and detach him functionally from the pressures arising from civil society.

Typical of the resistance encountered by the *Hegelsche Mitte* is an article published in 1971 by Karl-Heinz Ilting. Following Karl Popper, one of Hegel's most famous liberal detractors, Ilting concurred with the charge that Hegel's state was 'simply not a liberal state' (Ilting, 1971: 109). Ilting reaffirmed Popper's stance because he was not ready to dismiss what the *Hegelsche Mitte* had closed its eyes to, namely the authoritarian temper of Hegel's monarch. He found Joachim Ritter's liberal reading of Hegel flawed for he had not dispelled 'the doubts which arise from Hegel's deification of autocratic monarchy' (ibid.: 102, n. 31). Ilting evinced a clearer understanding of what Hegel meant when he declared the monarch to be 'the apex and the beginning of the whole' (§273). This affirmation, in Ilting's view, manifested Hegel's endorsement of the monarchical principle.[2] This principle was to be regarded as incompatible with a conception of the modern state and constituted, on the part of Hegel, 'a betrayal of his own principles' (Ilting, 1971: 106). Though Ilting, as is shown below, later absolved Hegel by circumscribing this charges to the *Philosophy of Right* (in his view an anomalous text produced under exceptional circumstances), I argue for the centrality of this text within the continuity of his work. The *Philosophy of Right* is the text he actually published, and this renders it authoritative. Emergencies and exceptional circumstances do not necessarily cloud one's understanding, but may render it sharper and better focused. A crypto-absolutist monarch dressed up in constitutional garb was not an optional extra in Hegel's political philosophy. Such a figure allowed him to preserve the separation of civil society from the state and ensure the relative autonomy of both spheres. The contrasting view of the *Hegelsche Mitte* dismissed this separation of civil society and the state as involving, in Pelczynski's words, an unnecessary 'splitting of public authority . . . into two spheres'. Pelczynski wished 'to view these two sets of authorities as just two facets of one and the same system of public authority' (1971: 11). But this harmonization may be accomplished only if the authorities recognized within civil society are drastically subordinated to the state.

The key to Hegel's social philosophy lies in his notion of civil society, which reflects his unerring understanding of the mechanism of modern market society. He perceives that the integration of its members is difficult to attain as long as the particularist and centrifugal forces generated within it are allowed free and spontaneous development. In turn, Hegel's political philosophy explores possible ways of moderating the impact of those social forces without altering them in any substantive manner and without curtailing the freedom of enterprise and trade. The freedom claimed by recalcitrant particularity demands universalist state authority. Business interests unavoidably invoke individual freedom against higher regulation, but the more freedom sinks into selfishness, the more it requires that higher regulation. As Marcuse sees it, 'the gist of Hegel's analysis is that liberalist society necessarily gives birth to an authoritarian state' (1968: 59).

The pressures and contradictions that afflict civil society, and which cannot be resolved by its own civil institutions, motivate Hegel's conservative, anti-democratic options. This ought not to be seen as a betrayal of the liberal principles that inform civil society, but as the fulfilment of its basic orientation. His conservative stance shows up in two places. First, at the level of civil society itself, Hegel introduces corporations – intermediate associations that satisfy the need for order and self-discipline required by business activities. Second, the prospect that these corporations may be unable to withstand the contradictions generated within civil society determines Hegel to postulate a strong independent state crowned by a self-generating monarch. This political solution is meant to control the social disruption brought forth by inevitable poverty and block the possibility that it be redressed democratically. Only after the monarch is defined by the monarchical principle, thereby invalidating popular sovereignty (see Heller, 1921: 110), does Hegel contemplate implementing forms of political representation and pluralism which cannot serve as channels for democratic participation (see Brandt, 1968: 156–7). This is as much as saying that Hegel in his *Philosophy of Right* extracts conservative implications from his liberal principles. This poses the question whether Hegel betrayed or obscured those principles. For my part I believe that a case can be made for showing that Hegel's liberal conception is not betrayed in his *Philosophy of Right*, but clarified and enhanced as a result of the Congress of Vienna's confirmation of the monarchical principle in May 1820, at the precise time when he was preparing the publication of that work.

I

Immediately after the outbreak of the Second World War, both T. M. Knox and Herbert Marcuse defended Hegel against non-liberal, fascist interpretations of his political philosophy. But they defended a liberal Hegel from opposed standpoints. Knox, writing in 1940 (1970), argued against regarding Hegel's social and political thought as a justification of Prussianism, particularly in light of the Prussian government's evolution after the Carlsbad decrees. Hegel's highest political institution, the state, ought to be seen as 'a description of the essence of modern political life' (ibid.: 22). According to Knox, Hegel did not plant an absolute monarch at the head of the state. On the contrary, his monarch was bound by a constitution so that the functions assigned to him were compatible with individual freedom. The monarch's 'functions are to be restricted; he is one organ of the body politic, the executive and the legislative being the other two' (ibid.). Knox acknowledged certain external similarities between Hegelian institutions, like corporations, and the practice of fascism. But these resemblances evaporated when one took Hegel's whole story into account. And by this Knox meant Hegel's constitutional monarchy. Knox became the first Hegelian scholar to have consciously defined and defended Hegel as a 'progressive liberal' and thus reaffirmed the *Hegelsche Mitte* (Ottmann, 1977: 282).

Marcuse, one year later, also argued against an uncritical identification of Hegel's political philosophy with fascism. In the preface to *Reason and Revolution* he stated that his intention was to 'demonstrate that Hegel's basic concepts are hostile to the tendencies that have led to fascist theory and practice' (1968: p. xv). He saw evidence of progressive liberal tendencies in Hegel's political philosophy, but restricted those tendencies to his conception of civil society. Paradoxically, it was the development of those progressive tendencies, expressed in the increasing antagonism among individuals within civil society, that finally led to an authoritarian political system. Marcuse stopped short and did not define Hegel's monarch as absolutist. He still thought that Hegel assigned some space to the idea of freedom by 'giving a strong constitutional flavour to monarchy' (ibid.: 218).

This was no longer the incipient *Hegelsche Mitte* of Knox. Hegel, in the eyes of Marcuse, was both progressive and reactionary. If his philosophy contained internal contradictions it was because 'its basic concepts absorb and consciously retain the contradictions of this society and follow them to the bitter end. The work is reactionary insofar as the social order it reflects is so, and progressive insofar as it is progressive' (ibid.: 178). Progressive and reactionary tendencies came together in Hegel, but they did not blend. Marcuse, following Engels, found that Hegel's inconsistencies were to be traced back to his discovery of a progressive *method*, which then was forced to yield a regressive *system* of thought. Hegel's method, according to Marcuse, could be read materialistically (ibid.: 148). If, at a certain point, Hegel betrayed 'his highest philosophical ideals' (ibid.: 218), this was the result of forswearing his initial materialism.

In 1949, Lukács published his study on the young Hegel, completed ten years earlier. Lukács again detected in Hegel a contradiction between progressive and reactionary tendencies. With Engels, he agreed that Hegel's dialectical method correctly moved from the particular to the universal, 'developing the universal starting from the particular by means of the dialectics proper to it' (1967: 483). This was the tendency Hegel developed when he examined the structure of civil society. Against this 'democratic' movement from below Hegel postulated a totally independent state, interrupting the embryonic dialectical drive. Particularity became the prisoner of a monarchical universal. Lukács quoted from Marx's critique of Hegel: 'Hegel proceeds from the state and conceives of man as the subjectivized state; democracy proceeds from man and conceives of the state as objectified man' (ibid.: p. 488; see Marx, 1975a: 87).

Following Marx, Lukács traced these perceived counterposed tendencies in Hegel's thought to a 'central philosophical weakness affecting his entire system: the problem of democracy' (1967: 487). This weakness appeared most clearly in Hegel's inability to grasp the 'movement towards democracy within the French Revolution' (ibid.: 488). But this weakness proved to be his strength when compared to Fichte's radical-democratic stance. Fichte adopted a revolutionary stance when there was no actual revolution in Germany and no objective conditions for a revolutionary onset (ibid.: 364). Hegel's objectivism allowed him to see that Germany's backwardness stifled democratic forces and that progress in that respect could only come riding on a white horse.

Avoiding a direct confrontation with either Marcuse or Lukács, Ritter in 1956 defended Hegel as a progressive liberal whose philosophy ought to be read as a 'philosophy of the Revolution, even in its inner

most impulses' (Ritter, 1977: 192).[3] As Knox before him, Ritter defended
Hegel against charges of Prussianism and conservatism. Studiously
ignoring the 'problem of democracy', he identified a progressivist
position with liberalism *tout court*. With Ritter, the *Hegelsche Mitte*
acquired philosophical maturity and became a well-defined position.
The novelty in Ritter's reading of Hegel was his initial agreement with
the interpretations advanced by Marcuse and Lukács. Such readings
placed the notion of civil society at the centre of Hegel's political
philosophy (ibid.: 219, 223). According to Ritter, Hegel obtained this
notion from classical political economists; its content was the need-
bound nature of individuals and the satisfaction of those needs through
labour and the division of labour (ibid.: 221). Classical political
economists did not proceed by deploying abstract principles from which
new political forms could be deduced. This was the path taken by the
French political revolutionaries, which Hegel clearly rejected. Classical
political economists evinced their empiricist method by deriving their
categories from a historically matured social reality, which gave rise to
a hermeneutic of social formations. The contradictions that arose in
their account of society and dashed its pretended universality, contradictions sharpened by the rise of the proletariat (ibid.: 222, 253), could
not be resolved by an abstract application of principles. They would
find their solution if the development of civil society itself were allowed
to proceed unimpeded. Universality was to be attained spontaneously
by increased production and colonialist expansion (ibid.: 222).

If civil society could achieve universality on its own, why then the
need for a state? Ritter argued that the state was required to prevent an
abstract political revolution, which could only disturb the spontaneous
revolution taking place within civil society. The natural constitution of
civil society dissolved the concrete historical ties that held traditional
society together. Individual subjective freedom generated a centrifugal
development, which Hegel identified as *Entzweiung*, and which ob-
structed the attainment of universality. Since Hegel would not allow
that the 'historical abstraction, which necessarily constitutes society in
itself, could result in contradiction with history' (ibid.: 230), the state
was a 'necessary correction for the naturalist theory of society' (ibid.:
230). Ritter thought that Hegel had thus eliminated the risks involved
in the emancipatory structure of civil society. Civil society could now
stand on the firm ground provided by the state, 'just as a spark thrown
on to a powderkeg is far more dangerous than if it falls on solid ground,
where it disappears without trace' (ibid.: 232; see §319).

With Hegel's authoritarian monarch out of the picture, the *Hegelsche Mitte* sought a place, somewhere between Locke and Mill, for the exhibition of Hegel's portrait (Ottmann, 1977: 225). In 1971, Karl-Heinz Ilting challenged the view that the *Philosophy of Right* could be read as a defence of progressive liberalism. Assuming a posture discordant with the *Hegelsche Mitte*, he manifested his agreement with Popper's charge that Hegel's state was 'simply not a liberal state' (Ilting, 1971: 109). In 1973, he edited and published the notes of Hegel's lectures on *Rechtsphilosophie* immediately before and after the publication of the *Philosophy of Right*. His research has been hailed as 'one of the success stories of Hegelian scholarship' of the twentieth century (Ottmann, 1979: 227).[4] The central thesis of Ilting's project is that the text published in 1821 represents a break in Hegel's continuous adherence to a liberal *Grundkonzeption*. The *Philosophy of Right* ought to be seen as 'only one, even if in certain respects one especially important moment within Hegel's complete work, and should thus be studied in connection with his lectures' (Hegel, 1973: 7). Ilting's argument is based on a comparison between the *Philosophy of Right* and the notes taken by Carl Gustav Homeyer, during the academic year 1818–19, and notes taken by other students, Hotho and Griesheim, on lectures held after 1821, when the political turbulences of 1819–20 had subsided. Ilting is able to detect changes in Hegel's internal argument of which perhaps the most important is a revision of the role he assigned to the monarch. In the *Philosophy of Right*, according to Ilting, the monarch was granted absolutist powers of decision, while the other elements of the constitution, the executive and legislative powers, were subordinated to the monarch who was now not only the apex of the state but also its beginning. This change in Hegel's political posture could be attributed, according to Ilting, to his accommodation to external historical events, the difficult times which followed the assassination of August von Kotzebue on 23 March 1819, and which gave the government the excuse to promulgate a state of emergency (the Carlsbad decrees) in October of that same year. Ilting interprets the change in Hegel's conception of the monarch as a major revision of Hegel's 'liberal-progressive *Grundkonzeption*' which he held before and after 1821. Ilting is not simply expanding the argument presented in his 1971 article, where he assumed a position discordant with the *Hegelsche Mitte*, by engaging in a Hobbesian reading of Hegel's political philosophy. Now his intentions are markedly different. In the esoteric lectures one finds the authentic voice of a progressive liberal thinker. The *Philosophy of Right*, his exoteric presentation, does not represent his true insights. Characteristically, Ilting does not align himself any more with Popper's interpretation, but with Thomas Knox, an early representative of the *Hegelsche Mitte* (Hegel, 1973: 103ff).

In order that Hegel could appear consistently to profess progressive liberal views, Ilting seeks to circumvent his conception of an autocratic monarch in the *Philosophy of Right*. This he tries to attain, first of all, by isolating that particular work and assigning it a unique position among Hegel's politico-philosophical expositions. To devote exclusive attention or attach excessive importance to what Hegel wrote there is to be avoided. The external pressures suffered by Hegel during the time he was redacting this work 'obscured' his internal arguments (ibid.: 106). Hegel's progressive liberal *Grundkonzeption*, in evidence immediately before and after 1821, cannot be forestalled by an understandable and only temporary obfuscation. Second, within the *Philosophy of Right* itself, Ilting finds evidence of views that are closer to classical republicanism, to Attic democracy and the Roman republic (Ilting, 1977: 125). Ilting acknowledges that 'Hegel's republican conception of the state comes into conflict with the historical powers of his day . . . [A]t the time of the restoration, the monarchs of the European states claimed that they exercised underived rights of sovereignty' (ibid.: 123). But Hegel 'circumvented this conflict by accepting the legitimacy of the "monarchical principle" ' (ibid.: 124). Acceptance of the monarchical principle, as will be shown below, is definitely not the way to circumvent the problem. On the contrary, it signals a renunciation of republican views and a shift towards monarchical absolutism (see Hocevar, 1968: 207). But Ilting maintains that in this 're-working' (Hegel, 1973: 64) of the *Philosophy of Right*, Hegel was not 'interested in bringing forth a new conception which could fit the policies of the Restoration, but only retouched the existing text, and tried to conceal its actual meaning' (ibid.: 82). When the danger subsided, Ilting surmises, the cosmetic plaster peeled off and the original *Grundkonzeption* came to light again, as is evident in the lectures Hegel later gave in Berlin.

Ilting's critics have objected to his attempts to restrict Hegel's conservative views to the *Philosophy of Right* of 1821. The authoritarian demeanour of Hegel's monarch is not merely a façade, a 'retouching' by means of which he attempted to conceal his original liberal *Grundkonzeption*, still breathing under the heavy conservative makeup. Hegel's critics have stressed the continuity of his politico-philosophical argument. Rolf-Peter Horstmann maintains that Ilting faced two options: either contend that Hegel's conception of an absolutist monarch, as presented in his *Philosophy of Right*, was incompatible with his earlier and later esoteric expositions; or state that those seemingly incompatible positions were merely two different applications or translations of one and the same continuous *Grundposition* (Horstmann, 1974: 242). Ilting opted for the first alternative. Horstmann thinks that the second one, defended earlier by Haym and Rosenzweig, is the right choice. Continuity is confirmed by the fact that the conception of an absolutist monarch cannot be restricted to the Berlin period, but extends to the Jena period. Hegel's own continuous *Grundposition*, he concedes, was not exempt from internal contradictions, notwithstanding possible accommodation to his changed circumstances in Berlin (ibid.: 244).

Henning Ottmann, for his part, opposes to Ilting what he refers to as the *Kontinuitäts-Argument* (Ottmann, 1977: 230, n. 8; see also n. 40). But Ottmann, unlike Horstmann, recognizes that Hegel, in his *Philosophy of Right*, envisioned a monarch who was a purely formal, empty instance of power: 'the monarchy of 1820 is explicitly a non-arbitrary instance of power' (1977: 234). The monarch could hold the power to decide in the last instance, but his decisions were always empty. Ottmann explicitly defends the continuity of Hegel's political thought from the Jena period right through the entire Berlin period, and denies that there was an accommodation on the part of Hegel to the crypto-absolutist policies of the Restoration. Specifically, Ottmann disputes Ilting's exoteric conception of the monarch by bringing to the fore clear instances showing that already in his 1818/19 Berlin lectures Hegel maintained the very same conception of the monarch he held in the *Philosophy of Right* (Ottmann, 1977: 234; see Kervégan, 2003: 19). In spite of the continuity Ottmann sees in Hegel's liberal *Grundkonzeption*, he recognizes that some logical inconsistencies subsisted within his systematic exposition, but did not further elaborate this point (ibid.: 235). One should also note that, in trying to defend a liberal reading of Hegel's political philosophy, Ottmann ends up turning Ilting's thesis upside down – the writings of the Jena period appear to him to be more illiberal than the *Philosophy of Right* (ibid.: 242).

Of these criticisms of Ilting's position, I find Horstmann's Hobbesian reading of Hegel the more compelling. Ottmann focuses on the notion of the monarch, without realizing that all formal inconsistencies would vanish were the monarch, and the rational state built around him, understood as derived from the irrational principle of particularity constitutive of civil society. Though Hegel criticizes the modern theory of natural rights, which he finds one-sided, abstract and thus incapable of assuming the holistic perspective furnished by *Sittlichkeit*, he acknowledges its capacity 'adequately to reflect the specific conditions under which the social reality of the modern age has developed' (Horstmann, 2004: 217–18). For this reason one ought to understand that the realm of civil society holds a central place in Hegel's political philosophy, 'and precisely for the purpose of demonstrating the necessity of the state' (ibid.: 232). If inconsistencies remain within Hegel's continuous *Grundposition*, they cannot be explained as prudential accommodations to changed historical circumstances.

Inconsistencies may be resolved when the role of the monarchy, and that of the state in general, is not allowed to monopolize one's attention. The centrality of Hegel's conception of civil society for the configuration of his political philosophy must be reaffirmed. Civil society is designed according to a liberal blueprint that acknowledges the subjective freedom of individuals. Subjective freedom translates into the abstract right to acquire property and enter into contractual agreements. Ilting evokes Macpherson's possessive freedom to define Hegel's subjective freedom (Ilting, 1971: 92).[5] Individuals belong to and actively participate in civil society qua possessive individualists.

Neither Ottmann nor Horstmann challenge the key theoretical assumption that underlies Ilting's argumentation. Ilting rightly recognizes Hegel's affirmation of the monarchical principle in his *Philosophy of Right* and interprets this both as a concession to Prussia's restoration policies and as a betrayal of his own liberal progressive views. He assumes that 'the doctrine of the monarchical principle is incompatible with the natural rights *Grundkonzeption* that defines Hegel's political philosophy' (Hegel, 1973: 108). My own reading of Hegel's political philosophy challenges this assumption. The modern theory of natural rights, particularly Hobbes's version of it, is not refractory to royalism. Ilting, following Carl Schmitt, distinguishes between liberalism and democracy,[6] but does not acknowledge that an affinity may be drawn between liberal premises and authoritarian conclusions (Ilting, 1971: 103; see also note 36; see Hayek, 1960: 103). Recognition of the possibility of authoritarian transcriptions of liberalism should allow one to see that Hegel consistently defends the authority of an absolutist monarch as the best safeguard against the revolutionary democratization of civil society.[7]

II

In 1983, two additional sets of notes from Hegel's lectures on *Rechtsphilosophie* imparted in 1817–18 (Heidelberg) and in 1819–20 (Berlin), were published by Ilting and Dieter Henrich (Hegel, 1983a, 1983b). According to Ilting, these lecture notes confirmed the view he had advanced earlier, namely that the esoteric, not the exoteric, was the authentic Hegel. His views on the role of the monarch as they appear in the Homeyer lecture notes coincided with the ones expressed by Hegel in the newly discovered ones. A novelty was the extent of Hegel's acquaintance with the political and constitutional events in Restoration France (see Hegel, 1983a: 156), and his agreement with the political strategy of the French liberal *doctrinaires* and the constitutional approach of Benjamin Constant (Ilting, 1983: 23–5). Presumably, the meetings he held with Victor Cousin during the latter's visit to Heidelberg in the summer and autumn of 1817 were his immediate source of information.[8] Interest in French affairs was not hollow curiosity on his part, but responded to shared experiences of ideological readjustment in post-Napoleonic Europe. Part of that readjustment was given urgency by the sight of a restored Bourbon monarch agreeing to be bound constitutionally. According to Hegel, Louis XVIII's constitutional Charte, issued by royal decree on 4 June 1814, was a 'beacon' which incorporated 'all the liberal ideas the national spirit had developed since the time of the Revolution' (Hegel, 1995: 240–1). Ilting is right in emphasizing the impact of French constitutional affairs on Hegel's political philosophy.[9]

This French Charte inaugurated the notion of a limited monarchy and for that reason liberals hailed it as a model constitution. Its first twelve articles consecrated advances made by the Revolution (legal equality, individual freedom, religious freedom, freedom of the press, inviolable private property). Also, because monarchical rights and duties were defined by the Charte, it seemed that the place assigned to the monarch was not above or beyond the constitution, but within it. Executive power was placed in the hands of the monarch (art. 13) and legislative power was to be 'exercised collectively by the king, the chamber of peers and the chamber of departmental deputies' (art. 15).

The separation of powers was made explicit by article 48 which stipulated that taxes could not be collected without the consent of both chambers. This introduced a severe limitation of the monarch's executive powers. More than a monarchy, the political system envisaged by the Charte appeared to be a 'dyarchy' (Prélot, 1984: 390–3; see Stolleis, 2001: 61–2).

Hand in hand with these liberal features, the Charte also espoused plain authoritarian views. To begin with, it recognized the monarch as the subject of sovereignty.[10] The monarch was in charge of appointing ministers (art. 14), who were responsible to him and not to a legislature elected on a very narrow property franchise. In its Preamble, the Charte determined that 'l'autorité tour entière réside en France dans la personne du roi' and that the monarch voluntarily conceded (*octroi*) his subjects a constitutional charta (Capefigue, 1843: 210).[11] It also stated that the foundation of monarchical power was not the people but divine providence (Rosanvallon, 1994: 250). All this was intended to rebuke revolutionary doctrine, and particularly the 1791 constitution, interpreted as an anti-monarchical document designating the nation as the subject of constituent power (see Boldt, 1975: 25). The monarchical principle, namely the assertion of 'the superiority and pre-existence of royal power with respect to the constitution' (Kaufmann, 1906: 42), was designed to offset popular sovereignty.[12] One should add that the Charte severely limited the franchise to approximately 100,000 voters in a country of thirty million inhabitants.

Criticized by both royalists and liberals, ideological support for Louis XVIII's constitutional design came from the liberal *doctrinaires*.[13] Two *doctrinaires*, Montesquiou and Beugnot, were involved in the redaction of the Charte, and the intellectual leaders of the group, Royer-Collard and Guizot, participated in the government in a ministerial capacity. *Doctrinaire* influence was conspicuous until the assassination of the Duc de Berry in February 1820, which led to the fall of the Decazes ministry and the beginning of ultra-royalist ascendancy. Ilting postulates that Hegel's political position in the period between 1817 and 1820, prior to the publication of the *Philosophy of Right*, coincided with that of the *doctrinaires*, but that his 'agreement extended only to their political strategy' (Ilting, 1983: 25). When it came to constitutional matters, he claims that Hegel abandoned the more cautious posture of the *doctrinaires*, and endorsed the 'radically liberal' reading that Constant gave of the Charte (ibid.: 25). His evidence rests on Hegel's attribution of a passive governing role to the monarch, and an active one to his ministers. In his lecture notes, Hegel acknowledged that 'rulers do almost nothing but merely add their signatures' (Hegel, 1983a: 163). He added that 'in a well-constituted monarchy, the choice of ministers is not a matter of arbitrary decision by the ruler' (ibid.: 167). On the basis of this, Ilting maintains that Hegel went beyond adopting the notion of constitutional monarchy and did embrace parliamentary monarchy in the British style (1983: 26). This coincides with what the *Hegelsche Mitte* has maintained all along.

But Ilting's attempt to approximate the esoteric Hegel to Constant's liberalism proves to be misguided (see Siep, 1986: 403–4). Constant proposed the separation of the passive power of the monarch from the active power of ministers, and conceived of the former as a mere *pouvoir neutre et intermédiaire*.[14] According to article 13, while ministers were responsible for their decisions, the neutrality of the monarch ensured his non-responsibility and inviolability. The main role attributed to the monarch was the preservation of the unity of the state in the face of conflicts arising between the executive and legislative powers. Constant thought that a figure that floated above human concerns, inhabiting a sphere reserved for majesty, would be its best guarantee.[15] But Constant did not think that granting the monarch a *pouvoir neutre* meant that he was a 'higher third', and not merely a 'neutral third'.[16] In his view, the monarch could not transcend the limits defined by the constitution. The monarch could not be seen as the subject of *pouvoir constituant*. Constant consistently defended the principle of popular sovereignty, unambiguously rejected by the *doctrinaires* (see Bagge, 1952: 101–2; Holmes, 1984: 150) and Hegel. This meant that he could move forward and accept a parliamentary democracy, something that neither the *doctrinaires* nor Hegel could agree to. The *doctrinaires* underscored the sovereign authority of Louis XVIII, and Hegel did the same with the prince he placed at the apex of his state. The *doctrinaires* were pragmatic politicians whose only principle was to avoid acting on principle. Ardent defenders of freedom, they defended monarchical authority with equal ardour. Their program may be summarized as follows: 'Établissez l'autorité d'abord, puis crées les libertés comme contrepois' (see Bagge, 1952: 99–101). Contrary to Constant, they attributed a political role to the monarch. Inviolability did not render monarchs impotent. Monarchs had a will and possessed the right to see it come through (Prélot, 1984: 401).[17] In this respect, the Hegel of the Heidelberg and Berlin lectures was, contrary to what Ilting asserts, much closer to the *doctrinaires* than to Constant. As Cousin recognized, Hegel was profoundly liberal and could not be said to be a republican. And he explicitly acknowledged that Hegel had great affinities with Royer-Collard[18] (Cousin, 1866: 616–17).

If Hegel had great affinities with the *doctrinaire* liberals, and if Ilting errs in assimilating his position to that of Constant's, the contrast between an esoteric and an exoteric Hegel, as Horstmann noted above, loses much of its force. It also follows that his exoteric conception of the role of the prince in the *Philosophy of Right* need not have been as insincere and opportunist as portrayed by the *Hegelsche Mitte*. The Carlsbad decrees (August 1819) and the assassination of the Duc de Berry (February 1820) may have impressed on him the need to actualize and reinforce the authoritarian potential of the *doctrinaire* position. In no case did this *doctrinaire* rapprochement of liberal and authoritarian themes seem paradoxical to Hegel. The deontological liberalism of Constant was refractory to these kinds of authoritarian tendencies. Evidence for this lies in his strict adherence to legal formalism and his rejection of utilitarian justifications that would allow violations of the constitution in order to save it (see Campagna, 2001: 570–1). By contrast, Hegel acknowledges that 'formalities should not impede right, and in the conflict between right and formalities, formalities are to take second place' (Hegel, 1995: 201). In the *Philosophy of Right* he also concedes that, in the face of contingencies, a decision should be reached 'no matter how this is done' (§214).

The monarchical principle, introduced by the Charte, was promptly adopted during 1818–19 by southern German states (Bavaria, Baden, Wurtemberg). It found its first and exemplary expression in article 1 of section 2 of the Bavarian constitution of 26 May 1818 (Boldt, 1975: 15). This article proclaimed that the king was the supreme head of state who unified all the powers of the state and was both sacred and inviolable (Huber, 1970: 156). The *Schlußakte* of the Congress of Vienna (15 May 1820) gave definitive sanction to this principle in its article 57, by stating that 'all governmental authority must remain concentrated in the head of state, and only in the exercise of certain specific rights may the sovereign be bound by a corporative constitution' (Huber, 1970: 99; see Huber, 1978: 156; Böckenförde, 1991: 90–1). Undoubtedly, these constitutional developments in France and Germany influenced Hegel's argument in the *Philosophy of Right*.[19] But one should also recognize that these political events were filtered by Hegel's own philosophical system of ideas and accommodated within an argumentative structure that in many respects pre-dated the circumstantial direction those events had taken at the time he was preparing the *Philosophy of Right* (see Boldt, 2000: 175). This criss-crossing of philosophical ideas and political realities meant that sometimes the political institutions adopted by Hegel could make little sense philosophically, and vice versa (ibid.: 182).

In relation to the influence that political events had on Hegel's systematic writing, Ilting presciently wrote, in his edition of the Heidelberg lectures, that 'in the future, whoever wants to study the *Philosophy of Right* will do well to begin with an investigation of these three lectures' (Ilting, 1983: 5). His advice has been followed without much controversy by contemporary adherents of the *Hegelsche Mitte* who dismiss the exoteric in favour of the esoteric Hegel. Lately, this view has been reasserted by Alan Patten who has defended the view that, in the Preface to his *Philosophy of Right*, Hegel admits that 'the book is meant to accompany his lectures, suggesting that he himself took the lectures to be an authoritative statement of his own views'. And he adds, reiterating Ilting's argument, that due to the censorship imposed by authorities in Prussia, the lectures 'offer a more authoritative statement of Hegel's view than do the published writings' (Patten, 1999: 6, n. 9; see Hegel, 1974b: 58).

Earlier, Mark Tunick offered a more guarded view. After summarizing Ilting's position according to which 'Hegel was no royalist, but a protestant, liberal, pro-French Revolution, pro-English freedom constitutionalist', and noting that this view has not become consensus, he refuses to dismiss the *Philosophy of Right* as a feigned and inauthentic document (Tunick, 1992: 10). In his own exposition he proceeds to rely on both Hegel's lectures and the published text of the *Philosophy of Right*. For my part I agree with Horstmann that, though the lectures notes greatly contribute to clarifying Hegel's own political interests and compromises (Horstmann, 1974: 250), they are subservient to the published text. One has to assume the responsibility of an author with respect to the text he or she decides to present to the public.[20] To do otherwise would be to fail to esteem their dignity as authors.

2 • Freedom and authority: *complexio oppositorum*

> . . . *it must be owned, that liberty is the perfection of civil society; but still authority must be acknowledged essential to its very existence.*
>
> (Hume, 1894)

> *Because I have been a man of order, my efforts were directed towards the attainment of a real, not a deceptive freedom.*
>
> (Metternich[1])

> *Et il [Hegel] ne séparait pas la liberté de la royauté.*
>
> (Cousin, 1866: 616–17)

My aim in this chapter is to probe the arguments presented by Terry Pinkard, Alan Patten and Frederick Neuhouser in favour of the point of view defended by the *Hegelsche Mitte*. According to Pinkard, Anglo-American philosophers have for the most part rejected Hegel and derided him 'as humbug, poppycock, maybe even fraud' (Pinkard, 2000: xiii). Surely the aspiration of clarity and rigour on the part of Russell's heirs is bound to be frustrated by the idiosyncratic, tortured style of Hegel's systematic works. But this is not the more serious charge. Hegel has been blamed 'for the German authoritarianism that led to the First World War, and for the nationalist worship of the state . . . that led to the Second World War' (ibid.: p. xii). In Popper's eyes, he is ultimately responsible for the rise of Nazi totalitarianism. Pinkard is particularly offended by this misrepresentation, and rightly so. Hegel, he argues, is the first great philosopher to 'make modernity itself the object of his thought' (ibid.: p. x). Since individual freedom is the goal of modern life, Hegel is first and foremost a philosopher of freedom. To prove this point Pinkard writes about the life and times of Hegel. If 'as a man is outwardly, so is he inwardly', his biography is quintessentially a philosophical defence of Hegel's philosophy of freedom.

This use of Hegel's biography as an argument for freedom coincides with recent systematic projects in which freedom is also represented as Hegel's central normative value. In *Hegel's Idea of Freedom*, Patten holds that freedom is the key value of Hegel's social philosophy. And Neuhouser thinks that the rationality of the institutions recognized in Hegel's social philosophy rests on the 'essential roles' they play 'in realizing the central value of freedom' (2000: 4). This should set the stage for an attempt to determine that Hegel's social philosophy acknowledges authority as a companion normative standard to freedom.

I

At 16, in his Stuttgart diaries, we get a glimpse of Hegel's fascination with the figure of the *Popularphilosoph* composing Enlightenment themes. In this capacity he sought to do philosophy in a manner accessible to the educated public and to participate in a project that he would never abandon – the creation of an enlightened, modern Germany. Later, as a theology student at the university in Tübingen, then no more than a Protestant seminary, the French Revolution gave more urgency to this liberal project. Together with his friends Hölderlin and Schelling, he welcomed the defeat of the duke of Braunschweig at Valmy on 20 September 1792, for it allowed the revolutionary winds of freedom to penetrate Germany. His commitment to the Revolution deepened as he saw in it 'a newer version of the older Protestant Reformation, destined to lead society to a better ethical condition' (Pinkard, 2000: 26). In Hegel's earliest essay on the religion of the people, Pinkard detects 'his devotion to the Revolution and its cause of freedom, and . . . his emerging love of ancient Greece, into which he [had] stirred various Rousseauian themes' (ibid.: 43).

Germany's pre-eminent liberal philosopher at the time was Kant. Though influenced by Kantian ideas in the seminary, Hegel continued to think he could accomplish his project as a man of letters, not as a philosopher in the strict sense. In 1795, he wrote that a revolution in Germany would proceed from the completion of Kantian principles. But at this point, in Berne, this meant for him 'only the *application* of Kantian philosophy in a "popular" way' (ibid.: 61). Later, in Frankfurt, influenced by Hölderlin's Fichtean orientation, he redirected his intellectual course and also his writing style. The intricacies of post-Kantianism and the pre-eminence it attained within universities, propelled philosophy to the very centre of academic life and forced Hegel to abandon his idea of becoming an unattached, free man of letters.

Seeking a university career he arrived in Jena on 21 January 1801, at Schelling's invitation. The university, under Fichte's leadership, housed the post-Kantian avant-garde. Inspired by a revolutionary need to advance freedom, Fichte sought to demolish Kant's thing-in-itself, the last substantive barrier faced by the free spontaneity of the Kantian subject. The Jena Romantics radicalized Fichte's subjective freedom with their theory of irony. Free from substantive ties, as ironic artists they could distance themselves from the authoritative rules of classical art and deconstruct the world. Hegel concluded that this kind of freedom (he would later refer to it as 'negative freedom' or 'abstract freedom') necessarily led to a frenzy of anarchy and destruction. By 1805–6, 'like many people in France, who had become tired of the anarchy, Hegel too continued at this time to be seduced by the idea of a strong leader, a "Theseus", a Napoleon of the Germans who would do the equivalent of founding a new Athens in Germany' (Pinkard, 2000: 195). Freedom's deconstructive upsurge was responsible for bringing down an old, oppressive social order, but history now called for a new authority and the fashioning of stable political institutions. The Code Napoleon that went into effect in France and parts of Germany on 21 March 1804 gave a rational foundation to the new authority. To think that freedom alone was Hegel's basic normative standard misses the attention he lavished on authority, elevated in his works to a status on a par with freedom's foundational quality.

The *Phenomenology of Spirit* is the final, decisive stage of the post-Kantian response to Jacobi's attack on Kant. Jacobi alleged that scepticism about the existence of things-in-themselves could only lead to wholesale, corrosive nihilism. To demonstrate reason's self-sufficiency, Hegel traversed the 'path of doubt' and hit upon a way 'in which a thoroughgoing skepticism undid itself, and reason's commitments were thereby established and secured' (Pinkard, 2000: 205). The itinerary guiding this path leads to the set of normative pre-conditions that determine our consciousness from its bare beginnings. The realization that those norms are constructs of our private understanding plunges us into the nihilism feared by Jacobi. The veritable state of nature that ensues ceases when one of the parties at war submits to the authority of the other by recognizing the normative value of survival. The precariousness of this standard, acknowledged by the slave but not by the master, indicates the normative failure of relations of mastery and slavery. The argument shifts to historical considerations and focuses on the 'cultural crisis that followed the demise of the slave-owning societies of antiquity' (ibid.: 207). After a number of failed attempts to harmonize authority and freedom, 'the discipline of Christian worship throughout the mediaeval period . . . prepared the way for an assertion of self-activity through the application of impersonal reason to the world' (ibid.: 208). This was a precarious equilibrium. Modern life saw a challenge to the authority of reason arising from reason's own reflective self-doubt. This disposition 'undermined the alternative claims of authority that appeared within that way of life' and placed us in the 'path of despair' (ibid.). Kant was able to rescue 'modern reason's claim to authority' (ibid.: 209). But the liberal self-sufficiency granted to reason was empty; its intrinsic negativity was incapable of producing anything worthy of allegiance. Kant's vindication of the authority of reason succumbed to Jacobi's challenge. The stage was now set for a new beginning. Hegel introduces the section on *Geist*, where he retraces his steps, restates the ancient failure to harmonize freedom and authority, and advances towards a final stage of 'fully modern Christian reconciliation', where we are all 'obligated to act on reasons that can be shared by all' (Pinkard, 2000: 216). Thus, the failed *Popularphilosoph* had become 'the systematic philosopher of *Geist* and modern life' (ibid.: 220).

Hegel wrote the *Phenomenology* hoping to secure a professorship at the university, but Napoleon's triumph at the battle of Jena in 1806 put an end to that prospect. When he secured a job as editor of a Bamberg newspaper, he continued to endorse its pro-Napoleonic editorial line (Pinkard, 2000: 247). The 'liberal monarchical constitution' (ibid.: 245), sought by Napoleon for Germany, was congenial to Hegel's idiosyncratic liberalism. In 1808, he accepted a position as rector of the Nuremberg Gymnasium. Pinkard observes that a 'philosophical emphasis on freedom' determined his pedagogical practice, which was marked by a 'characteristic philosophical junction of discipline . . . and freedom' (ibid.: 305). To avoid the appearance of inconsistency, Hegel did not accept the 'fully specious point that discipline and obedience are really freedom' (ibid.: 305), seemingly oblivious that, in his *Philosophy of Right*, he would recognize that 'the individual finds his liberation in duty' (§149).

In 1816, after eight years as a schoolteacher in Nuremberg, Hegel finally secured a position at the University of Heidelberg. His fame being well-established, he then received a fateful call from Berlin, where he arrived on October 1818. He was hard at work on his book on political philosophy when a theology student murdered the conservative publicist Kotzebue on 23 March 1819, precipitating a major crisis in German politics. The tragic events that followed would turn Hegel into a controverted *Popularphilosoph* until his death in 1831 and beyond. The Kotzebue affair concerned the end of the Stein and Hardenberg reform era in Prussia and the onset of Metternich's repressive, authoritarian policies. These included a strict censorship on all university publications, the persecution of students and the expulsion of Hegel's colleagues de Wette and Fries. When his *Philosophy of Right* passed the censors and appeared in 1820, had Hegel renounced his liberal views? Was he now endorsing Metternich's version of the monarchical principle, the authoritarianism reviled by his Anglo-American critics? Did the powers of his monarch extend much beyond 'dotting the "i's" on legislation presented by his ministers' (Pinkard, 2000: 486)? Pinkard's philosopher of freedom responds negatively to all these queries.

At the same time, Pinkard detects a dualism in Hegel's personality. 'He defended the government's dismissal of de Wette and Fries, *and* he openly drank to the storming of the Bastille. He led a cozy, Biedermeier life, *and* he went to the Faschings balls decked out in a Venetian cape and mask' (ibid.: 453). Pinkard traces this dualism to two very different features in his personal experience: 'the *universalism* of his upbringing . . . and the *particularism* of hometown life' (ibid.: 198). And he hints that Hegel thought that this either–or could not be overcome 'except through the intervention of some "Theseus" ' (ibid.: 199). This is a view Hegel shared with French *doctrinaires* like Cousin and Mignet (with whom he also shared a dinner during a visit to Paris in 1827), who espoused Louis XVIII's constitutional monarchy, a free society along with a strong 'Theseus' as apex and beginning of the political whole.

If Hegel could successfully combine contradictory elements in his personality, it seems plausible that his political thought could embrace both liberalism *and* authoritarianism, as is evident in his last essay *The English Reform Bill*. Pinkard rightly identifies Hegel's 'big issue' at stake in the Reform Bill, namely 'whether modern political life necessarily undermines the very authority it needs to make good on its promises' (ibid.: 651). He recognizes that true freedom can be sustained only if concrete authoritative institutions are acknowledged as valid. And he is also aware that attainment of this aim is beset by immense difficulties, of which Hegel is also much aware. The condition for the possibility of true freedom is authority, but 'obedience to law . . . when demanded by the authorities . . . is seen to run counter to freedom. The right to command . . . is contrary to equality' (Hegel, 1964b: 329). Pinkard thinks that Hegel's solution lies 'in the recognition that for the government of a free people, "more is needed . . . than principles" ' (2000: 651). But the 'more' that Hegel recommends, namely the monarchical principle, escapes Pinkard's attention unnoticed. Hegel thought that the Reform Bill was popular in England because it further weakened the influence of the Crown. 'Jealousy of the power of the throne [is] that most stubborn of English prejudices' (Hegel, 1964b: 300). In his view, liberalism would be able to withstand the challenge posed by the abstract egalitarian principles by boldly asserting the monarchical principle. In Germany, true freedom did not subvert the very authority it required to make good on its promise. This is the example England needed to follow.

II

Hegel's most quoted definition of freedom appears in H. G. Hotho's lecture notes taken in 1822–3, two years after the *Philosophy of Right* appeared in print. After describing the initial two moments in the development of the will, Hegel states: 'Then the third moment is that "I" is with itself (*bei sich*) in its limitation, in this other . . . This, then, is the concrete concept of freedom' (§7A; see Wood, 1990: 45–6; Williams, 1997: 126–7; Patten, 1999: 43; Neuhouser, 2000: 19–20). To be with oneself conveys the idea of lack of determination, which corresponds to a conventional view of freedom as absence of impediments and openness to unlimited opportunities. But to be with oneself and simultaneously be 'in this other' implies a limitation to freedom. The presence of this 'other' introduces a determining, authoritative element that is external to the self. By advancing to the third unifying moment, Hegel intended to reconcile the free self with the determining other. The preceding moments define two separate aspects of the will – the will as freedom and the will's authoritative other – both moments abstractly facing each other as opposites. The third moment brings them together and constitutes 'the concrete concept of freedom'. In H. G. Hotho's lecture notes we read: 'While [the will] limits itself, it yet remains with itself, and does not lose its hold of the universal. This is, then, the concrete concept of freedom, whereas the two previous moments have been found to be thoroughly abstract and one-sided' (§7A). Concrete freedom reconciles not two configurations of freedom, but freedom and its opposite – authority.

An accurate reading of how Hegel defines the two abstract moments of the will is essential for an understanding of his concrete concept of freedom. The first abstract moment presents a purely internal realm of the will where it is with itself alone. This conveys a picture of the self enjoying the full autonomy that results from complete detachment and the absence of guidance by an alien authority.[2] Hegel refers to this moment of the will as 'subjective freedom', which he also characterizes as 'negative freedom' (§5) and 'abstract freedom' (§149).

> The will contains (α) the element of pure indeterminacy or the 'I''s pure reflection into itself, in which every limitation, every content, whether present immediately through nature, through needs, desires and drives, or given and determined in some other way, is dissolved; this is the limitless infinity of absolute abstraction or universality, the pure thinking of one self. (§5)

In the second moment the self ceases to be with itself and appears to be fully determined and saturated by otherness and externality. Hegel does not refer to this stage as a moment of freedom, but as a moment of the will under the weight of determination.

> (ß) In the same way, 'I' is the transition from undifferentiated indeterminacy to differentiation, determination, and the positing of a determinacy as a content and object. – This content may further be given by nature, or generated by the concept of spirit. Through this positing of itself as something determinate, 'I' steps into existence (*Dasein*) in general – the absolute moment of the finitude or particularization of the 'I'. (§6)

Robert Williams detects an authoritative undertone in the description of this second moment. He writes: 'In identifying itself with its object, the will "loses itself" as freedom or is not yet aware of its freedom; immersion in its object is an entanglement that corresponds to naïveté, loss of perspective, and so on. It is a will without a will of its own' (1997: 126).[3] Yet Williams still refers to it as the moment of 'positive freedom' (ibid.: 126). Similarly, Alan Patten thinks that concrete or absolute freedom 'consists in the unity of two one-sided forms of freedom' (1999: 43) and defines the second moment as 'objective (or occasionally substantive) freedom', and does not see it as a sort of authoritative determination. Objective freedom is the companion piece of the first moment which manifests Hegel's conception of 'subjective freedom' (ibid.: 43). As separate moments, they constitute 'the two elements of freedom' (Patten, 2003: 389). This is not a minor point. What is at stake here is the significance of freedom in Hegel's political philosophy. If the moment of determination and differentiation were to be defined in terms of authority instead of freedom, this would substantively alter the concrete result attained by Hegel in his dialectical deduction. The third moment, the synthesis of the preceding ones, would bring about the reconciling of freedom and authority, and not simply the distinction between two elements of freedom. It would mean that the holistic concept of the will, defined by Hegel as being at home in determination in §7, reconciles freedom and authority:

> (γ) The will is the unity of both these moments – particularity reflected into itself and thereby restored to universality. It is individuality, the self-determination of the 'I', in that it posits itself as the negative of itself, and at the same time remains with itself (*bei sich*), that is, in its identity with itself and universality; and in this determination, it joins together with itself alone. (§7)

Patten acknowledges that, in a few marginal texts, Hegel recognized an 'important tension between freedom and authority' (1999: 67). He maintains that, if Hegel was attempting to reconcile freedom with the authority of the state, he did so 'only in a very weak sense' (ibid.: 68). That is, on condition that the authority of the state were rational, and recognized as such by those who obey its orders. But this cannot be thought of as a reconciliation, even in a very weak sense. Patten does not take into account that recognition of the rationality of state authority obtains when the synthesis of freedom and authority (the third moment of the dialectic of the will) has already taken place. In this case, recognition is the result of reconciliation, not its premise. A reconciliation of the already reconciled is pointless.

My argument rests on the assumption that the second moment of the will, its particularization, occurs as an external determination. To the subjectively free will this determination appears as an 'other', as the manifestation of an objectively alien power. Together with freedom, this yet unrecognized power or authority is one of the components of ethical freedom or *Sittlichkeit*. Later on, when Hegel expounds the many meanings of subjectivity and objectivity, one of the meanings of subjectivity coincides with the notion of subjective or negative freedom defined in §5. This is subjectivity as the 'absolute unity of the self-consciousness with itself, in which the self-consciousness, as "I = I", is totally inward and abstractly dependent upon itself' (§25). Correspondingly, one of the meanings of objectivity coincides with the authority imposed by alien determination. Hegel writes: 'the objective will, inasmuch as it lacks the infinite form of self-consciousness, is the will immersed in its object or condition, whatever the content of the latter may be – it is the will of the child, the ethical will, or the will of the slave, the superstitious will, etc.' (§26). This is not objective freedom, but a will that is totally immersed in its external object. Hegel illustrates this situation with the example of the child under the authority of its parents, or the slave under the authority of a master. In H. G. Hotho's lecture notes, Hegel expands and clarifies the meaning of these examples. The will of the child is said 'to be founded on trust and lacks subjective freedom'. Similarly, the slave is said to be 'a will with no will of its own'. In both cases their 'actions are guided by an alien authority *(fremde Autorität)*' (§26A). This should show that Hegel cannot conceive of concrete or absolute freedom as the synthesis of subjective and objective freedom, as Patten postulates. Concrete ethical freedom or *Sittlichkeit* is the *complexio oppositorum* of freedom and authority.

In §258, Hegel explicitly argues that concrete or absolute freedom is the synthesis of subjective and objective freedom. Patten takes this to be the lynchpin for his contention that freedom is the sole central notion of Hegel's political philosophy. Hegel writes:

> Considered in the abstract, rationality consists in general in the unity and inter-penetration of universality and individuality. Here, in a concrete sense and in terms of its content, it consists in the unity of objective freedom (i.e. of the universal substantial will) and subjective freedom (as the freedom of individual knowledge and of the will in pursuit of particular ends). And in terms of its form, it consists in self-determining action in accordance with laws and principles based on thought and hence universal. (§258)

This must be read in the context of Hegel's exposition on the state. The state is the end result of the dialectic of will which has now reached its goal – the concrete notion of freedom, or substantive freedom, the definitive synthesis of freedom and authority.[4] The state is where the individual 'has objective freedom for the first time' (Hegel, 1983b: 209–10). What interests Hegel in §§257 and 258 is to show that substantial freedom does not mean the annihilation of subjective freedom, but merely its overcoming in the sense of *Aufhebung*. Patten connects this passage with his interpretation of §7A, where Hegel, as we have seen, defines freedom as the being with oneself in an other. Patten writes:

> for this state of being with myself to be achieved, Hegel thinks that two distinct conditions must be satisfied. I must be both (i) subjectively free, and (ii) objectively free with respect to my end (§258). When these conditions are both satisfied, then I am with my self in my end or 'concretely' (subjectively + objectively) free. (2003: 387)

Patten clearly interprets 'objective freedom' as the second moment in the development of the will, which, conjoined with subjective freedom, yields concrete or absolute freedom. But for Hegel 'objective freedom' is not one of the elements of concrete or absolute freedom. Objective freedom by itself is concrete or substantial freedom – the synthesis of freedom and authority.[5] The state, as the 'actuality of concrete freedom' (§260), represents the authoritative other recognized by individuals as their own, where individuals now feel at home and with themselves. When Hegel, in §258, postulates the 'unity of objective freedom (i.e. of the universal substantial will) and subjective freedom (as the freedom of individual knowledge and of the will in pursuit of particular ends)' what he means is that *Sittlichkeit* (or concrete absolute freedom) contains subjective freedom as one of its elements.

III

In his book *Foundations of Hegel's Social Theory*, Neuhouser uses the term 'foundations' to refer to the basic normative standards that sustain arguments in favour of a rational social order. He maintains that in the case of Hegel's political philosophy the basic normative standard is freedom. In Neuhouser's view, Hegelian freedom has three manifestations: personal abstract freedom, free moral subjectivity and social (or ethical) freedom. The latter is the object of his foundational study. Neuhouser postulates that Hegel's notion of social freedom has 'deep affinities' with Rousseau's own conception of freedom and its two-part structure (Neuhouser, 2000: 6). The objective component (or objective freedom) takes into account the republican conditions necessary to realize individual freedom. The subjective component (or subjective freedom) responds to a liberal criterion which requires that individuals be able to affirm those freedom-realizing institutions 'as coming from their own will' (ibid.: 8). He, then, raises the question – why is it necessary to regard social freedom or *Sittlichkeit* as composed of two elements (subjective and objective freedom), and why must each of these elements 'be regarded as a kind of freedom in its own right' (ibid.: 53–4)?

In the wake of Wood, Hardimon, Patten and the *Hegelsche Mitte* generally, Neuhouser tries to mollify liberals who recoil at the sight of social freedom, a notion they associate with ominous collective interests and the authoritarianism that stems from the general will. He valiantly defends the view that Hegel is a liberal thinker who has 'important affinities' with Rawls (ibid.: 228). It is therefore important for him, as it was for Patten, to eliminate every possibility that Hegel's *Sittlichkeit*, the central notion of his political philosophy, may be constituted by elements that may not be regarded as a kind of freedom in their own right.

Neuhouser raises the stakes by bringing Rousseau's general will into the picture in an effort to prove his point. In his *Second Discourse*, Rousseau deploys an evolutionary conception of the state of nature which advances through stages of increased personal dependence. While natural individuals remain free, cooperation renders them progressively interdependent. When conflicts arise which lead to a horrible social war, the rich propose rules of justice and peace, and the accumulation of all power in a supreme power. Rousseau's liberal state of nature is surpassed and an authoritarian state is born. Seeking to redress this calamitous conclusion, the *Social Contract* suggests a republican solution to the problems posed by liberalism. Rousseau proposes to harmonize the freedom enjoyed by primitive and savage individuals, with the required but intolerable degree of personal dependence brought forth by civilization. This is attained, in Neuhouser's view, by a 'restructuring of dependence' which involves 'transforming the dependence on individual persons into the dependence on the community as a whole' (ibid.: 73). In acquiring a general will, which becomes their own true will, individuals are able to leave the state of nature behind without loss of freedom. They surrender natural freedom but acquire social freedom. The general will is both an embodiment of freedom and its precondition. From a subjective point of view, in obeying the general will, individuals gain moral freedom and continue to obey only themselves. Objectively, they gain civil freedom. The general will corresponds to the republican rule of law that 'mitigates the freedom-endangering consequences of dependence' (ibid.: 79).

Hegel, according to Neuhouser, formulates a 'conception of social freedom' that has precisely the structure he attributes to 'Rousseau's understanding of political freedom' (ibid.: 81). He acknowledges that central to his investigation is finding an answer to the question, What is social freedom? (ibid.: 52–3). He believes that the answer is to be found 'in Hegel's statement that *Sittlichkeit* consist in "the unity of objective . . . and subjective freedom" (§258)' (Neuhouser, 2000: 53). Like Patten, Neuhouser believes that each of these 'two components' of social freedom or *Sittlichkeit*, is to be understood as a kind of freedom in its own right. He seeks to relate them to the objective and subjective moments of *Sittlichkeit* described by Hegel in §§144 and 146. But the moments of *Sittlichkeit*, objective and subjective, are not two kinds of freedom that can be equated to objective and subjective freedom respectively. The whole of *Sittlichkeit* is social or objective freedom, synthesizing an objective authoritative moment and a subjective moment of liberty.

The following are the two moments of *Sittlichkeit* defined by Hegel. (α) The objective moment 'takes the place of the abstract good' (§144). The abstract good is proper to the moral sphere, and corresponds, therefore, to an empty and purely formal duty, lacking a particular content or a particular end (see §133). In contrast, with *Sittlichkeit* we obtain a concrete duty, which can be 'exalted above subjective opinions and preferences'. We face 'laws and institutions which have being in and for themselves' (§144). Strictly speaking, these laws and institutions are not instances of freedom, but authority. The objective moment of *Sittlichkeit* is not objective freedom, but the objective authority of the concrete duties that emanate from laws and institutions. *Sittlichkeit* as a whole is both freedom *and* authority, that is, 'freedom . . . as a circle of necessity whose moments are the ethical powers which govern the lives of individuals' (§145). Ethical substance is objective in the sense that its laws and powers have 'an absolute authority and power, infinitely more firmly based than the being of nature' (§146). (ß) The subjective moment corresponds to the inner disposition of the members that populate those ethical institutions.

These are not 'something alien to the subject'. Subjects 'bear witness to them' as to their own essence, in a relation, stronger than faith or trust, that becomes constitutive of their own 'identity' (§147).

Socially free individuals do not just identify subjectively with the rational institutions they endorse. Those institutions must be worthy of their endorsement and be so independently of their conscious knowledge. This means, in the first place, that rational ethical institutions, taken holistically, must embody a self-determined will. According to Neuhouser, this is the distinctively Hegelian meaning of objective freedom. Second, the Rousseauean conception, for which 'explicit textual evidence . . . is very difficult to find' (ibid.: 120), defines objective freedom as the social conditions of individual freedom. The ethical institutions envisaged by Hegel make possible or realize 'the more individualistic forms of freedom, most prominently those associated with personhood and moral subjectivity' (ibid.: 120).

Neuhouser acknowledges that Hegel's rejection of the idea of social contract is a stumbling block in his design to bring about a rapprochement with Rousseau. Social contracts are typically liberal devices which assume methodological atomism, namely, the reducibility of collective to individual goods. Contractarianism takes the 'interests of individuals as such' to be the 'final ends of political association' (ibid.: 176). The sovereignty and primacy of individual interests implies that collective goods can retain only an instrumental value for individuals.

To surmount this difficulty Neuhouser postulates that Rousseau's methodological atomism is compatible with the view that individuals may regard their social participation 'as having more than merely instrumental value' (ibid.: 184). This harmonization is brought about by the major 'reconfiguration' undergone by individuals when they leave the state of nature. Upon entering the civil state they are 'transformed' into morally free citizens who 'consistently will the common good because they recognize that their own fundamental interests are best served by doing so' (ibid.: 191). According to Neuhouser, the same educational transformation occurs in Hegel's social theory. One ought to dismiss his critique of Rousseau's social contract for it wrongly assumes that methodological atomism requires the reduction of collective interests to the interests of individuals as such.

Neuhouser's absorbing defence of Hegelian liberalism draws our attention to the 'substantial critical potential' of his social theory (ibid.: 8). Hegel is not an antiquated or inherently reactionary author, and most definitely not totalitarian. On the contrary, Neuhouser shows how Hegel enriches our understanding of a freedom-procuring social order. But it seems odd to base a defence of Hegel's liberalism on Rousseau, whose overtly republican conception of freedom involves a decisive critique of liberalism. An interpretation of the social contract which suggests that the contracting parties undergo a fundamental transformation does not accord with the strictures of methodological atomism. Methodological atomism demands that the legitimate pre-social and fixed attributes of individuals be preserved when they enter society. But by distinguishing between natural and moral freedom Rousseau subverts methodological atomism and de-legitimizes natural claims (see Gauthier, 1977). In his hands, the social contract becomes a republican device meant to transcend the problems generated by the *Second Discourse*'s atomism.

Again, Neuhouser does not clearly identify what counts as Hegel's liberal moment. On the one hand, he acknowledges that Hegel 'does not appear to be (and indeed is not) a methodological atomist' like Rousseau (Neuhouser, 2000: 199). He postulates the 'irreducibility of collective goods' (ibid.: 203) which distances him from the liberal camp. On the other hand, he believes that Hegel omits 'an antecedent account of the fundamental interests individuals have as such' (ibid.: 199), and therefore does not need to deploy a state of nature. This does not take into account the extent to which Hegel's treatment of abstract right represents a veritable state of nature situation, preserved and not simply negated within the theory of *Sittlichkeit*.

By dismissing the concept of the monarch as a mere 'institutional detail' (ibid.: 3) devoid of normative content, Neuhouser disregards the issue of political legitimacy. By forsaking the democratic legitimacy espoused by Rousseau and granting his monarch a dignity that is entirely self-originating, Hegel recognizes the notion of authority as a companion normative standard on a par with freedom's foundational quality. But then Hobbes, rather than Rousseau, ought to be invoked if one is rightly to apprehend the dialectical intent of this *complexio oppositorum*.

3 • The epistemology of freedom and authority

What is looked for here is the effort to give up this freedom, and to sink this freedom in the content, letting it move spontaneously of its own nature, and then to contemplate this movement.

(Hegel, 1979: 35–6)

The structure of Hegel's argument in the *Philosophy of Right* contains two basic movements: one whose point of departure is freedom, and another whose point of departure is authority. The first movement, in agreement with liberal canons, takes abstract rights as its premise, and deduces the rights of legal and moral subjectivity.[1] The second movement responds to a conservative disposition, and presents institutional order and authority as conditions for the possibility of freedom. The family, the etatist institutions that develop within civil society, the corporation and a monarchical state unfold as the natural ground that sustains the rights of freedom and the spontaneous order they generate. The dialectical articulation of these two movements preserves the continuity of Hegel's argument and confirm that he is a liberal much aware of the limits of liberalism. As Ilting puts it,

> although he starts from the liberal principle of autonomy, Hegel (unlike Kant) is not a theoretician of the liberal state which guarantees and respects the rights and liberties of the individual . . . [H]e does not think that liberal principles alone are sufficient for a comprehensive theory of the modern state (Ilting, 1971: 95)

The reconciliation of freedom and authority is mediated by recognition. Subjectively free individuals come to recognize that their freedom can only be sustained and preserved if realized 'in the realm of the substantial' (Preface, 22). According to Hegel, a substantive authoritative order is the condition for the realization of subjective freedom. A similar point was made by Locke in his *Second Treatise*, when he wrote: 'the end of law is not to abolish or restrain, but to preserve and enlarge freedom: for in all the states of created beings capable of laws, where there is no law, there is no freedom' (Locke,

1980: 32). There is hardly any novelty in these assertions. Hegel acknowledges that 'the truth concerning right, ethics (*Sittlichkeit*), and the state is at any rate as old as its exposition and promulgation in public laws, public morality and religion' (Preface, 11). The truth concerning right, ethics and the state may be old and established, but it still needs to be recognized as such. As a content that is 'already rational in itself', Hegel maintains that it still needs to 'gain a rational form and thereby appear justified to free thinking' (Ilting, 1971: 11).[2] This assertion identifies free thinking as the epistemological topography where the reconciliation of freedom and authority may take place. Free thought 'does not stop at what is given . . . but starts out from itself and thereby demands to know itself as united in its innermost being with truth' (ibid.). In Hegel's mind, 'what is given' has authoritative standing. The 'given' may be the external authority of the state, or the external authority that arises from the mutual agreements entered by individuals; or it may be the internal authority of personal convictions. But as given or established, either internal or external, it cannot bind if free thinking does not 'start out from itself and thereby demands to know itself as united in its innermost being with the truth' (ibid.).

This unity of content and form, of 'what is given' and free thinking, prefigures the reconciliation of authority and freedom. My aim in this chapter is to probe Hegel's epistemology of freedom and authority.[3] This requires an examination of his critique of both empiricism ('what is given') and idealism ('free thinking'), and the dialectical method that supersedes their opposition. Combining a 'development according to historical grounds' and a 'development according to concepts', the dialectical method allows the derivation of the historically concrete institutions, experienced as 'what is given', from the categories of abstract free thinking postulated by idealism. The key to Hegel's dialectical derivation lies in the spontaneous order that springs naturally from the self-seeking behaviour of free individuals. This order safeguards the freedom of individuals and, at the same time, disciplines and reconciles their divergent aims. In the end, Hegel's realization of the negative ethical value generated by that spontaneous order, prompts the pre-eminent role he confides to the state and its monarch. *Hegelsche Mitte* interpreters have placed too much emphasis on Hegel's *constitutional* monarchy, a *Rechtsstaat* designed to channel and chasten the authority of the state. This is mistakenly to assume that the monarch is an optional extra in Hegel's system. The monarch, an individual like any other in his particularity, but 'universal because first' (Aristotle) is, I submit, what can ultimately sustain the formal universality of a *Rechtsstaat*.

I

Though freedom and authority are eminently practical notions, Hegel extends their employment to the theoretical realm (see Inwood, 1983: 470–82). Moral duties and legal rules may be regarded as authoritative encroachments on our freedom in the sense that they can be understood as external and alien intrusions. Projecting this view on to the theoretical realm we see that the same can be said of our perceptions. Perceptions occur when an alien content authoritatively forces its way onto our sensory organs. In the theoretical realm, the highest expression of freedom is thought (*Denken*). Hegel calls thought (or reason) the 'principle of freedom' (Hegel, 1991b: 107). He credits Kant with asserting 'the principle of thinking and of freedom' (ibid.) against empiricism, which he characterizes as a 'doctrine of unfreedom' (ibid.: 79). Hegel credits early Greek philosophers with the discovery of thought. They were interested in knowing about God, nature and the state, and through their unprejudiced thinking they gravely compromised their authority. 'Thinking deprived what was positive of its power. Political constitutions fell victim to thought' (ibid.: 48). Greek philosophers also contradicted traditional religion and subverted the old faith. This led citizens to exile and crush philosophers for undermining state and religion, which they thought to be essentially inseparable. Because of its enormous strength, the claims of thought were closely scrutinized and found to be exaggerated when compared with what it actually accomplished.

Thought has many features that relate to the notions of freedom and authority. The product of thought, first of all, is the 'universal, the abstract in general' (ibid.: 49). According to Hegel, the self, in its abstraction and its retreat from an alien world, is the paradigm case of universality. ' "I" is the universal in and for itself' (ibid.: 51). The abstraction by which the self asserts a relationship solely to itself is constitutive of its freedom. The self is what is 'abstractly free' (ibid.: 51), in the sense that it is stripped from all determination and is thus exempt from the authority of perception. Self-identity is seen by Hegel as the maximal expression of freedom and reason. 'In the expression

I = I is expressed the principle of absolute reason and freedom. Freedom and reason consist in my raising myself to the form I = I, in my knowing everything as mine' (ibid.: §424Z). At the same time, thought imposes or rather discovers itself in the world. And because it represents the true nature of human beings, it is acknowledged as having 'a certain authority' over the other human faculties.

Second, thought is active, and the product of its activity is the value of things, namely what is 'essential, inner, true' (Hegel, 1991b: 52). What is inwardly essential of things is not given by first impressions, but by the 'thinking-over of something' (*Nachdenken*). Children learn to think over or to reflect when they remember universal rules which they then apply to particular cases. In general, the ends pursued by activity constitute the universal, the 'governing factor' (*das Regierende*). Again, this applies most definitely to moral concerns. In this case, thinking-over (or reflective thinking) means evoking our duties, the universals that serve as a 'fixed rule' in moral life (ibid.: 53). From these examples one gathers how thought 'always seeks what is fixed, persisting, and inwardly determined, and what governs (*dem Regierenden*) the particular' (ibid.: 53). They confirm that Hegel assigns an authoritative role to thought.

Third, Hegel is aware that to bring 'thinking-over (or reflective thinking)' to the fore implies the alteration of the object of knowledge. He acknowledges that it is 'only through the mediation of an alteration that the true nature of the object comes into consciousness' (ibid.: 54). Though this coincides with the activity that is proper to thought, it does not mean that thought is subjectively free to force its coincidence with things. This is not the rule of conviction whereby 'conviction as such, the mere form of being convinced, is already good (whatever its contents may be), since no criterion is available for its truth' (ibid.: 54). The alterations brought about by reflective thinking respect the true nature of objects. In no case will Hegel give in to subjectivism. This is not what he understands by freedom.

Finally, the foregoing statement makes it clear that reflective thinking or *Nachdenken* brings to light the true nature of things. But reflective thinking is still thinking, which is definitely '*my* activity' and, therefore, the '*product of my* spirit' (ibid.: 55). This means, according to Hegel, that thinking should be understood as 'my *freedom*' which he defines as the self 'being simply at home with itself (*bei sich seinden Ichs*)' (ibid.: 55). How then can Hegel postulate the objectivity of thought? How can thought respect the true nature of things and maintain a humble or modest attitude towards them? Hegel recognizes that freedom resides in thought because it constitutes an abstract 'relation of the self to itself' (*Sichaufsichbeziehen*), a 'being with oneself' (*Beisichsein*).[4] Free thought, in its abstract relation to itself, implies first, in terms of form, that thought 'is no particular being or doing of the subject', and second, in terms of content, that thought is 'in the matter (*Sache*) and in its determinations', that it is 'immersed in the matter (*Sache*)' (ibid.). Thought opens up an abstract space, freed from all particularities, from all qualities and circumstances – a veritable *tabula rasa*. Because of this it 'does only what is universal, in which it is identical with all individuals' (ibid.). This conception of thought is reminiscent of Aristotle's passive intellect, which he conceives as pure potency awaiting the actualization of the intelligible forms illuminated by the active intellect.[5] Hegel explicitly names Aristotle and praises his idea of sweeping away all particular opinions and prejudices, so as to allow 'the matter [itself] to hold sway over us' (ibid.).

In the *Encyclopedia* §24, Hegel explains in greater detail the identity of thought and self.

> We can say that 'I' and thinking are the same, or, more specifically, that 'I' is thinking as what thinks . . . 'I' is this void, this receptacle for anything and everything . . . Everyone is a whole world of representations, which are buried in the night of the 'I'. Thus, the 'I' is the universal, in which abstraction is made from everything particular. (1991b: 57)

The abstraction of thought and the abstraction of the self go hand in hand. Abstraction is what determines the universality of thought and the self, and allows Hegel to ascribe freedom to both. But abstraction by itself is a defective condition. If we go no further than abstract universality and abstract freedom, we remain at the level of the understanding (*Verstand*) and the categories of essence. At that level, we may distinguish between the universal and the particular, the essential and the inessential, but are unable to reconcile them. 'As mere understanding, thinking is restricted to the form of the abstract universal, and is unable to advance to the particularisation of this universal' (ibid.: 76). Hegel postulates the need to advance towards concrete thought or the concept (*Begriff*). Once this level is attained, we do not have to deal with merely formal thought, but with the content appropriated by thought.

This passage from abstract to concrete thought is parallel to the passage from abstract to concrete freedom examined above in Chapter 2. In §24 of the *Encyclopedia*, Hegel defines the object of logic as 'pure thought'. In logic, thoughts are understood in such a way 'that they have no content other than one that belongs to thinking itself, and is brought forth by thinking' (1991b: 58). Hegel adds: 'spirit is here purely at home with itself (*bei sich selbst*), and thereby free, for that is just what freedom is: being at home with oneself in one's other (*in seinem Anderen bei sich selbst zu sein*)' (ibid.). To be determined by one's desires and instinct is not to be 'with oneself' (*bei sich selbst*), for this content is not one's own. Freedom, in this case, is only formal. But then 'when I think, I give up my subjective particularity, sink myself in the matter, let thought follow its own course; and I think badly whenever I add something of my own' (ibid.). To become immersed in the thing, to be able to acknowledge the 'authority of outward perception' (ibid.: 106) is the value of empiricism. Its defect is the renunciation of freedom as the possibility of remaining with oneself. To affirm the authority of thought is to remain with oneself and be free. This is the value of Kantian critical philosophy. Its defect is that thought, or reason, is deprived of all determination, and is thus 'set free from all authority' (ibid.: 107). The virtues and failings of both empiricism and Kantian criticism are explored below.

II

At first sight, empiricism appears to promote freedom. Its principle, that 'whatever is true must be actual and present for perception', contradicts the authority of the 'ought' (*Sollen*) which only shows contempt for what is actual and present (1991b: §38). Empiricism is right in its acknowledgement of what is, and also in not delving in to utopian considerations. Subjectively, it also accords with the 'principle of freedom' for it demands that what someone admits as valid must have first been seen and owned by that same person (ibid.). At the same time, Hegel believes that empiricism is the 'doctrine of unfreedom' because it remains a prisoner of the given. Freedom consists in not having an 'absolute other' confronting us. For this reason Hegel shares the effort displayed by German idealism to move beyond empiricism, particularly beyond Hume's sceptical approach to general ideas. Hume denies our understanding's access to universal and necessary principles, indispensable for eliciting a rational order within the realm of particularity. According to Hume, 'the scenes of the universe are continually shifting . . . [but] the power or force, which actuates the whole machine, is entirely concealed from us' (1977: 42). Thoughts or ideas, in themselves neither universal nor necessary, have no other function than to represent or copy particular impressions. As such they are captives to an epistemological mandate issuing from particulars, and lack the capacity to impose an order of their own. Events, admits Hume, 'seem entirely loose and separate. One event follows another; but we can never observe any tie between them' (ibid.: 49). The political translation of this epistemological model was made by economists like Adam Ferguson, for whom authoritative establishments are 'the result of human action but not the execution of any human design' (see Hayek, 1973: 150).

Under Humean assumptions, philosophy adopts conservative attitudes. Reason, admittedly the slave of preferences, lacks the authority to dictate categorical regulations that conform to its universalist claims. Reason is reduced to instrumental reason and becomes subservient to the needs of civil society. Functioning as a market system, civil society observes the spontaneous rise of an authoritative order whose normative foundations lie in the freedom claimed by its economic agents. But their freedom is only preferential freedom and not any form of rational self-determination. Because agents are moved by their preferences, and not by any autonomous set of rational ideas, the spontaneous order generated by the market is seen as self-sufficient, and not in need of interventions by an external power or authority acting on its own. Governments, though not denied prerogative, are seen as inert instruments deferential to the needs of civil society.

Germany's backward social conditions, still encumbered by the remnants of a feudal order, but with hopes of revolutionary change sparked by events in France, destined its philosophers to assume constructivist rather than the more acquiescent attitudes of the British. Not satisfied with allowing the gratification of preferences and desires to define the parameters of freedom, Kant underscores autonomy and rational self-determination. Governance of the passions is to be guided by the categorical, not the hypothetical imperatives of instrumental reason. For Fichte, the epistemological translation of rational self-determination means a rejection of knowledge viewed as a mirror of the natural order. He thus paves the way for the constitution of idealism as an epistemology of freedom. According to Schelling, philosophy is inconceivable 'without construction'. Theoretical philosophy ought to bring forth Ideas, for 'only Ideas provide action with vigour and ethical meaning' (Schelling, 1965: 299). Idealism aims at securing the autonomy of concepts and at cancelling the mandate arising from particularity. Reason is now empowered to dictate its terms to particularity and avoid the Philistine demands of empiricism and the traditionalist attitudes it fosters.

Hegel is aware that idealism relieves our minds from the heavy cargo of custom and tradition. But the price to be paid for instituting the universality and necessity of ideas is high. An insurmountable separation arises between the universality of our understanding and particularity, between the a priori and the empirical. Hegel is critical of Kant, for whom 'thoughts, although they are universal and necessary determinations, are still *only our* thoughts, and they are cut off from what the thing is *in-itself* by an impassable gulf from the thing in-itself' (Hegel, 1991b: 83). But Hegel's reservations go beyond mere epistemological considerations. The isolation in which thoughts are placed by idealism stimulate an intellectual posture contemptuous of hard facts and given to the refashioning of social and political institutions according to an abstract, preconceived logic. Hegel shares the perennial concerns voiced by conservatives of all times.[6] More than this, he also traces the actions of terrorists, who do not hesitate to sacrifice the rights of particularity to the demands of abstract reasonings, to the same source.

This critical view of idealism does not lead Hegel to retrieve empiricism's instrumentalist stance. He acknowledges the value of empiricism, but is also fully aware of its limitations. The value of empiricism resides principally in its respect for natural and spontaneous formations. In the *Encyclopedia* he celebrates its battle-cry: 'Stop chasing about among empty abstractions, look at what is there for the taking, grasp the *here and now*, human and natural, as it is *here* before us, and enjoy it!' (1991b: 76). Empiricism, starting from concrete historical standpoints, employs analytical tools in its search for the proper determinate abstractions. The determinations that ensue from this resolutive process are then subjected to a minimum of artificial construction. Empiricism is seen by Hegel as 'rightly sticking to its obstinate opposition to an artificial framework of principles' (1975b: 69). Purely abstract principles and laws are to be challenged because they lack perceptual warranty. At the same time, Hegel is aware of the limitations of empiricism. Its unreflective acceptance of the concrete undermines the universality and necessity demanded by scientific knowledge. Empiricism sees these properties as mere mental accidents and explains them away as the product of customary connections. Spontaneously generated institutions acquire a substantiality that makes them intractable to reason. In its struggle against the demands of abstract reason, empiricism is at the heart of conservative perceptions and attitudes. Hegel adopts a Kantian view of scientific knowledge which demands a procedure that moves from the abstract to the concrete. In the *Science of Logic*, the point of departure of Hegel's argument is being, conceived as a most abstract notion. The argument then proceeds from simple determinations to those which are richer and more concrete. But Kant not only rejected empiricism's claim to explain universality and necessity by an appeal to custom. He went on to say that conceptual abstractions were determinations which could be derived from experience. Universality and necessity were spontaneous products of our free thinking. Hegel's concern in this case is the unbridgeable gap that opens between concepts and the things in themselves. For Kant the closing of this gap lay in the hands of an hypothetical *intellectus archetypus*. The search for this figure would become a programmatic undertaking for Hegel (see Kroner, 1921: 287).

Hegel's dialectical method is meant to supersede the limitations of both empiricism and idealism, bringing together the ever-changing empirical manifold and the unity and stability of abstract concepts. He rejects both the one-sided 'development according to historical grounds' proper to empiricism and the one-sided 'development according to concepts' (§3) typical of idealism. Empiricism starts from ordinary experience in search of a modicum of principles that may introduce order and structure into the chaos of experience. The method employed by idealism starts from a priori principles that aim at the reconstruction of experience. Hegel's dialectical method articulates these two moments. This is the conclusion reached in §§31–3 of the *Philosophy of Right*, which contain a succinct review of his methodology. Hegel justifies the paucity of this elaboration by referring to the *Science of Logic*, where these matters are supposed to be dealt with in detail. A reading of these paragraphs, in light of the *Science of Logic*, confirms Hegel's distinction between a procedure that follows the scientific development of a concept and one that follows its temporal, historical development. These procedural aspects should be distinguished, but it is a mistake to separate them, for this would just reiterate the one-sidedness of both empiricism and idealism.

The dialectical method synthesizes the scientific development of concepts with their temporal formation.

In the *Philosophy of Right*, Hegel first pursues the scientific flow of determinations that issue from the concept of freedom. This movement is interpreted as a synthesis of the multiple determinations that proceed from within that concept. The concepts which the dialectical method has availed itself of are not abstract universals, mere genera that passively receive their specific determinations *ab extrinseco*. Those specific determinations are seen, on the contrary, as internal to their genus, so that a manifold is to be found within unity. Concepts thus represent a priori syntheses of determinations. They are still abstract because they are prior to experience, but at the same time they are concrete clusters of determinations. In his *Science of Logic*, Hegel writes that a concept is not an 'empty identity or abstract universality which is not within itself a synthesis' (1989: 589). And in the *Philosophy of Right* he adds: 'the concept develops itself out of itself' (§31). This conceptual development has affinities with Aristotle's conception of generation and organic growth (see Ilting, 1975: 38). Aristotelian resonances are audible in Hegel's description of the synthetic phase of dialectics as 'the immanent progressing and engendering of the concept's determinations'. This development, he adds, is not 'an external action of a subjective thinking, but represents the proper soul of a content which brings out organically its branches and fruits' (§31). What this means in the context of the *Philosophy of Right* is that the abstract concept of freedom, the point of departure of Hegel's scientific exposition, is also the concrete result of a historical process embodied by the *Zeitgeist*. This determines that the radical autonomy espoused by Kantian liberals, and fully adopted by Hegel, rests on a transcendental condition for its possibility. The conservative component of Hegel's political philosophy provides such condition.

The synthetic moment in the development of the concept of freedom articulates with an analytic moment.[7] Analysis is consonant with a conservative approach that takes its cue from what is given empirically. The determinations that issue forth from the concept of freedom are seen as concretely existing forms. They are formations and institutions already constituted in experience (§32). The same formations and institutions appear as synthetical results in the scientific development of the concept. In the analytical phase their existence is acknowledged as forms already given, with a development and history of their own.[8] The initial determinations of the concept should be seen then as quasi-hypothetical steps leading to the transcendental conditions that make them possible. This dialectical progression determines the institutional sequence exposed within the *Philosophy of Right*. The family and the state, both mature synthetic determinations of the concept of freedom, are the ground on which stand respectively the synthetically prior categories of property and civil society. Hegel is able to play the analytic keyboard and assume its realistic consequences. At the same time, by developing the concept of freedom synthetically he can vouch for the rationality of reality. Reality is rational because it is actualized by that conceptual synthesis. As a dialectical enterprise philosophy is the synthesis of analysis and synthesis. Philosophy fully and without any reservation embraces the authoritative demands of particularity. Still, once that infinite mass of scattered particularities has been collected under general principles, as stipulated by the method of political economy (§189), a philosophical reconstruction of reality can take effect. In that abyss of dissociation and dislocation we recognize the rise of a consortium of hearts and minds, the matrix of rationality. 'To recognize reason as the rose in the cross of the present and thereby to delight in the present – as this rational insight is the reconciliation with actuality' (Preface, 22).

This programme of dialectical thinking certifies the systematic value of Hegel's political exposition. Political philosophy has no value as such if it assumes a given authoritative content that remains recalcitrantly alien to reason, that is, if it gives up on its claim to apprehend the absolute. This is the plight of empiricism. Empiricism in morals and politics considers the authority that emanates from traditional institutions which are regarded as things in themselves. They may be recognized as stemming from human conventions, but then inexplicably these establishments acquire a life of their own, stolidly appearing as substantive bulwarks impenetrable to synthetic reason. Subjective freedom suffocates in their presence. Hegel, committed as he is to authoritative institutions that may only be actualized by subjectivity, rejects that form of crude empiricism. But a commitment to subjective freedom, on the other hand, determines a pure *Sollen*, or, worse still, it may assume Fichte's positing reflection which presupposes nothing and exhausts itself as the pure constructivist striving of the absolute ego. Subjective idealism sees the natural non-ego as an unreduced adversary that has to surrender to reason. Fichte never explained the positing or production of the non-ego. And once again one was left to confront an inexpugnable authoritative barrier. Dialectical thought sweeps these difficulties aside by allowing individuals 'to preserve their subjective freedom in the realm of the substantial, and at the same time to stand with their subjective freedom not in a particular and contingent situation, but in what has being in and for itself' (Preface, 22).

The dialectical method is meant to bring about the reconciliation of freedom and authority. For Hegel this means postulating an institutional embodiment as the condition of possibility for his Kantian commitment to rational self-determination and free subjectivity. The scenario where this dialectical sublation plays itself out is civil society. Here dialectical thought shows how a spontaneous authoritative order naturally arises from the intersection of conflicting individuals' interests, and how the entrenched affirmation of particular rights does not prevent the rise of a form of universality. Classical political economists spoke of an order that arose spontaneously from the casual and universal-blind striving of individuals. Early in his intellectual development, Hegel refers to such an authoritative order as the 'system of universal mutual dependence' or the 'system of reality' (Hegel, 1975b: 94). In his *Philosophy of Right*, this system translates into the notion of civil society. But in contrast to classical political economists, Hegel does not trust the blind spontaneous authority generated within that sphere. Some limitations and controls are to be imposed on it, because the operations of the hidden hand represent a mere form of universality. The hegemony of the principle of particularity continues unabated within civil society, which exhausts itself in the particularity of individuals. In his *Natural Law*, Hegel concludes that absolute *Sittlichkeit* can only take 'a negative attitude to that system' (1975b: 98), while in the *Philosophy of Right*, the externality of relations in civil society is perceived as the 'demise of *Sittlichkeit*', as the mere 'phenomenal world of the *Sittlichen*' (§181). A fully conscious identification of individual and universal aims is attained only when the ethical state upholds that blind spontaneous order. By playing the analytic keyboard Hegel is able to bring forth the ethical grounds that sustain civil society. The people as a whole, embodying the individuality and character intuited by Montesquieu,[9] can bring patriotic animation and historical continuity to the drab prose of business. But 'the nation (*das Volk*), taken without its monarchs and the articulation of the whole which is necessarily and immediately concomitant to them, is a formless mass and no longer a state' (§279). Thus, only when a people unfolds as a state and the particularity of one individual is allowed to rise to its apex, would universality be concretely attained.

In his *Natural Law*, Hegel developed a detailed exposition of the epistemology that sustains this argument. Here, the limitations of subjective idealism and scientific empiricism are sublated by the pure empiricism of eminent individuals. Their action is guided by a pure intuition of the whole, by an intuition of the individuality and character of nations. Hegel offers an apology for the incapacity shown sometimes by these individuals to 'elevate into the ideal form' the content of their praxis. Their rambling expositions may often be incoherent and sometimes even self-contradictory, but as long as they remain true to their intuition, 'the ordering of the parts and the self-modifying facets will betray, the rational, though invisible, spirit' (Hegel, 1975b: 67–8). This access to pure intuition, made possible by averting any contact with abstract concepts, defines Hegel's understanding of the praxis of great monarchs, politicians and field-commanders. Their actions should not be seen as irregular and non-synthesized effusions of energy, but as spontaneously following natural, undesigned plans (see Hyppolite, 1968: 74). Kant, in his *Critique of the Power of Judgement*, admitted that what was particular was always casual and accidental, so that a genuine barrier was raised between particularity and universality. It was only for a hypothetical intuitive understanding, an *intellectus archetypus*, that this opposition between particularity and universality did not arise.[10] The practical knowledge of the political genius concentrates the dispersion of particularity into a unitary whole (Hegel, 1975b: 67). The limitations of both German idealism and British empiricism, the Gordian knot of modern philosophy, are transcended by one single blow of a French sword, Napoleon's. As an actual non-hypothetical *intellectus archetypus*, Napoleon embodies a concrete universal. He possesses the pure intuitions that bring forth the synthesis of particularity and universality. Great individuals are still individuals, but in their eminence and principality they attain a universal stance. Plato, according to Hegel, had wisely determined in his *Statesman* that 'the best thing of all is not full authority for laws but rather full authority for a man who understands the art of kingship and has wisdom' (Plato, 1957: 66; see Hegel, 1975b: 96). In the *Philosophy of Right*, this role is taken over by the monarch. As the beginning and apex of the whole, his individuality is the synthesis of particularity and universality.

Hegel's state and his choice of a strong authoritarian monarch reflect civil society's inability to generate politically stable and secure institutions. Institutions can maintain a stable course only if they express the tranquil animus of their members. If this is not possible, it is due to Hegel's particular conception of civil society. The subjectively free individuals who populate it are only contractually related, thus loose and separate like Humean events. This is why Hegel has to search for stability and unity in a sphere external to civil society – the ethical state.

III

The argument delineated by Hegel in his *Philosophy of Right* combines idealist and empiricist epistemological strands. By dialectically sublating their one-sidedness Hegel is able to bring about a reconciliation of freedom and authority. Hegel's liberal commitment to individual freedom requires that his argument synthetically deduce authoritative institutions compatible with that freedom. His conservative demand that those institutions not be reduced to arrangements arbitrarily designed by individuals requires a purely analytical deduction. Accordingly, he conceives two separate points of departure for each deductive argument. His argument for liberal institutions has to be deduced from the abstract rights of persons understood as free from all empirical encumbrances and lacking every determination. Only idealism can supply such an abstract point of departure. Conservatism is incompatible with this type of enlightened logic. The conservative side of Hegel's argument requires that a natural institution, like the family, serve as the foundation for the development of individuality. This time empiricism provides the concrete facts for analysis. The *Philosophy of Right* displays an argument that brings these two approaches together.

1. The synthetic deduction of legal and moral institutions assumes the priority of the self over its natural ends. A hiatus separates the self from anything external to it. This externality is constituted primarily by the natural and social worlds, but it extends to the self's own thoughts, affections and dispositions. Self-identity takes place independently of any such relations. This distancing of the self, by which its dignity and integrity are preserved, allows Hegel to advance the case postulated by liberalism. Liberalism articulates the claims of individuals as abstract persons. Persons have an immediate right to

property, one that does not require a naturalist justification since it is not based in our instincts (§§18 and 19). The elimination of all external points of reference confirms the priority of an abstract will by which 'an individual person (is) related only to himself' (§40). Contract partially abrogates this seclusion of individuals within themselves. With contract the argument moves for the first time from self-centred rights to other-regarding obligations. But individuals will only accept non-natural obligations, that is, those obligations that they impose on themselves as liberalism demands. Hegel develops his arguments on the basis of the liberal injunction: 'no obligation on any man which ariseth not from some act of his own' (Hobbes, 1968: 268). Even if passions have been, at this point, excised from the self, universality is still not available, for nothing prevents the emptiness of the abstract self from falling prey to arbitrariness (*Willkür*). Grounded as they are in the contingency of subjective freedom, contractual obligations fail to attain a stable true universality. Contracts, guided by arbitrariness (§§75 and 113), give rise to injustice (§81). The free self confronts a situation similar to that faced by Hobbes's passion-driven individuals in the state of nature. Injustice, remedied momentarily by vengeful justice, is seen by Hegel as leading to an endless cycle of retribution (§102). This unbearable state of affairs forces a transition to morality.

The moral point of view takes hold of the terror-stricken consciousness of individuals as a redeeming condition. Individuals acquire the capacity to surrender their rights and 'as particular wills, will the universal as such' (§103). Hegel restates the liberal creed – individuals have duties in proportion as they have freely renounced or transferred their rights. In Hegel's own words: 'only by means of my conviction may a law become a law that obliges and binds me' (§140R[e]). This conclusion, entailed by the liberal premises of the synthetic deduction, appears to Hegel as profoundly perverse. Abstract rights give rise to abstract duties, and so the same distance that was found to exist between the self and its rights exists now between the self and its duties. Morality, duly expressed by formal conscience (as opposed to true ethical conscience), ascends to the pinnacle of absolute subjectivity and of itself 'dissolves all determinations of right, duty and existence' (§138). At this point, Hegel unfolds the configurations of absolute subjectivity. They lead the liberal mind from Kant's idealism to Fries's 'superficiality', and ultimately to the empty convictions of Robespierre. Accordingly, Hegel thinks that no state can be founded on the basis of the radical subjectivism and formalism of Kantian morality. Nothing prevents this sort of morality from ending up positing personal conviction as the ultimate criterion. But when this occurs the 'authority of my individual conviction' will be set against, and be stronger than, the 'authority of God and the state' (§140). With this the synthetic deduction of freedom has reached a cul-de-sac. Pursued on its own it cannot yield the conditions that will ensure the realization of freedom. But this deficiency is not a complete loss. Hegel is now ready to demonstrate that a higher institution, the state, must guarantee the rights of the subjective will (§§124 and 132; compare §137). Hegel's recognition of liberal individualist principles does not mean that he accepts them without reserve. Legality and morality are confined to the consideration of the individual existence of human beings. This basis must be overcome in order to arrive at the state in which individuals pursue not the individual but the common good.

2. The point of arrival of the synthetic deduction of freedom opens the way for the analytical deduction of the authority claimed by *Sittlichkeit* and the ethical state. Hegel has come to terms with the liberal notion of individuals as primordial bearers of rights. Abstract personality is defined by the primacy of rights, so that abstract persons have duties because they have rights. *Sittlichkeit* now introduces individuals who have rights only because they have duties. Subjective freedom yields to substantive freedom, defined by Hegel as 'a circle of necessity whose moments are the ethical powers which regulate the life of individuals' (§145). The presence of these authoritative powers, the 'other' that confronts abstract freedom, is constitutive of substantive or concrete freedom. This agrees with Hegel's definition of freedom according to which a concretely free subject is with itself in its institutional limitation, in its 'other' (§7). By advancing to substantive freedom, as the unifying third moment, Hegel has laid the ground for the reconciliation of freedom and authority.

In *Sittlichkeit*, individuals appear as accidents attached to an ethical substance (§§145 and 163), which possesses 'an absolute power and authority, infinitely more solid than the being of nature' (§146). *Sittlichkeit* stands as an unmoved mover with the power to command the obedience of its subjects while being devoid of any obligation (§152). Hegel's intention is not to present his notion of ethical substance as the lion's den from which no one returns. On the contrary, ethical laws and institutions are not 'something alien' to individuals. In them they are able to find their own essence and live as in their own element

(§147). An identity between duties and rights obtains in *Sittlichkeit* – a human being 'has rights in so far as he has duties, and duties in so far as he has rights' (§155). This formal identity should not obscure the fact that it obtains within the conservative context of the ethical primacy of duty and authority. Individuals have rights only because 'they belong to ethical actuality' (§153). *Sittlichkeit* and the institutions that grow under its shadow are not themselves subject to any duties.[11]

(a) The institution that primarily embodies the ethical spirit is the family. Within the sphere of the family there are no persons who can claim to be subjectively free. According to Hegel, one is present in it 'not as an independent person (*eine Person für sich*) but as a member' (§158). The genesis of a family is marked by subjective freedom. The free consent of the persons that have decided to marry is demanded in virtue of the right of subjectivity proper to all moral agents. Accordingly, Hegel recognizes that marriage begins as a contract. But because this is an ethical institution, he also acknowledges that its purpose determines that its members supersede the standpoint of contract (§163). Only when the family dissolves do its individual members regain their full personality and independence (§159). One form of the dissolution of the family union is divorce, which Hegel readily accepts as a legitimate possibility. From this it becomes clear that Hegel conceives ethical institutions as regulative powers and authorities that loom over and above its individual members. In his view, when a couple has become 'antagonistic and hostile', but not 'totally estranged' (§176), the 'ethical substantiality of marriage' is upheld by avoiding the possibility of divorce on the basis of a transient mood or attitude. Hegel invokes the intervention of a 'third ethical authority', presumably the Church or a court of justice, to assess the total estrangement of a couple, and on that basis grant the divorce. The introduction of this 'third ethical authority' sets the stage for other higher authoritative interventions required to arbitrate conflicts between free agents.

(b) The family disintegrates into externally related 'self-sufficient concrete persons' (§181). Hegel considers this to be a 'loss of ethical life' (§181) which ushers the inception of civil society. In this sphere the main player is neither the abstract subject of rights, nor the moral subject of duties, nor the individual as a family member, but concrete persons who seek to satisfy their needs and preferences. The satisfaction of needs and preferences, mediated by market mechanisms, is mired in contingency and arbitrariness. Hegel detects the emergence of a residual state of nature, which marks the dissipation of all institutional authority (§200). At this point, Hegel's analytical deduction yields authority in the guise of two etatist formations: the administration of justice and the *Polizei*.

The administration of justice, or judicial state, aims at the protection of property. For this it retrieves the universality of abstract right and conducts itself as an authoritative institution which guarantees 'the undisturbed security of persons and property' (§230). A legal system is not 'an improper use of force, a suppression of freedom and a rule of despotism' (§219), but is instrumental to the cause of freedom. Hegel presents it as an instance of authority acting in the service of freedom. 'The administration of justice should be regarded both as a duty and as a right of the public authority (*Macht*), and as a right, it is not in the least dependent on whether individuals choose to entrust it to an authority or not' (§219). Though authority is instrumental to freedom, it is not the result of free choice. This assumes that authority is the 'other' of freedom. Accordingly, Hegel presents the prosecution and penalization of crime undertaken by a court of justice as punishment. Punishment is a 'genuine reconciliation of right with itself' and not merely the 'subjective and contingent retribution of revenge' (§220). Just as revenge is a manifestation of subjective freedom, punishment is a manifestation of authority. Hegel can now say that civil society returns to its concept, namely 'the unity of the universal which has being in itself with subjective particularity' (§229).

Apart from the harm caused by crime, other contingencies inherent to the market system may also cause harm (§232). The regulation of otherwise rightful actions, and the 'private use of property' within the system of needs, is placed by Hegel in the hands of an administrative state. This state secures that the subsistence and welfare of individuals be actualized as a right. But the authority of this state cannot safeguard individuals from every contingency. Hegel is aware that arbitrariness haunts the system of needs (§241) and refers back to §200 where he recognized that the 'sphere of particularity [i.e. civil society] imagines that it is universal, but in its mere identity with the universal, it retains both natural and arbitrary particularity, and hence the remnants of a state of nature' (§200). The authority of this etatist formation is gravely compromised by being a merely imagined universality. As such it remains an 'external order and arrangement' (§249). But, like the administration of justice, the *Polizei* actualizes the universal contained within the particularity of civil society. The stage is therefore set for the emergence of a strong authoritarian state which assumes the protective functions demanded by liberalism. The step that Hegel undertakes next is to ensure the full restoration of *Sittlichkeit*. This will happen only when the authority required by civil society is not seen just as an external universal order, but particularity makes that order 'the end and object of its will and activity' (§249). This introduces the corporate spirit which, together with the family, comprise the ethical roots of the state.

The authority of the judicial and the administrative state is not up to the task of overseeing the disruptive social effects brought on by market society. The corporate spirit envisaged by Hegel is supposed to tame the natural selfishness of the business classes, agents of disunity and instability because 'essentially drawn towards the particular' (§250). Corporations instil a spirit of solidarity amongst the members of that class and eliminate conspicuous consumption, which Hegel interprets as a compensation for the modern loss of status and sentiments of honour (§253). Corporations 'come to the scene as a second family for its members' (§252) aiming to preserve the ethical values exhausted in civil society. Within corporations the universal becomes 'the object and end of the will and activity' of individuals, so that 'the ethical circles back and appears immanent to civil society' (§249). This new disposition curbs the 'luxury and extravagance of the business classes' which, according to Hegel, 'goes together with the creation of a proletariat (*Pöbel*)' (§253). But the corporate spirit by itself is unable to solve the problem. The recognition of a still higher sphere, an ethical state, with distinctive executive and legislative functions, is needed to strengthen the corporate ethos and elevate the administration of justice and the *Polizei* above strife and faction. The principle of universality that transforms the purely external ties between individuals into ethical corporate bonds, unfolds only when the ethical state is recognized as the principle of the whole. As 'what is first' (§256), the ethical state sustains the corporate spirit, and lends full authority to the etatist formations within civil society. This represents the culmination of the analytical procedure.

(c) The highest expression of *Sittlichkeit* is Hegel's ethical state: 'The state is the actuality of concrete freedom' (§260). The state is the end result of the dialectic of the will which has now reached its goal – the concrete notion of freedom. In my discussion of §258 in Chapter 2 above, I concluded that concrete or objective freedom is the synthesis of (subjective) freedom and authority. This is no longer the external authority of the judicial and administrative states. The ethical state re-enacts the corporate spirit at the highest political level. Authority appears now fully internalized. This is what defines the strength of modern states – the rights of subjective freedom are now fully recognized.

> The principle of modern states has enormous strength and depth because it allows the principle of subjectivity to attain fulfillment in the self-sufficient extreme of personal particularity, while at the same time bringing it back to substantial unity and so preserving this unity in the principle of subjectivity itself. (§260)

This recognition of subjective freedom does not push us back to abstract right and the moral point of view with their one-sided affirmation of the priority of rights. The ethical state is presented as the synthesis of the internal privileges and claims of freedom and the external constraints that necessarily determine its demands. Hegel postulates a perfect balance between rights and duties. The family, and not abstract right or morality, is now the point of reference.

> In relation to the spheres of civil law (*Privatrecht*) and private welfare, the spheres of the family and civil society, the state is on the one hand, an external necessity and a higher power to whose nature their laws and interests are subordinate, and on which they depend. But on the other hand, it is their immanent end, and its strength consists in the unity of its universal and ultimate end with the particular interests of individuals, in the fact that they have duties towards the state to the same extent as they also have rights. (§261)

This identity between duties and rights is analogous to the synthesis between freedom and authority. But it remains a formal identity. The content of rights and duties is determined by the function Hegel assigns to the ethical state. In civil society, as a result of the ethical dissolution of the family, individuals plumb the abyss of particularity in a resurgence of subjective freedom. The ethical state reverses this process. Subjective freedom is superseded by ethical duties towards the whole. Only this can reinforce the authority exercised by the judicial and administrative states within civil society. *Sittlichkeit* has a 'fixed content' which is exalted above the inherent instability of opinions and preferences, and forms the basis for stable institutions and laws (§144). In an ethical institution like the family, rights and duties do not match in respect to content. Father and son are concrete persons, and so 'the duties of the son do not have the same content as his duties towards his father' (§261). Their relations cannot be situated at a level of formal equality.[12] A substantive content, filial subordination in this case, neutralizes the unsettling effect of abstract rights. The family transmits to the social and political institutions analytically derived from it, a stability and firmness based on that natural dependence and subordination. '[T]he rights of the citizen are not the same in content as the citizen's duties towards the prince and government' (§261). This is no longer the priority of rights, but the priority of duties.

> The individual, whose duties give him the status of a subject (*Untertan*), finds that, in fulfilling his duties as a citizen, he gains protection for his person and property, consideration for his particular welfare, satisfaction of his substantial essence, and the consciousness and self-awareness of being a member of the whole. (§261)

This is no longer abstract liberalism, but a liberalism open to the demands of authority.

The point of view of abstract right and contract coincides with modern natural law theory. Proof that Hegel acknowledges the limits of liberalism is his rejection of contract as a foundation for the authority of the state, just as he rejected contract as a foundation for the family. For Rousseau, the social contract that generates the union of individuals is 'based on their arbitrary will and opinions, and on their express consent given at their own discretion' (§258). But this implies the destruction of 'the divine [element] which has being in and for itself and its absolute authority and majesty' (§258). Of itself, liberalism cannot invoke the authority required to channel and control subjective, arbitrary freedom. Hegel raises the spectre of the French Revolution, that 'most terrible and drastic event', which attempted the overthrow of the state and the creation (*anzufangen*) of its 'constitution from first principles and purely in terms of thought' (§258). Forswearing the *pouvoir constituant* of the people is Hegel's decisive philosophical decision, for now the prince, conceived not only as the apex of the constitution but also as its beginning, is recognized as its subject. The *princeps* is essentially *principium*. Hegel is able to secure a central role for the prince and comply with what is entailed by the monarchical principle.

4 • Property and recognition

Si le droit de propriété n'est pas sacré, la liberté est violée, car c'est la propriété qui est le rempart de la liberté.

(Chateaubriand, 1987: 405)

Contemporary readers of Hegel typically characterize his conception of property as social. This relativization of property, which justifies subjecting it to higher regulation by civil society and the state, follows from understanding property not as a real right (*ius in rem*), but as a personal right (*ius ad personam*), namely as a relation between persons who recognize each other. Original occupation, a possessive relationship between an individual and a thing, is not sufficient ground for the constitution of property. Absent is the recognition by others and their consent to the duties imposed by property claims. What this view assumes is summarized by Waldron's apt phrase: 'property relations do not exist between persons and objects; they exist between persons and other persons' (1988: 267; see Cohen, 1933: 45). Waldron follows Plamenatz, who writes that in Hegel's view '[t]o make a claim is not to give vent to an appetite. It is to make a moral gesture understood by others capable of making them, a gesture that has a meaning only between persons who recognize one another as persons' (Plamenatz, 1971: 40–1). This same view inspires Avineri when he argues that

> not an individualistic but a social premise is at the root of Hegel's concept of property, and property will never be able to achieve an independent stature in his system . . . Property always remains premised on social consensus, on consciousness, not on the mere fact of possession. (Avineri, 1972: 88–9)

In this chapter, I argue that this progressive social conception does not capture Hegel's account on property. He does propound such an account in his early political works, where he ties property to recognition. But in his *Philosophy of Right* this conception is amended, and Hegel now presents a view of property defined as a subjective right.

As a subjective right, abstract and immediate property dispenses with recognition and bears all the marks of a possessive individualist conception. In opposition to Marx, who 'comprehends property exclusively in social terms in accordance with his concept of society itself as the "true nature of man," ' Joachim Ritter rightly observes that, in the *Philosophy of Right*, 'the freedom that is based on property . . . still finds all the substantial relations of human existence outside itself' (Ritter, 2004: 123 and 106; see Hüning, 2002: 257–9).[1]

As Hegel's argument advances, this individualist concept of property is joined by a social concept defined by the recognition of others. This takes place initially within the section on abstract right when the argument moves from property to contract. Contractual relations are constitutive of *iura ad personam* and therefore involve recognition by others. But this relativization of property is not meant to weaken individual appropriation. On the contrary, Hegel intends its reinforcement. Individual property is duly safeguarded only when social property re-emerges within civil society and a legal system contributes the required institutional context. Ultimately, a strong state is the best protection for property when defined in possessive individualist terms.[2]

I

In the *Philosophy of Right*, there are five indications that mark Hegel's individualist conception of property: (1) the priority he assigns to subjective rights; (2) his rejection of Kant's reduction of real to personal rights; (3) his identification of possession and property; (4) the confinement of recognition to the sphere of contract; and (5) his agreement with the dissolution of the distinction between *dominium directum* and *dominium utile*, which marks the transition from feudalism to capitalism. Below I will explore these five points in more detail.

1. Hegel adopts the modern notion of subjective rights and conceives them as logically and temporally prior to objective law and the constitution of a legal system. In this respect, Hans Kelsen's rejection of the notion of subjective rights may serve as an adequate counterpoint to clarify the assumptions underlying the Hegelian conception. In Kelsen's view, the modern legal conception assumes that subjective rights are primordial and do not presuppose recognition by other individuals. He writes: 'subjective rights emerge first, and property

constitutes their prototype' (Kelsen, 1934: 41).[3] He also acknowledges that the modern conception admits that 'objective law, manifested as a political order, emerges only later for the purpose of protecting, recognizing and guaranteeing the independently generated subjective rights' (ibid.: 41).[4] This conception of independent subjective rights is rejected by Kelsen as a fictitious and ideological scheme, an attempt merely 'to protect the institution of private property from its abrogation at the hands of the legal order' (ibid.: 44). What Kelsen disavows is a modern individualist conception of subjective rights and property which coincides point for point with Hegel's own individualist notion of abstract right.[5]

2. Hegel rejects Kant's distinction between real and personal rights (Kant, 1966: 70).[6] 'Personality alone confers a right to things, and consequently . . . personal right is in essence a real right . . . This real right is the right of personality as such' (§40). Hegel's abstract and immediate notion of property, one that is not mediated by recognition, requires the reduction of personal to real rights. By definition, a real right is in no need of such mediation, for it is constituted by the immediate possessive relation between a person and a thing.[7] The thing that is taken into possession is owned by nobody. In contrast, Kant reduces real to personal rights. Personal rights, Hegel admits, are 'rights that arise out of a contract' (§40). They presuppose an original system of ownership where all things belong to everyone. For Kant, 'the right to a thing is the right to the private use of a thing. With respect to that thing I have a community of possession (original or established) with all other individuals' (Kant, 1966: 71). In order to claim the property over any one thing, agreements have to be reached that extinguish the existing property rights claimed by other persons and identify the portion to be appropriated. Hence contract precedes property. 'Strictly speaking, there is no (direct) right to a thing. What we call right is what we hold against a person who shares with all others (in civil society) a community of possession' (ibid.: 72).

According to Hegel, property as an abstract right can only be conceived as a *ius in rem*. Contrary to Kant, for whom an individual who existed alone in the world would not be able to own anything, Hegel thinks that such individual may, without previous agreement, come to own things (see Hüning, 2002: 248–9). Property precedes any agreement of any kind, a clear indication that Hegel operates here with an *in rem*, that is pre-social, concept of property.[8]

3. The most visible sign of Hegel's individualist concept of property

is the argument where he collapses the classical distinction between possession and property.[9] In doing so Hegel retreats from his earlier political writings where he affirms that distinction.[10] Avineri, for instance, interprets Hegel's views in the *Realphilosophie II* (1805/6) as supporting a 'trans-subjective' and 'non-individual' conception of property.

> Property pertains to the person as recognized by others, it can never be an intrinsic quality of the individual prior to his recognition by others. While possession relates to the individual, property relates to society; since possession becomes property through the other's recognition of it as such, property is a social attribute. (Avineri, 1972: 88–9)

Avineri is not aware that Hegel collapses this distinction in his *Philosophy of Right* in order to make room for an individualist concept of property.

Hegel introduces the distinction between possession and property in §45. But the terms of this distinction are defined in a manner that ensures the collapse of possession into the logical space defined by property.

> To have external power over something constitutes *possession*, just as the particular circumstance that I make something my own out of natural need, drive, and arbitrary will is the particular interest of possession. But the circumstance that I, as free will, am an object to myself in what I possess and only become for the first time an actual will by this means constitutes the genuine and rightful element in possession, the determination of *property*. (§45)

Possession, defined as 'external power', does not constitute a right. As an expression of our natural will possession is a matter of fact devoid of prescriptive value. By contrast, property involves a rightful or lawful relation of the will to the thing. Our external power over a thing ceases to be merely possessive and becomes property. The sphere of right lies beyond that of natural or arbitrary will. Hegel adopts the traditional distinction between possession and property, which defines possession as a mere factual or physical taking of a thing, and property as legally recognized possession.

Hegel's next step is to undermine this traditional distinction at the level of abstract right. Possession, which should serve as the point of departure for the process that leads to rightful appropriation, is unable to retain logical priority over property. Possession manifests the arbitrary, subjective will of an individual, whereas property expresses our own free will. But why is it possible for 'free will', and not for 'subjective will', to appropriate a thing rightfully? Since it is inconceivable that the thing itself, which is pure externality by definition, may oppose a kind of measured resistance to the advances of the human will, arbitrary or free, why is property not constituted immediately? Why does its realization need an intermediate possessive stage? What this indicates is that, in the absence of objective limitations, there is nothing to prevent the will from fully appropriating the thing entirely. This leaves no logical space for a possessive stage constituted prior to property. Just as the subjective will collapses into the free will, so possession collapses into property.

After the collapse of the logical priority of possession over property, Hegel turns to the question of its temporal priority. His argument shows that appropriation follows first occupancy immediately so that the possibility of a transition from possession to property is abrogated. Hegel addresses the issue of first occupancy in the following terms: 'That a thing belongs to the person who happens to be the first to take possession of it, is an immediately self-evident and superfluous determination, because a second party cannot take possession of what is already the property of another' (§50). In the first place, since the first occupant finds no objective limitations in the thing itself, he is not required to stay for an unspecified period of time suspended in the stage of mere possession. When a second person steps forward and claims that same thing, that person will discover that the first occupant is *already* its proprietor. When did his appropriation first take place? When did the first occupant or possessor of a thing assert full proprietorship? Since there are no conditions imposed by the thing itself and, as Kant stipulates, there is no 'accompanying genie to protect it from external attacks' (Kant, 1966: 71), no objective grounds exist for a waiting period at the end of which his property would take effect. Even when the time stretching between one's first possessive apprehension, that is, the time when one was a mere possessor, and the claim raised by the second person were to be decreased *ad infinitum*, this person would never be able to catch the first possessor in the stage of mere possession. At no time may the first possessor be seen as mere possessor. Appropriation takes effect immediately, leaving no room for a purely possessive stage. In the second place, if the second person were to take effective possession of the property of the first person, that person would not maintain a merely possessive relation in regards to it. The thing can serve as the term of only one relationship, the property relationship. Taking possession of that thing immediately extinguishes the proprietary rights of the first person and institutes those of the second. Between property and non-property there can be no intermediate stage. Possession is unable to assert a temporal space of its own. The temporal distinction between possession and property collapses in favour of property. Property is possession, that is, an immediate relation between a person and a thing.[11]

In the paragraph that follows Hegel appears to introduce a social moment that would confirm a communitarian stance.

> My inner idea (*Vorstellung*) and will that something should be mine is not enough to constitute property, which is the existence (*Dasein*) of personality; on the contrary, this requires that I should take possession of it. The existence which my willing thereby attains includes its ability to be known (*Erkennbarkeit*) by others.[12] – That a thing of which I can take possession should be ownerless is a self-evident negative condition; or rather, it refers to the anticipated relation to others. (§51)

Is the knowledge of others an essential requirement for the constitution of property? Can I claim that a thing is rightfully mine only when other persons are able to know that it belongs to me? In my view, §51 makes clear that possession does not antecede property. Possession serves merely as a sign attached to property to manifest previously constituted ownership and required as a forewarning to third parties. Their presence and their acknowledgement is not a condition for the constitution of property. Though recognition is not essential for the constitution of property, property may be essential, as Patten maintains, for the recognition of autonomous and independent personality.[13]

4. The definition of property as an abstract and immediate subjective right cancels the possibility of mediation. This precipitates the collapse of the distinction between property and possession, and property is reduced to the monological possessive relation between a person and a thing. No other person is required to witness the constitution of this individualist possessive linkage. Hegel's analysis of the three moments of abstract right in §40 is most instructive in this respect. The first moment explicitly assumes the identity of possession and property. Property is thus defined as 'the freedom of an individual

person who relates only to himself' (§40; see 1991b: §490). This leaves
no room for recognition in the configuration of pre-contractual
property (see Siep, 1982: 256; Hüning, 2002: 249, n. 38). Recognition
shows up when the argument advances to the sphere of contract, the
second moment of abstract right. Contract allows the formation of a
'common will' for it makes it possible for an individual proprietor to
relate 'himself to another person' (§40). The formation of this
common will is what allows the mediation of property through mutual
personal recognition. The reinstatement of the distinction between
possession and property signals the introduction of this new conception
of property. In §78, Hegel declares that someone who intends to
acquire property by means of a contract need not take the thing thus
acquired into immediate possession. Possession is defined as a purely
'external' circumstance that does not alter the 'substantive' aspects
involved in property (§78).

5. Hegel's individualist conception of property becomes again visible
when he examines the notion of use as a determination of property.
Use, which goes beyond mere detention or apprehension, represents the
completion of the process of appropriation. It constitutes, therefore,
the 'real aspect and actuality of property' (§59). This does not mean
that use is required for property to become an accomplished fact. A
thing that is not being used may appear to be dead, to lack the vivifying
presence of a proprietor. But use is only a phenomenon which presupposes as its 'primary substantive basis' the free will of a proprietor
(§59). Still, use or possession is to be seen as a sign of the capacity of
the will entirely to penetrate and saturate a thing. If I am entitled to
the totality of the use of a thing, this is a clear indication that I am the
full proprietor of that thing. Partial or temporary use or possession is
not an indication of property (§62). In this case, my free will appears
fully to saturate the thing and, at the same time, not to do so. Hegel
inserts here a reference to §52, where taking possession of a thing is
said to imply total lack of resistence on the part of the thing to my will's
penetrating agency. This is so because, when I own a thing, my free will
fully penetrates and saturates it, leaving nothing residual for the thing
to claim on its own. 'In the face of the free will, the thing does not
retain any distinct property for itself, even if possession, as an external
relationship, still retains an external aspect' (§52). Hegel may now
conclude: 'ownership is therefore essentially free and complete ownership' (§62). Use follows property immediately, and must necessarily do
so once the property relationship is established. If one could think of a

property relationship where use was permanently removed, that relationship would cease to be a property relationship. This clarifies why Hegel rejects the notion of *dominium utile*. Only *dominium directum* is full property or *dominium in plenum* (see Heineccius, 1729: 112). Otherwise the same thing would have 'two owners in a mutual relationship', and a transition to 'common ownership' would be 'very easy to make' (§62). Hegel intends to offset this dreaded possibility by warning us that the *dominium* claimed by individuals must be conceived as eminent or *in plenum*. If not, it will cease to be *dominium*.

Rosenzweig rightly interprets this aspect of Hegel's conception of property as in conformity with modern individualism and the abolition of feudalism. He thinks that Hegel has the night of 4 August 1789 in mind, when he writes: 'It must be one and a half millennia since the *freedom of personality* began to flourish under Christianity . . . But it is only since yesterday, so to speak, that the the *freedom of property* has been recognized here and there as a principle' (§62; see Rosenzweig, 1920: 109–10). This explains Hegel's rejection of the distinction between *dominium directum* and *dominium utile*, essential to feudalism, but not found in Roman law (§62).[14] In Rosenzweig's view, when Hegel admits that 'active use, and not a dead juridical title, makes someone the proprietor of a thing', he remains faithful to Adam Smith and stands in agreement with the 'foundations of economic individualism' (Rosenzweig, 1920: 109).

II

Hegel's individualist concept of property loses its immediacy and abstract nature when he introduces recognition. He does so in the paragraph that marks the transition from property to contract.

> This relation of will to will is the true distinctive ground in which freedom has its existence. This mediation whereby I no longer own property by means of a thing and my subjective will, but also by means of another will, and hence within the context of a common (*gemeinsamen*) will, constitutes the sphere of contract. (§71)

I become a proprietor and my will attains exclusive right to possess, use, enjoy or dispose of a thing, when I am recognized as such by another party. I am a proprietor in the presence of the will of another person. I own property not as an abstract will, but as a will mediated by the recognition of others. In the pre-contractual stage, property was constituted solely by the relation of my subjective will to a thing. The transition to contractual property makes recognition an essential moment, for 'contract presupposes that the contracting parties recognize each other as persons and owners of property' (§71; see Cristi, 1978; Landau, 1973: 180; Hüning, 2002: 251).

Despite the social aspect involved in contract, the contractual relation itself remains abstract and ruled by arbitrary will.[15] The agreements attained constitute merely a common will. 'The identical will which comes into existence through the contract is only a will posited by the contracting parties, hence only a common (*gemeinsamer*) will, not a will that is universal in and of itself' (§75). Hegel contrasts the common will attained by means of contract with the universal absolute will that sustains institutions like the family and the state. He strongly denounces the intrusion of abstract property and contract within the state. This wrests the state of its autonomy and reduces it to a purely instrumental role, a view shared by both feudalism and social contract liberalism. To transfer the determinations of property and contract to the political sphere would bring down the state to the level of civil society.

In view of this poverty of property and contract, many have overlooked the social context that contractual recognition provides to property. It is held that, only when Hegel ascends to the standpoint of *Sittlichkeit*, is possessive individualist property rightfully transcended and social property attained. Peter Stillman, for instance, maintains the 'major institutions of ethical life are rooted in community, impose obligations, and so overcome the atomism and individualism of property and contract' (Stillman, 1991: 208). This is only partly true. When Hegel examines the notion of property within the confines of civil society, it is contract which is said to actualize property. Of course, contract itself is now mediated by a legal system, which is again part of the etatist institutions introduced by Hegel within civil society.

> Just as right *in itself* becomes law in civil society, so too does my individual right, whose existence was previously *immediate* and *abstract*, acquire new significance when its existence is recognized as part of the existing universal will and knowledge. Acquisitions of property and transactions relating to it must therefore be undertaken and expressed in the *form* which that

existence gives to them. Property is now based on contract and on those
formalities which make it capable of proof and valid before the law. (§217)

In the remark in the same paragraph, Hegel adds: 'The original, i.e.
immediate, modes of acquisition and titles (see §§54ff.) are in fact
abandoned in civil society, and occur only as individual accidents or
limited moments.'

Hegel retrieves the notion of property as an abstract right to compare
it with the social significance it acquires in civil society. Individualist
property 'whose existence was previously immediate and abstract' is
now recognized as existing within a concrete institutional context.
Property was initially socialized by the mediation of contract. But
contract, viewed abstractly, is only sustained by a *common will*. The
absence, at that stage, of a *universal will* means that legal claims are
'multiple and mutually external'. Multiple exclusive claims on any
particular thing naturally result in a 'collision of rights' (§84). Since
the merely common will of the contracting parties is unable to
adjudicate these collisions, this leads to the rule of vengeful justice
dispensed randomly by individuals. This inference from abstract
freedom is Hegel's version of the state of nature. By contrast, the legal
system that is put in place within civil society expresses an 'existing
universal will'. This means that the modes of appropriation that
seemed early on to be in accordance with right are now abandoned in
civil society, even though they may reappear in exceptional circumstances.[16] It also means that we have moved away from the state of
nature. Hegel recognizes that, in the system of needs, 'the remnants of
a state of nature' are retained (§200). This is due to the fact that the
system of needs contains the 'universality of freedom, but only
abstractly and hence as the right of property' (§208). Within the legal
system, the right of property is 'present no longer merely in itself, but
in its valid actuality' (§208). For Hegel this means that property is now
fully socialized for it is protected by a universal will.

III

The dual conception of property held by Hegel in his *Philosophy
of Right* betrays a duality of aims. In order to override egalitarian
aspirations and redistributive claims by the state, Hegel prioritizes and
entrenches an individualist concept of property as a real right or *ius in*

rem. At the same time, he observes that the legal protection of private property implies its socialization. A social concept of property first emerges within the sphere of abstract right. Then, the establishment of a protective legal system within civil society introduces a political factor that moves us even further away from the meagre socialization provided by abstract contract. Finally, with Hegel's state we reach the apex of this process of socialization. But the effectiveness of the state as a protective agency cannot be guaranteed if its sole function is the protection of property. To avoid turning it into an instrument in the service of sovereign property owners, Hegel reinforces the state's autonomy and underscores its priority with respect to civil society.

Hegel is fully aware of the dangers involved in the socialization of property. A social concept of property and the concomitant distinction between possession and property clear the way for thinkers like Rousseau[17] and Fichte whose aim is the relativization of private ownership. Hegel is particularly concerned about Fichte's radical proposals. In his *Grundlage des Naturrechts*, Fichte distinguishes between possession and property and defines the latter as a social institution grounded on the reciprocal recognition of individuals.

> When an individual is posited in relation to others, his possession becomes rightful only insofar as he is recognized by others. In this manner, he attains for the first time external *common* legitimation, common to him and the parties that recognize him. Thus possession becomes property for the first time. (Fichte, 1845: 130)

Mediated by recognition, property acquires a social function and ceases to be an absolute right. There is no room left for pre-contractual property. This means that an individual is justified in holding a certain amount of property 'on condition that all citizens can make a living on their own. Civil property is cancelled when citizens cannot make a living on their own; it becomes their property. Obviously, this must be determined by the power of the state' (ibid.: 213). This is a clear expression of Jacobinism on the part of Fichte. His liberal views of earlier years have now taken a sharp turn towards radical democracy.

Possibly as a response to Fichte,[18] Kant acknowledged that individuals held property rights within the state of nature, but he defined them as provisional and not as peremptory rights. In his *Metaphysik der Sitten*, Kant detected the radical consequences implicit in the distinction between possession and property, and associated the latter with the existence of a state of right. 'To have something external as one's own (*das Seine*) is possible only in a state of right, under a public legislative power, i.e. in a civil state' (Kant, 1966: 64). This statement is followed by one which extended the holding of property to the state of nature. 'In the state of nature there can be a real, if only provisional external ownership (*Mein und Dein*)' (ibid.: 65). Kant sought to refute Fichte's radicalism and in so doing he prefigured Hegel's aim in the *Philosophy of Right*.

> Natural right in the state of a civil constitution . . . can not suffer attacks from statutory laws. Thus, the following legal principle maintains its validity: 'Whoever follows the maxim according to which it is impossible for me to own the object of my arbitrary will (*Willkür*), does injury to me.' For the civil constitution is only the state of right, through which ownership (*das Seine*) is merely secured, but not, properly speaking, constituted and determined. (1966: 65)

Ownership secured by right is not constituted or determined only when the state of nature is left behind and the sphere of right is attained. On the contrary, it is properly constituted and determined within the state of nature. A state of right can only guarantee protection and respect for property that is already constituted. 'A guarantee', writes Kant, 'presupposes one's ownership' (ibid.: 65). Firmly anchored within the state of nature, property is not liable to interference arising from positive legislation. Kant rehabilitates property as a natural right and distances himself from Fichte.

> Therefore, prior to the civil constitution, ownership must be regarded as possible. A right to compel everyone with whom we could engage in any sort of trade to enter with us in a constitution where ownership is secured, must also be regarded as possible. (ibid.: 65–6)

Kant thus distinguishes between provisionally rightful possession and peremptory possession. The former ensues within the state of nature, which he conceives as of itself capable of leading towards a state of right. Peremptory possession (or rightful possession) follows upon provisionally rightful possession and perfects it. Provisionally rightful possession anticipates peremptory possession and prepares us for its inception. Kant, therefore, sees a transition to a state of right as already happening within the state of nature. Within the state of nature I stand as a mere person defined only by my particular will. But before I become involved in civil interaction with other persons in a state of right, the possibility of such interaction precedes its actualization. This is because, within the state of nature, I have a right to compel other individuals to recognize themselves, and all others, as subjects of rights. Kant is careful to preserve the distinction between state of nature and state of right. He prevents the breakdown of this distinction by defining the state of nature as a provisional (or potential) state of right. For this he allows acquisition of property within the state of nature. If the state of nature was defined as a mere privation of right, there could be no property qua rightful possession within it. Because the state of nature contains the idea of a civil state, property may be provisionally acquired within it.

> The state of a universal, real, unified will to legislate is the civil state. And it is only in conformity with the idea of a civil state, i.e. in view of it and its realization, but prior to its reality . . . that something external can be acquired originally, even if only provisionally. Peremptory acquisition takes place in the civil state exclusively. (1966: 76)

Kant traces the civil state, and therefore the right of property, back to the state of nature. This is much firmer ground for its justification than the purely conventional status defined by Rousseau and Fichte. But by defining property as provisional within the natural state, Kant detracts from its sanctity and exposes it to legislative interference. The interventionist window, opened by Rousseau and Fichte, Kant has not been able to close.[19] A liberal conception of property cannot outlive the relativization imposed by public consent and supervision. Hegel's notion of pre-contractual property in the *Philosophy of Right* seeks to ward proprietors from Fichte's radicalism. For this he defines property as a *ius in rem* and assigns it both logical and temporal priority.[20]

   In sum, Hegel is aware of the fact that the establishment of a protective legal system implies the socialization of property. He is also aware that the figure of contract, and the embryonic socialization it implies, is completely inadequate as a means of protection. Contractual recognition, due to its abstract nature, is a bare gesture that lacks institutional backing. Infringements of contractual property are adjudicated under the strictures of vengeful justice (§102). This is an inherently unstable procedure that mirrors the ineptitude of executive justice in Locke's state of nature. Individual property is duly safeguarded only when social property re-emerges within Hegel's civil society, and a legal system contributes the institutional setting directed specifically towards 'the protection of property' (§188 and §208). The protection of property, in Hegel's view, must be understood in its most liberal sense. It cannot involve redistribution by taxation or any other egalitarian intervention, for this is contrary to the principle of civil society which requires that the livelihood of the needy be mediated by work (§245). Hegel's social concept of property does not leave private property exposed to state interference. He does not intend to follow Hobbes and declare that property consists in the right to exclude all other individuals, 'and not to exclude their sovereign' (Hobbes, 1968: 297). On the contrary, socialization is proposed only as a way to expedite the protective role assigned to the state and the judicial institutions it strongly supports. Socialization cannot in any way be interpreted as taking away a proprietor's rights against the sovereign state. Hegel's concept of property makes a much stronger claim. In spite of demanding the supremacy of the state he asserts a natural pre-contractual right to individual property aimed at excluding redistribution. At times, Hegel reads like a Prussian Locke.

Contrary to Locke, Hegel places judicial institutions within the confines of civil society and distinguishes sharply between civil society and the ethical state. He does so in order to avoid the notion that the 'sole function [of the state] is to protect and secure the life, property and the arbitrary will of everyone', for this would mean that 'the state is merely an arrangement dictated by necessity' (§270). The ethical state, Hegel reiterates, 'is by no means a contract, and its substantial essence does not consist unconditionally in the protection and safe-guarding of the lives and property of individuals as such' (§100). An instrumental state whose sole function was the protection of private property would be contractually bound to civil society. This is the mistake made by empiricist natural law theorists like Hobbes and Locke. When contractualism is allowed to infiltrate the sphere that properly belongs to the ethical state and to sap its autonomy and neutrality, it substantively impairs the state's capacity to protect private property. Paradoxically, the ethical state, a strong state that rises unconditionally above civil society, is the condition that sustains the possibility of Hegel's individualist conception of property. This is a paradox only for empiricists who conceive the state as a 'result', and not as the metaphysical 'primary factor' (§256). Instead, a political thinker like Hegel, who has made peace with Aristotle, may proceed

confidently to affirm that only 'a state which is strong . . . can adopt a
more liberal attitude' (§270).

5 • Liberal civil society

Water stagnates and corrupts when it is closed in by banks on all sides; when it is open on all sides it spreads, and the more outlets it finds the freer it is. So with the citizens.

(Hobbes, 1998: 151)

. . . the movement of the winds preserves the sea from that stagnation which a lasting calm would produce – a stagnation that a lasting . . . peace would also produce.

(Hegel, §324)

Wealth and speed are the things the world admires and for which all men strive . . . Railways, express mails, steamboats, and all possible means of communication are what the educated world seeks.

(Goethe, 1967: 147)

Hegel is said to be the first philosopher to have distinguished systematically between civil society and the state. In so doing he broke with a tradition, stretching from Aristotle to Kant, that conflated these notions. Traditionally, the state did not claim a monopoly over the political, and civil society did not see itself confined to a purely societal status (see Riedel, 1970: 146).[1] Hegelian civil society, posited as a distinct and separate entity, claims a relatively autonomous status. In similar fashion, Hegel's state, separate from civil society and defined by a monarchical constitution, also claims independence and autonomy. This separation of societal and etatist realms coincides with the demands of classical liberalism which tries to reconcile them while keeping them in strict separation. Unlike traditional philosophy, classical liberalism does not subordinate civil society to the state; and unlike nineteenth-century liberalism, it does not subordinate the state to civil society.

Since the end of the Second World War, a concerted effort has been made to secure Hegel's liberal credentials by highlighting the distance that separates his thought from totalitarianism (see Avineri, 1972; Pelczynski, 1984; Franco, 1999; Patten, 1999). Time and again, Hegelian scholars have pointed out that Hegel's notion of civil society includes a spontaneously generated market order. Nothing can lie further away from totalitarianism than societies with markets that operate fully undisturbed. More recently, a 'civil society argument' has been added to the defence of Hegel as a liberal philosopher. He is said to be 'both first and most successful in unfolding the concept of civil society as a theory of a highly differentiated and complex social order' (Arato, 1991: 301). This view equates Hegel's conception of civil society both with a corporatist network of intermediate associations where individuals can learn the virtues of civility and cooperation, and with the functions of a market economy. Societal integration of this kind is seen as requiring minimal interventions by the state, which minimizes the dangers of totalitarian etatism (Arato, 1991; see Smith, 1995).[2]

A preference for societal integration, generated either by a spontaneous market order or by the activity of autonomous intermediate associations, has been a key element in the defence of Hegel's liberal credentials. Though no one disputes that Hegel also considers an etatist manner of integration – the soaring presence of the Hegelian ethical state cannot be easily overlooked – the distinction he introduces between state and civil society warrants a secure space for a purely societal moment whether corporatist or market oriented.

This defence of Hegel as a liberal philosopher ignores the fact that the egoistic competition and conflict discernible in his conception of civil society thwart the operation of a purely societal order. Hegel understands civil society as a system of needs initially ruled by what he calls the 'principle of particularity' (§182). This centrifugal principle replaces the solidaristic family and allows individuals to satisfy their contingent arbitrariness and subjective caprice (§185). In the satisfaction of subjective needs 'universality asserts itself' (§189), but this remains merely formal. Formal universality constitutes the mere semblance of rationality (*Scheinen der Vernunftigkeit*) from which reconciliation could be forthcoming. But then Hegel recognizes that this semblance of rationality '*is* the understanding', and in this sphere of finitude 'the understanding, with its subjective ends and moral opinion, gives vent to its discontent and moral irritation' (§189). This plunges individuals, he acknowledges, into a residual state of nature (§200).[3] Like Hobbes, Hegel's argument gains impulse and acceleration from the social disintegration afforded by this scenario. The reintegration of society is premised on the centripetal impulse to move away from an unrestrained system of needs (*exeundum est e statu naturae*) and towards forms of integration that cannot be secured socially and require etatist mediation.

Hegel conceives of two generic forms of etatist mediation. One occurs within civil society itself and is brought about by two specific state configurations: a judicial state (the Administration of Justice), and an administrative state (the *Polizei*).[4] The other generic form, the ethical state, develops outside the sphere of civil society and is specifically embodied by an executive state (which combines the power of the sovereign and the executive power) and by a hybrid sort of legislative-corporatist state.[5] Paradoxically, Hegel refers to the state internal to civil society as 'external state' (§183). The other state, the typical Hegelian ethical state, is presented as external to civil society, but, because it stirs up the republican dispositions and ethical habits of citizens, must be characterized as internal.

Hegel's critique of liberalism is first and foremost his critique of the state configurations that develop *within* civil society. These state configurations fail to offset the social disintegration that unfolds within the system of needs.[6] Concerned only with the protection of property and redistributive welfare policies, both of them fail to secure a stable 'form of universality', and consequently cannot solve the problem of poverty inherent to the system of needs. To complement the functions discharged by the judicial and administrative states, Hegel proposes an embryonic corporatist system whose aim is the societal integration of the business classes. The corporations envisaged by Hegel at this point are not autonomous and, therefore, their functioning is dependent on etatist directives issued from above. This does not match the kind of societal integration espoused by the 'civil society argument'.

The aim of this chapter is to show that Hegel's conception of civil society proves him both to be a liberal philosopher and critic of liberalism. Evidence for his liberal commitment is to be found in his recognition of a spontaneous order or system of needs. He observes how the 'principle of particularity' manifests the unrestrained demands of selfish individuals. Those demands must run their course for the most part unrestrained. Hegel's critique of liberalism does not negate this fundamental feature of the system of needs. It simply notes that the form of social integration generated by the spontaneous market order (social classes or *Stände*) leads to a more serious form of social disintegration. This befalls some actors in the market who are mired in stubborn poverty. The ship of civil society founders on the shoals of poverty (see Williams, 1997: 259). To prove his case Hegel does not engage in a wholesale refutation of liberalism, but merely argues for the need to limit the range of its application. He postulates a sphere of human activity which must remain absolutely untouched by market forces. Only his ethical state can rise above civil society and the instrumental state formations (judicial and administrative) it engenders. The standard liberal argument seeks to separate state and civil society in order to protect the market from undue state intrusion. Hegel also believes that the liberal argument should emphasize the separation of the state to prevent manipulation by the market. Only a strong executive state, strengthened in Hobbesian fashion, may adopt a more liberal attitude.

I

In the prelude to the section devoted to civil society (§§182–7), the main actor is neither the abstract person who claims property rights, nor the subject of moral duties, nor the member of a family. Hegel introduces a 'concrete person . . . as a particular person, as a totality of needs and a mixture of natural necessity and arbitrariness' (§182). This particular person endowed with rights and duties cannot be envisaged within the family. Children are incapable of holding their own free property and therefore cannot not constitute fully juridical (*rechtliche*) persons (§177). Parents are not fully autonomous either. Married persons give up their natural and individual personalities and transcend the point of view of contract. The proprietors and contractors of abstract rights take to the scene again in civil society, but this time as concrete private persons who bear bundles of subjective desires and needs. They represent what Hegel calls the 'principle of particularity' (§186).

A 'form of universality' (§182) develops as a result of the external interactions (contracts) of these concrete persons (proprietors). The 'principle of universality', which seeks the integration of centrifugal and atomized individuals, is at first barely perceptible. Equated by Hegel to Smith's invisible hand, it generates a spontaneous order that arises out of the selfish needs and wants of individuals (see Avineri, 1972: 146–8). Individuals reach for and attain their own particular ends. In so doing they automatically contribute to the subsistence, welfare and rights of everyone else (§183 and §199). This spontaneous order or system of needs, though self-regulated to a certain point, is intrinsically unstable (§185) and needs to be supplemented by an external and visible organization – a state that rises above particularity, as a 'power (*Macht*) standing over it and as its final end' (§184). Crimes against property and personality must be annulled so as to guarantee an 'undisturbed security of persons and property', and the 'livelihood and welfare of individuals' must be protected (§230). Hegel characterizes this form of etatist integration as the 'external state' (§183), which is made instrumentally to serve the needs of individuals. In the realm of civil society, this external state[7] is described under two headings: 'Administration of Justice' and *Polizei*.

The interaction between two basic principles – of particularity and universality – propel the whole movement of civil society. At first, these principles lie separate and lost in their division (§184). But eventually 'the principle of particularity passes over into universality' (§186). Hegel acknowledges that this coalescence cannot be described as 'ethical identity, because at this level of division the two principles are self-sufficient' (§186). This self-sufficiency determines that the state configurations that embody the principle of universality within civil society remain purely external agencies. They can appear as mere means to the self-sufficient aims of individuals.

The last paragraph of this prelude (§187) examines the final destination of the movement of civil society – the ethical state. There, the principles of particularity and universality attain their ethical identity. Division (*Entzweiung*) within civil society was necessary because 'spirit attains its actuality through internal division' (§187). Only in overcoming that division can spirit attain its objective existence. This ethical state is the concrete form of universality attained when individuals themselves 'determine their knowledge, volition and action in a universal way and make themselves links in the chain of this continuum' (§187).[8] The concrete universality of the ethical state transcends civil society. It represents the ethical peak towards which civil society is led as the result of a process of education (*Bildung*). To become the appropriate tool for lifting human beings towards ethical life, this educative process cannot be conceived as external instruction, superadded to one's natural being. The notion of a state of uneducated Rousseauean innocence and simplicity of customs is entirely incorrect. If this were the case, education would have to be seen as an 'ally to corruption' (§187). Education does not merely enhance the satisfaction of our need for comfort and refinement. Hegel views education as the absolute point of transition towards the ethical state. The immediate, natural substantiality of the family is not what is achieved in that higher sphere. The ethical state allows the attainment of 'infinite subjective substantiality' (§187) elevated to the form of universality. The subjectivity of feeling and conviction and the arbitrariness of inclination are definitely cancelled. But one does not arrive at the ethical state immediately. Subjectivity must be 'educated in its particularity' (§187).

To sum up. Civil society is marked by the tension between a centrifugal principle of particularity and a centripetal principle of universality.[9] But as the argument unfolds, it becomes evident that particularity is the leitmotiv and universality its instrumental accompaniment. (i) Hegel first notices that particularity, in its infinite expansion, spontaneously generates a universal order of needs. This spontaneous system helps initially to explain the social configurations of particularity. But what appears as a form of societal integration (social classes or *Stände*) leads to utter social disintegration. The hegemony of particularity determines a society infinitely torn between the extremes of luxury and poverty.[10] Hegel discerns in this a relic of the state of nature.[11] (ii) Universality is able to gain authority by restoring social integration through state action. An administration of justice protects property owners and the *Polizei* takes measures to alleviate poverty. But etatist integration fails to tame the recalcitrance of particularity and the extremes of luxury and poverty resurface. (iii) The quintessential aim of Hegel's critique of the liberal state is to expose the failure of this instrumental universality and its lack of an ethical dimension. His argument now turns away from the type of etatist integration proposed by liberalism and focuses on the societal integration provided by corporations. Universality becomes 'the end and object of the will and action' of corporate members. The ethical is able to 'return to civil society' (§249). But the aim of corporations is 'limited and finite' (§256) and serves only to show the way towards the Hegelian ethical state. The ethical state is no longer the instrumental state of liberalism, but 'the end which is universal in and for itself' (§256). Not societal but etatist forms of integration constitute Hegel's solution for civil society's problems. My exposition will examine the unfolding of these three moments in Hegel's exposition on civil society.

II

The principle of particularity multiplies the needs of human beings *ad infinitum*. Compared to the restricted range of animal needs, human beings transcend their instinctual fixations and become the subjects of infinite desires (§§190–1). Hegel retrieves this view from Hobbes, Locke and the English economists, who define human beings by their capacity to maximize their individual utilities. This endless expansion of particularity is initially checked by a form of universality represented by the phenomenon of recognition. In my needs, and the means that satisfy them, I recognize the needs and labours of others. My natural needs are first and foremost social needs (§192). A manifestation of this takes place even in trivialities such as the acceptance of fashions or the determination of fixed social times for eating.

The socialization of our needs betrays the presence of the principle of universality. This implies a demand of equality with others by the imitation or the equalizing of oneself with others. At the same time, there is the need to manifest one's particularity and distinctive features (§193). The demand of equality is thus tied to a demand of inequality required by the principle of particularity. These two demands cannot be balanced. Our social needs, declares Hegel, combine natural and spiritual needs. But spiritual needs, because they can claim the universality of representational thought, become paramount. Individuals may now 'refer to their own universal opinion and to a necessity that is of their own making' (§194). Up to now, individual opinions and other individual manifestations fell under the principle of particularity. But after Hegel has recognized the universal moment of socialization, individual opinions attain a universal character, by which the demand of equality may be bypassed. Socialization does not compromise individual freedom. On the contrary, Hegel admits that 'this social moment contains the aspect of liberation' (§194).

Having exorcized egalitarianism, Hegel retrogresses to his point of departure in §191. There he established that the infinite multiplication and division of individual needs gives way to *refinement*. In §195 that same development of particularity leads to *luxury*. But with one notable difference. Particularity has now been tied, through socialization, to the interaction with other particularities. This means that when some individuals advance towards luxury, others are inevitably drawn towards an 'infinitely' expanding poverty,[12] for they confront 'a material which offers infinite resistance' (§195). That 'resistance' is constituted by external things characterized by the fact that 'they are the property of the free will [of others] and are therefore absolutely unyielding' (§195).

Next, the system of needs evolves into two successive configurations that confirm the hegemony of particularity and the tension between luxury and poverty. The first yields a division of labour and education; the second collects the variety of needs and satisfaction, and the division of labour and education, into 'particular systems of needs'. Individuals are then 'separately assigned' to them (§201). They constitute social classes or *Stände*.

(a) Human beings qua consumers encounter mainly human productions (§196). Labour is the universal basis for social interdependence. But Hegel does not focus on this generic character of labour. Instead he considers its division into irreducible kinds. 'The kind of labour' is the title of the subsection that follows his study of human needs and the mode of satisfaction. Labour is presented as the mediation between particularized needs and particularized means for their satisfaction. Matter is given a form by the activity of human beings. What they consume is the product of human effort (§196). Labour is a social activity and its specific articulations follow a pattern determined by history. Labour is thus divided into intellectual and mechanical labour. This division is reinforced by the two types of education envisaged by Hegel: theoretical and practical. Theoretical education is the education adapted to the business class and its fluctuating ethos. Practical education coincides with that element in civil society that remains tied to immediate labour.[13]

(b) The second configuration is presented by Hegel in much greater detail. Individuals are assigned to 'particular systems of needs' or social classes (§201).[14] This assignment to a particular class is again the result of the hegemony retained by the principle of particularity. Hegel recognizes that civil society is the 'sphere of particularity', where individual differences manifest themselves in every direction and at every level. In conjunction with other contingent and arbitrary circumstances, those differences 'necessarily result in inequalities in the resources and skills of individuals' (§200). Hegel explains this arbitrariness as a residue of nature. The sphere of civil society, in its particularity, constitutes a rudimentary or residual state of nature (§200). The naturally conditioned inequalities refer to every aspect of social interaction, making particularity appear impermeable to any form of universality. A demand for equality belongs to the empty understanding (§200). Particularity is the domain where equality finds no place (compare §49).

The social classes envisaged by Hegel are three: the class of land-owners, the business classes and the class of civil servants. The substantiality and sluggishness of the landowning class prevents it from falling under the domination of the principle of particularity. The patrimony of this class is independent 'of the uncertainty of trade, the quest for profit and all variations in property' (§306). No menace to social integration can arise from it. Standing firmly on its landed estates, this class is essentially associated with stable property and its protection through the administration of law (§203). Similarly, the universal class or bureaucracy takes care of the universal tasks charged to the state and cannot constitute a hindrance to the social integration fostered by the principle of universality (§205). Governed by the principle of particularity and refractory to the form of univer-sality by its own disposition, only the business classes can be said to represent the spirit of civil society and its fluctuating nature (§308). Only the bourgeois,[15] the main actor in civil society (§190), can feel at ease in this Hobbesian 'field of conflict in which the private interest of each individual comes up against that of everyone else' (§289).

III

The time is ripe for introducing a more effective manifestation of the principle of universality. The exuberant bourgeoisie, 'the changing element in civil society' (§308), and the type of property it owns, requires an increase in the powers of government.[16] Hegel introduces the *state of civil society*.

(a) The first embodiment of the state of civil society is the judicial state – the Administration of Justice. This state borrows its temper from the calm disposition and the feeling of independence of the landowning class. And rightly so, because the landowning class, the substantial class, presided historically over 'the proper beginning and original foundation of states' (§203). The cultivation of the soil was the scenario where private property and civil law were initially introduced. The right of property is affirmed in its 'valid reality' and not abstractly. It is affirmed 'as the protection of property through the administration of justice' (§208).

The judicial state is the first step on the educational ladder that steers civil society towards the ethical state. With calm disposition and elevated independence the judicial state contemplates each person as a universal person. Everyone shares this identity. 'A human being has worth because he is a human being, not because he is Jewish, Catholic, Protestant, German, Italian, etc.' (§209). The principle of particularity is overcome when each individual recognizes other individuals as persons with the same capacity for rights. The objective universality that emerges establishes itself as an equality of all before the law. This is only a formal universality, for it only makes explicit what is right and determines it as law. Law illuminates what is right in the consciousness of all. Formal equality before the law means that all individuals must be presumed informed of the legal system valid in a society.

What law must provide to each individual are the necessary formalities to make their properties recognizable. This constitutes an essential prerequisite for a system of ownership that has acquired such a degree of mobility.[17]

> Acquisitions of property and transactions relating to it must therefore be undertaken and expressed in the *form* which that existence gives to them. Property is now (*nun*) based on contract and those formalities which make it capable of proof and valid before the law. (§217)

The right of property is legally recognized in civil society. To secure private property, firm and objective signposts must be attached to it, making its demarcations visible.[18] Education allows individuals to recognize and respect those signs.

Crime ceases to be a purely natural and individual offence. Individual victims of crime are no longer isolated individuals. The reciprocity of recognition wrought by the objective organization of the principle of universality creates a web of social ties which, rising beyond the blind system of needs, constitutes an integrated social body. A crime against the property of an individual becomes a crime against society as a whole. Compulsory etatist interventions, and not automatic societal integration, bring about social cohesion and integration. By introducing this effective counterbalance to the principle of particularity and the centrifugal forces it unleashes, a judicial state preserves the societal moment intrinsic to the system of needs and does not obstruct self-regulatory market processes.

(b) The judicial state annuls the crimes against personality and property and thus guarantees 'the undisturbed security of persons and property' (§230). In this respect the administration of justice may be regarded as a boon to the rich and a bane to the poor. Considerations like these may prompt Hegel's concern with poverty and the introduction of an agency committed to welfare. Apart from the harm caused by crime, as an arbitrary 'evil contingency', other 'permissible contingencies' inherent to the system of needs may also cause unwanted harm (§232). The regulation of otherwise rightful actions, and the 'private use of property' within the system of needs, is placed by Hegel in the hands of an administrative state – the *Polizei* or *Polizeistaat*.[19] This state secures that the subsistence and welfare of individuals is actualized as a right (§230).

The organizational function assigned to the administrative state is the regulation and control of contingent economic distortions that cannot be resolved automatically and could lead to social disintegration. 'The differing interest of producers and consumers may come into collision with each other, and even if, on the whole, their correct relationship re-establishes itself automatically, its adjustment also needs to be consciously regulated by an agency which stands above both sides' (§236). Normally, the market should be allowed spontaneously to regulate its dysfunctions. Hegel is invariably distrustful of any form of higher regulation. But if it appears unavoidable that external controls must be imposed on the system of needs, regulation can never 'provide for everything and determine the work of everyone' (§236). The enforced allocation of labour does not allow the mediation of activity by one's particular arbitrary will and particular interests. The pyramids in Egypt were built under such conditions. More recently, a similar regulatory system determined the Jacobin policies in France and Fichte's proposals for a closed commercial state (Hegel, 1974a: 85–6). Hegel is scornful of this kind of state intervention.

Still, if particularity gets the upper hand and the market is abandoned to the rule of pure economics, societies that include a system of needs are endangered. Controls must be imposed on the freedom of enterprise and trade. Price controls on articles vital for subsistence, quality controls, protectionist measures on international trade, care for the poor, public health services, public illumination of streets, etc. – these are some of the measures that Hegel places in the hands of the administrative state. Not that Hegel has abandoned his faith in a spontaneous market order. But when the freedom of enterprise and trade blindly . . . immerses itself in its selfish ends, the more it requires regulation to bring it back to the universal, and to moderate and shorten the duration of those dangerous convulsions to which its collisions give rise, and which should return to equilibrium by a process of unconscious necessity. (§236)

Hegel admits that only exceptionally may the system of needs require some correction. The *Polizeistaat* cannot safeguard individuals from every harmful contingency. Individuals, through their extravagance, may squander their family livelihood and personal capital. But, more importantly, Hegel is aware of other harmful contingencies inherent to the system of needs (§241). Here, he refers back to §200, where the system of needs was seen as spontaneously bringing about 'inequalities in the resources and skills of individuals' which point to a residual state of nature. This is the dilemma faced by the administrative state. For it can either support the poor through taxation, or create job opportunities. In the first case, the 'livelihood of the needy would be ensured without the mediation of work', which is 'contrary to the principle of civil society' (§245). In the second case, increased production leads to overproduction and lack of consumers. Hegel reports that in England, and particularly in Scotland, the best way of trying to deal with this problem has been 'to leave the poor to their own fate and direct them to beg from the public' (§245). This sobering reflection on poverty proves the narrow and confined universality of the etatist bodies within civil society. It also demonstrates that, in this sphere, the abstract right of individuals necessarily trumps the welfare of individuals and groups. Pace Siep, nothing appears to distinguish Hegel's civil society from a possessive market society (see Siep, 1982: 273).

IV

When the system of needs functions as it is supposed to, the two regulatory agencies Hegel puts in place cannot remedy the social disintegration brought about by the extreme accumulations of wealth and poverty endemic to that system. The problem is actually compounded by the introduction of those two state configurations. While the judicial state successfully protects the property of the rich, the administrative state cannot alleviate the plight of the poor. The failure of the external state devised by liberalism prompts the return of the ethical[20] and explains the attention Hegel pays to corporations.

Hegel understands that the business classes are to blame for the dislocations and collisions within civil society. The excessive wealth they amass, due to the overproduction generated by the system of needs, is responsible for the creation of a *vulgus* of propertyless.[21] Hegel introduces corporations as a way ethically to curb the selfish particularity of the business classes and their resistance to external administrative controls. Corporations are designed to integrate only the business classes; the other two classes are part of the solution, not of the problem (§250). By becoming members of a corporation, business agents pursue their own self-interest, but recognize that their fellow members have interests common to theirs. This promotes a special sense of community which prefigures the higher solidaristic dispositions typical of the ethical state.

Hegel believes that entrepreneurs ought to be allowed to attend to their own business in autonomous fashion, with as little interference from the *Polizei* as possible. The primary purpose of the administrative state is 'the actualization and preservation of the universal which is contained within the particularity of civil society' (§249). The control this state exercises over civil society takes the form of 'an external order and arrangement for the protection and security of the masses of particular ends and interests which have their subsistence in this universal' (§249). Hegel designs corporations as an alternative form of control. They activate internal dispositions not taken into account by the judicial and administrative states and thus announce the return of the ethical.

> In accordance with the Idea, particularity itself makes this universal, which is present in its immanent interests, the end and object of its will and activity, with the result that ethical returns to civil society as an immanent principle to civil society; this constitutes the determination of the corporation. (§249)

Hegel's faith in the spontaneous order imposed by the system of needs is unshaken. Market society showers the rich with abundance and luxury, but spells ever-increasing misery for the poor. The series of measures displayed by the administrative state were meant to alleviate poverty, but its burden remains a hard, recalcitrant fact. No solution to poverty is to be found in Hegel's theorizing, which is not swayed by Adam Smith's optimism (Avineri, 1972: 148). Still, corporations bring about indirect relief to the poor by curbing the luxurious consumption exhibited by the business classes. The fluctuations of business produce increased social mobility which diffuses and relaxes the old traditional ranks. The exhibition of wealth becomes an important means by which individuals assert their social standing. If social rank and honour are guaranteed, the alienation and lack of recognition fuelled by social mobility are nullified.

> When complaints are made about the luxury and love of extravagance of the business classes (*gewerbwetreibenden Klassen*) which is associated with the creation of a rabble (see §244), we must not overlook . . . its ethical basis as implied in what has been said above. If the individual is not a member of a legally recognized corporation (and it is only through legal recognition that a community becomes a corporation), he is without the honour of belonging to an estate, his isolation reduces him to the selfish aspect of his trade, and his livelihood and satisfaction lack stability. He will accordingly try to gain recognition through the external manifestations of success in his trade, and these are without limit . . . (§253)

Corporations offer a meagre solution to the problem of poverty. The help received by the poor now loses its 'contingent and unjustly humiliating character' (§253).

All in all, corporations, much like the administrative state, are not supposed to interfere with the freedom of enterprise and trade of the business classes. They share the ethical temper fostered by medieval guilds, but also contain the rudiments of a modern corporatist state. Traditionally, the interstices left between individual producers and public authority were filled by guilds and corporations. They presided over the societal integration of entrepreneurial, professional and labour activities. Scorned by Hobbes, who compared them to 'wormes in the entrayles of naturall man' (1968: 174),[22] guilds and corporations were abolished in revolutionary France (Law of Chapelier) and dismantled in Prussia in 1811.[23] Hegel does not retrieve these traditional institutions without modifications. He requires them to operate under higher state supervision, with express prohibition to act independently. His corporations cannot be assimilated to the abolished guild-system; they herald the corporatist movement of the early twentieth century.

The function ascribed to corporations requires the formation of habits and dispositions that curb the typically selfish particularity of agents operating within the system of need. The development of an *esprit de corps* preludes the more comprehensive and demanding dispositions that are required of the citizens of the ethical state. The etatist integration promoted by the judicial and administrative states fails because of their inability to evoke those internal attitudes. Even though corporations signal the return of the ethical, they do so on a very limited scope. Hegel's ethical state promises to expand the corporate spirit to cover the polity as a whole. But the monarchical executive state, which Hegel includes in his ethical state, is more Hobbesian than republican. The forces of particularity have expanded to such a degree that only freedom, not virtue, can be the source of duty.

V

The distinction between civil society and the state is drawn explicitly for the first time in Hegel's Heidelberg lectures on *Rechtsphilosophie* (Hegel, 1983a: 93), and henceforth becomes a permanent and visible feature in his expositions on political philosophy. Horstmann has shown that the role played by the notion of civil society, even if there is no terminological evidence of its use, can be traced back to the first systematic presentations on political philosophy of the Jena period (Horstmann, 1973: 211–18). He explains that this distinction is made explicit by Hegel much later, when he felt the need to clarify his public statement concerning the constitutional disputes at Wurtemberg in 1817 (Horstmann, 1997: 211). While in principle he favours the position of the King and objects to that of the Estates, Hegel criticizes both parties. First, he is critical of the Estates for not living up to the new political and social realities that had arisen subsequent to the French Revolution. The new times had demonstrated that old positive law and privileges had to give way to the principles of rational law.

> One might say of the Wurtemberg Estates what has been said of the returned French émigrés: they have forgotten nothing and learnt nothing. They seem to have slept through the last twenty-five years, possibly the richest that world-history has had, and for us the most instructive, because it is to them that our world and our ideas belong. (Hegel, 1964b: 282)

Second, he is also directing this same criticism to the King, who appeared to have dozed off through a decisive phase of the French

Revolution – the terror unleashed by Jacobins. His constitutional project envisaged granting voting qualifications to 25-year-old men who possessed an income of at least 200 gilders from real estate. This shy opening up of the franchise is seen by Hegel as a dangerous democratic give-away:

> If a constitution nevertheless makes him something, a voter, it grants him a lofty political right without any tie with other civic bodies and introduces in one of the most important matters a situation which has more in common with the democratic, even anarchical, principle of particularization (*Vereinzelung*) than with that of an organic order. (1964b: 263)

Hegel, to be sure, is very much awake to the dangers posed by 'the French abstractions of mere number and quanta of property' (ibid.). If an organic order is to be preserved, the democratic principle, even the King's restricted formulation, ought to be discarded, or at least no longer 'made the dominant qualification or, all over again, the sole condition for exercising one of the most important political functions' (ibid.).

The democratic principle, expressed at this point as a limited opening of the franchise by extending voting privileges to a portion of the population, convinced Hegel about the need to secure a space in his political theory for a single political authority whose final decisions could withstand the pressures rising from atomistic particularity. This is the space he assigned to the state. Civil society, by contrast, defined as the domain where particularity would roam free, could only support subordinate and strictly dependent authorities.

Once the spheres of civil society and the state had been thus separated, it may be seen as appropriate for Hegel to justify public authority as one and universal (Horstmann, 1997: 213–14). The separation of civil society and the state meant the division of public authority into two spheres, civil and political. Pelczynski feels that it would be more natural 'to view the two sets of authorities as just two parts of one and the same system of public authority, just as their activities could be viewed as phases or stages of the same governmental process' (1971: 11). But this ought not to be seen as constituting a problem for Hegel. The unity of political authority was not in need of being justified, for the duality that Pelczynski detects did not actually arise. Hegel's constitutional monarch is the guarantee that this would not occur. Pelczynski's misconception arises from the fact that he misses the affinity that may exist between the liberalism espoused by Hegel and authoritarianism. If instead of trying to approximate Hegel to Bentham, and even to Paine, Pelczynski had taken into account the viability of conservative liberal postures, he would have seen that an authoritarian monarch might be the solution for the problem posed by an individualistic liberal society (Hegel, 1964: 55; see Avineri, 1967: 260). The introduction of Hegel's constitutional monarch depoliticized the judicial and administrative authorities that had emerged within civil society. As non-political instances, they proved too weak to withstand the pressures of particularity. Their political function had to be assumed, within the sphere of the state, by instances that could be placed directly under the discretionary power of the monarch. From this high point, the highest in the political realm, power could irradiate to these re-constituted spheres of subordinate authority – the lawcourts, the *Polizei* (supervised now by the state's executive power) and the corporations (placed under the tuition of the legislative power).

Hegel intended to make sure that the autonomy of the state was absolute, so that there could be no gaps through which civil society's particularity could seep through and withdraw their consent, for example, from taxation required to confront political emergencies (Hegel, 1964b: 267–8). The authorities generated within civil society appeared as mere *results* of conflicts brought forth by the hegemony of particularity. The universality that they represented was empirical, purely derivative and a function of the subjective freedom of individuals. If Hegel's state was to attain autonomy and independence, it had to prove its original, underived universality, one that was thought to be a starting point and never a mere *result*. For this to be so, the state had to appear as the primary factor, 'what is first' (*das Erste*). It is precisely this that Hegel placed beyond doubt when making the transition from the sphere of civil society to that of the state.

This development of immediate ethical life through the division of civil society and on to the state, which is shown to be their true ground, is the scientific proof of the concept of the state, a proof which only a development of this kind can furnish. Since the state appears as the *result* of the development of the scientific concept in that it turns out to be the *true* ground [of this development], the mediation and semblance already referred to are likewise superseded by immediacy. In actuality, therefore, the state in general is in fact the primary factor (*das Erste*); only within the state does the family first develop into civil society, and it is the idea of the state which divides itself into these two moments. (§256)

Absolutism, which revived Roman law and its distinction between civil and public law, *ius* and *lex*, helped to overcome the contradiction between the decrees of absolute imperial sovereignty and the absolute rights of property. Under Napoleon, the pursuit of public policy lay in imperial hands, on the understanding that the private lives of free and equal citizens would be duly recognized and safeguarded. Royer-Collard summed it all up: 'Establish authority first, and then create liberties as a counterbalance' (see Bagge, 1952: 100). And Hegel follows suit by postulating the state as 'what is first'. He confronts Hobbes and the natural law tradition which seeks a philosophical justification of the state that conceives of it either as the result of a contract or as a utilitarian calculus. The claim that the state exists primarily to safeguard civil society invests it with a purely commissarial role. Only a non-contractual, non-utilitarian state is strong enough effectively to withstand the forces of particularity and preserve its existence. By postulating the state as 'what is first', Hegel reaches back to the republican disposition that animates Aristotle's state and presents it as the foundation of his own philosophical conception. Ultimately, republican virtue, which Hegel equates with Montesquieu's feudal aristocratic ethos, proves to be insufficient. Modernity demands the monarchical principle and postulates the prince as the primary factor.

6 • Hegel's constitutional monarchy: monarchical rather than constitutional

En 1814, le pouvoir royale se plaçait en quelque sorte en dehors et au-déssus de la Constitution.

(Alexis de Tocqueville[1])

The concepts of sovereignty and absolutism have been forged together on the same anvil.

(Maritain, 1969: 64)

Hegel's point of departure in the *Philosophy of Right* is the notion of free, abstract personality from which he deduces the fundamental right of private property and other derivative rights. The emphasis falls on a person's freedom and self-determination, and implies that only self-given duties may be validated, a conception shared by all liberals. Hegel's point of arrival is a conception of the state he defines in one place as 'constitutional monarchy' (§273).[2] Use of this term has invited liberal interpreters, like Allen Wood, to assert that his conception 'may be assimilated to presently existing parliamentary systems with a nominal hereditary monarch, as in Britain, Holland, Belgium, or Sweden' (Hegel, 1991a: p. xxiv). This interpretation appears problematic for it does not take into account the monarchical principle, a key element in Hegel's constitutional monarchy. By adopting the monarchical principle Hegel embraces not only the logic of sovereignty, but also lends support to the Hobbesian notion that sovereign power is indivisible and can only be held by a person. This is incompatible with contemporary parliamentarianism, constitutionalism and the doctrine of separation of powers on which it rests. Hegel rejects this doctrine and harshly criticizes its champion, Montesquieu, whom he interprets as espousing a return to feudalism. In his view, only the unified authority of the state, brought about by the monarchical principle, can contain the forces of particularity unleashed within civil society.

In order fully to understand Hegel's idiosyncratic notion of constitutional monarchy, I discuss his notion of princely power and its three moments – individuality or princely power proper, particularity and universality (§§275–86). In Constant's view, princely power, or *pouvoir royale*, is the neutral instance that stands between the executive and legislative powers and mediates any conflict that may arise between them. But Hegel's monarch, contrary to what Yack and Ilting maintain, cannot be assimilated to this notion of neutral power.[3] Constant espouses a genuine separation of powers, while Hegel thinks that princely power embraces the other governing powers. Princely power itself is constituted by three moments – legislative, executive, and princely power proper (Boldt, 1975: 119) – moments that may be distinguished, but in no case separated. The Hegelian prince is not a neutral, but a higher third.

If Hegel's constitutional monarchy is more monarchical than constitutional, this is primarily due to his conception of princely power proper (§§276–82). This determines that the monarch, and not the people, is sovereign and subject of constituent power. Espousal of hereditary monarchy presents a challenge for Hegel because he insists that this arrangement is not derived from consequentialist reasoning. This would relativize and debase majesty to the sphere of mere reasoning. Hegel is intent on demonstrating its conceptual necessity. Hereditary monarchy manifests the unity and continuity of the state. It confirms that the state is not 'a contractual relationship between monarch and the people' (§281).

By comparing Aristotle's classical conservative views and Hegel's conception of sovereign authority, I attempt to demonstrate the thoroughly modern nature of that systematic synthesis. According to Aristotle, the struggles within traditional societies do not challenge the substantial unity and existence of the polity. These occasional upheavals require only ad hoc solutions. By contrast, Hegel's hereditary monarch must permanently thwart the revolutionary challenge posed by modern civil society. The figure of the monarch, who takes his decisions beyond the confines of civil society, determines the authoritarian bent of Hegel's liberalism.

I

Much of the confusion surrounding the role assigned to the Hegelian prince stems from the introduction of the notion 'constitutional monarchy' in §273 of the *Philosophy of Right*. The *Hegelsche Mitte* apologists have made use of this notion, mentioned only in this particular paragraph, to negate Hegel's authoritarianism and reaffirm his liberal credentials. But faced with evidence that, in the paragraphs that follow §273, Hegel's monarch appears to be more monarchical than constitutional, even his liberal apologists concede that his conception appears apocryphal and hard to pin down.[4] Paragraph 273 reads as follows:

> The political state is therefore divided into three substantial elements:
>   *(a) the power to determine and establish the universal – the* legislative power
>   *(b) the subsumption of* particular spheres and individual cases under the universal – the *executive power*,
>   *(c) subjectivity as the ultimate decision of the will* – princely power, in which the different powers are united in an individual unity which is thus the apex and beginning of the whole, i.e. of *constitutional monarchy*.

This text manifests what M. M. Goldsmith has identified as 'the logic of the concept of sovereignty' (1980: 38; see Wilks, 1969). According to Goldsmith, sovereignty involves two defining notes: hierarchy and closure. A system of sovereign authority or rules is a closed hierarchical order – 'each subordinate rule or authority owes its validity to, or is derived from, a superior authority. But to "close" the system, to prevent it from being infinitely regressive, a highest or supreme norm or authority is required' (1980: 38). In Hobbes's *De Cive*, sovereign power is defined as 'the greatest power that men can confer, greater than any power an individual can have over himself' (Hobbes, 1998: 82). *Imperium summum* is the *terminus ultimus* in the sense that there is no superior power from which it could be derived.

Modern constitutionalism is determined by the same logic. Kelsen's *Grundnorm* and Hart's secondary rule of recognition are ultimate rules that cancel the possibility of an infinite regress. By standing at the top of a hierarchical order of subordinate rules, the sovereignty of the constitution validates the whole legal system (see Wilks, 1969: 201–2). Constitutionalism can be traced back to Aristotle, for whom, as Hobbes acknowledges, 'sovereign authority in the commonwealth should be lodged in the laws alone' (1998: 134). But precisely on this point Hobbes breaks with Aristotle and veers towards anti-constitutionalism. Like Bodin, he asserts that sovereignty is indivisible and therefore its subject must be one person or one assembly (Goldsmith, 1980: 39). In *Leviathan*, he writes: 'Subjection, Command, Right and Power are accidents not of Powers, but of Persons', and thereby rejects the rule of constitutional law (Hobbes, 1968: 601). Hegel adopts a similar conception. For him the moment of closure proper to the logic of sovereignty is assigned to princely power, 'the apex and beginning of the whole' (§273). Princely power constitutes, for Hegel, the personality of the state, which 'has actuality only as a *person*, as the *monarch*' (§279).

In the Remark to §273, Hegel has two things to say about constitutional monarchy, both confirming the view that for him this notion has more to do with monarchism than constitutionalism. First, he acknowledges that 'the development of the state to constitutional monarchy is the achievement of the modern world'. Second, though he introduces constitutional monarchy in the context of the separation of powers (legislative, executive and princely powers), he proceeds to discuss it in terms of the forms of government (monarchy, aristocracy and democracy), and writes that those forms 'are reduced, in constitutional monarchy, to [the status] of moments'. I will examine these two points in greater detail.

(i) When Hegel says that constitutional monarchy is the achievement (*Werk*) of the modern world, he has in mind developments in post-Napoleonic France. Constant had first defined this notion in 1814 and it was subsequently employed to describe the regime installed in France under Louis XVIII. This became the model for the constitutional experiments conducted in Germany's south-western states from 1815 onwards. Hegel probably does not mention Constant by name because of the latter's affirmation of popular sovereignty, a view strongly rejected by Hegel. Instead, he chooses to highlight the modernity of his own proposal by setting it against the purported feudal characteristics of the forms of government discussed by Montesquieu in book 3 of *De l'esprit des lois*. Praise is due to Montesquieu's depth of insight, but at the same time Hegel feels he has to distance himself from backward-looking institutions that do not square well with modern circumstances. In this exchange with Montesquieu, Hegel raises the issue of democracy and virtue. Montesquieu maintained that a democratic constitution depended on the virtue of citizens, and illustrated this view with a reference to revolutionary England in the seventeenth century and the vain efforts of its citizens to establish a democratic government. He blamed their failure on their lack of virtue.[5] Ambition and avarice had crept into their hearts, a favourable occasion for the state to grow weak. In such circumstances, Hegel acknowledges, the state 'falls prey to universal exploitation and its strength resides solely in the power of a few individuals and the unruliness of everyone' (§273).

Hegel brings up the issue of democracy as a foil to justify his rejection of popular sovereignty. This becomes clear in his response to Montesquieu:

> To these remarks, it must be replied that, as the condition of society grows more advanced and the powers of particularity are developed and liberated, it is not enough for the heads of state to be virtuous; another form of rational law is required apart from that of the [individual] disposition if the whole is to have the strength to maintain its unity and to grant the forces of developed particularity their positive as well as their negative rights. (§273)

Montesquieu retained a notion of monarchy that was neither ancient nor constitutional, but feudal. In feudal monarchy 'the relationships covered by its constitutional law (*inneren Staatsrechts*) have become firmly established as rights of private property and privileges of individuals and corporations' (§273). When public offices become privileges and the property of designated individuals, rank and honour are needed to hold the state together. Modern, post-revolutionary Europe has experienced the eruption of the forces of particularity to such a degree that freedom, and not honour or privilege, becomes the only source of duty. In this context a different 'form of rational law' is required. The virtue of citizens is not something one can depend on to safeguard the unity of the state. Only the authority of an absolutist state, not medieval democracy, can guarantee the exaction of duties from all citizens equally. Hegel observes that democracy is not alone in demanding the formation of virtuous citizens. Virtue, he admits, is not superfluous to monarchies. But after his recognition of the extent to which particularity has now been liberated, this recommendation, tempered as it is, sounds hollow.[6]

(ii) Hegel's option for constitutional monarchy has been hailed as proof of his commitment to constitutionalism, the hallmark of political liberalism. Constitutionalism is the procedure which seeks to limit and chasten the authority of the state and make it responsive to the demands of civil society (see Cristi and Ruiz-Tagle, 2004). The essential function of a constitution aims at protecting private property and contract freedom. Wherever individual rights are not constitutionally recognized, and no division of governmental powers exists, liberals deny the existence of a constitution. This is forcefully postulated by the Declaration of the Rights of Man and Citizens of 1789 which identifies constitutional rule with the entrenchment of rights and the division of powers. The Declaration, in its article 16, avers: 'Toute société dans laquelle la garantie des droits n'est pas assuré, ni la séparation des pouvoirs déterminée, n'a pas de constitution.'

Characteristic of the Hobbesian state was a rejection of the separation of powers. 'For what is it to divide the Power of a Commonwealth, but to dissolve it; for Powers divided mutually destroy each other' (Hobbes, 1968: 368). Hegel appears to agree with this statement when he writes:

> The basic determination of the political state is the substantial unity or ideality of its moments. In this unity, the particular powers of the state are both dissolved and preserved. But they are preserved only in the sense that they are justified not as independent entities, but only in such a way and to such an extent as is determined by the Idea of the whole. (§272)

Support for the monarchical principle explains this rejection of the division of powers – division of powers and monarchical principle are incompatible. Hegel explains that 'the political state is . . . divided into three substantial elements', and then adds that constitutional monarchy is the whole that issues from the organic union of these elements, with princely power at the pinnacle. His interest lies in magnifying the monarchical, not the constitutional aspects of constitutional monarchy. Instead of focusing on the division of powers, he shifts his attention to the division of forms of government (monarchy, aristocracy, democracy). From a pre-modern point of view it makes sense to distinguish between monarchical, aristocratic and democratic constitutions. The criterion of division is given by the number of individuals participating in the tasks of government – one in monarchical regimes, several in aristocratic regimes, all in democratic regimes. Pre-modern governments had citizenries that were substantially homogeneous and compact, so that the type of regime available did not impinge on the unity of the state. As Hegel puts it, the old division of forms of government presupposed 'a still undivided and substantial unity'. Modernity has brought with it the dissolution of the substantive unity of classical polities. States are now populated by subjectively free individuals who do not naturally cohere and do not spontaneously constitute political unities. Hegel introduces constitutional monarchy as a way to preserve the state's substantive unity assailed by the forces of modern subjectivity. The classical forms of government are to be subsumed within constitutional monarchy as organic moments, so as not to endanger a unified political order. In agreement with Montesquieu, Hegel conflates the classical division of forms of government with the modern division of powers. 'The monarch is one; several participate in the executive power, and the many at large participate in the legislative power.'

By proceeding in this manner Hegel is able to link the division of forms of government to the division of powers and thus restricts democracy to the legislative function, turning the executive function into an aristocratic domain, and creating a unique role for the monarch.[7] The division of powers does not correspond to a balance of equal powers, but, in accordance with the logic of sovereignty, a hierarchical order is introduced, which is meant to secure the authoritative role of the monarchical summit and the subordination of other spheres of authority. The aim here is not constitutionally to check and chasten the authority of the state, but to enhance it.

The monarch becomes the holder of princely power, a newly devised function to be distinguished from the executive power. Princely power is Hegel's much enhanced rendition of Constant's *pouvoir royal*.[8] As the 'apex and unity of the whole', the monarch fuses the legislative and executive powers in 'an individual unity'. Hegel resurrects Polybius's idea of a *status mixtus* only to refashion its interior design. The architecture of government may now safely combine monarchy, aristocracy and democracy because one of the elements of the mixture, monarchy, has become its hierarchical pinnacle. Hegel's concern is the possibility that democratic constituencies may gain access to the legislature and from there try to overrun and revolutionize the whole system of government. As we saw earlier, this was precisely the concern he manifested in his discussion on the English Reform Bill. Only princely power, guided by the monarchical principle, may effectively tame and chasten democracy.[9]

Hegel's aim is to negate *political*, not economic liberalism. His proposal strives to ensure a fully functional civil society.[10] He confronts political or constitutional liberalism because he feels that it posits the state as an 'abstraction' and leaves undecided the question 'whether this state is headed by *one* or *several* or *all*'. There is danger in leaving the democratic floodgates wide open. Democracy can only cripple the state by diluting its unity and authority. Hegel blames what he calls 'the superficial conception of the state' for unlocking those floodgates. In §272, Hegel analyses this 'superficial' standpoint. This he does after

defining (in §271) what he understands by the 'internal constitution' of
the state as opposed to its external configuration. Externally, the state
faces other states as a single individual whole. Internally, this single
individual whole exhibits a complex articulation of parts. The internal
constitution of the state expresses its organic design. The constitutive
parts are the distinct faculties or powers of the state, functioning like
the integrated and inseparable members of a living organism. According
to Hegel, 'each of the powers in question is in itself the totality, since
each contains the other moments and has them active within it' (§272).
Superficiality interprets the division of powers abstractly. It conceives
the 'self-sufficiency of each power in relation to the others' (§272R).
Mutual checks and balances are supposed to protect public freedom
by weakening the unity of the state and chastening its unified authority.
The result is an equilibrium or balance of powers that brings about the
demise of the state as a 'living unity'. Hegel's verdict is foreboding. 'If
the powers . . . attain self-sufficiency, the destruction of the state, as
has been witnessed on a grand scale [in our times], is immediately
posited.' But even more ominous is the remedy he thinks can prevent
the destruction of the state. Only if one power is able to subjugate the
others will that destruction be avoided. This restores the unity of the
state and ensures its continued existence. Hegel is aware that this can
also bring about the collapse of governmental powers into one dominant, despotic power. This was the recipe employed by absolutism. The
ancien régime imposed absolutist dictatorships which precipitated
the destruction of the constitution.[11] But this harsh procedure meant the
salvation of the state. To avoid this messy outcome, Hegel introduces
princely power effectively to abolish a balanced division of power. As a
manifestation of the monarchical principle, princely power places
constituent power in the hands of the prince and grants him a monopoly on sovereignty (see Thiele, 2002: 163). Hegel thinks that only an
absolutist moment somehow ensconced within the constitution will
ensure its preservation.[12]

II

Paragraph 273 contains the blueprint that guides the construction of
Hegel's authoritarian state. On the one hand, Hegel's argument
reveals how much his state depends on a modern conception of civil
society. While centrifugal civil society accelerates mobility and pluralism,

the authority that emanates from a monarchical state offers the centripetal counterforce needed to maintain stability and unity. This is an argument that Hegel shares with Hobbes, who similarly built his state atop the anarchy and chaos of the state of nature. On the other hand, it reveals that Hegel is aware that post-Napoleonic restored monarchy could not reclaim the *plenitudo potestatis* of its predecessors who happily emulated Hobbes's sovereign. Overt absolutist policies were now out of the question. The French Restoration and prescriptions emanating from the Congress of Vienna were living proof that monarchism required a compromise with constitutional rule. The formula 'constitutional monarchy' was a manifestation of that compromise. Hegel's effort to strengthen the hierarchical unity of the state and dilute the division of powers has to be understood as part of that process.

In §275, Hegel summarily introduces princely power, the moment of closure required by the logic of sovereignty. Princely power contains three moments which correspond to the three governing powers: (i) legislative power ('the universality of the constitution and laws'), (ii) executive power ('consultation as the reference of the particular to the universal') and (iii) princely power proper. What interests Hegel the most is to show how the hierarchical unity of the state derives from the subjectivity of the prince, as the mainspring of ultimate, final decisions. 'This is the individual aspect of the state as such, and it is in this respect alone that the state itself is one' (§279).[13] In order to preserve the philosophical value of this derivation, he retrieves the synthetic deduction of the will he developed in the introduction (§5 onwards). Accordingly, he infers the entire content of princely power from the concept of the will. 'One and the same concept – in this case the will – which begins by being abstract . . . retains its character yet [at the same time] consolidates its determinations, again through its own exclusive agency, and thereby acquires its own content' (§279). The novelty of this transition, with respect to the dialectic of the will that developed in the introduction, is that the determinations of the monarch's will do not seem to require an external content. This cannot but reflect Hegel's push towards the elevation of the prince qua individual to inviolable heights. This conforms with his conception of the monarch's majesty (§281) and the moment of closure demanded by the logic of sovereignty.

Hegel first develops the moment of individuality – princely power proper. What most clearly defines princely power is the need to avoid an infinite regression and close the hierarchical system of authority. The unity of the state can be traced back to the subjective will of the prince and his power to render the ultimate, final decisions. This view he shares with Hobbes, for whom there must be a sovereign, an actual personal sovereign, and not just abstract sovereignty (Goldsmith, 1980: 40). It takes Hegel seven cumbersome paragraphs (§§276–82) to unpack the meaning of this key function. I will examine this in detail in the third section of this chapter.

The second moment is defined by particularity (§§283–4). According to Hegel this corresponds to the advisory body in charge of assisting in the prince's deliberations. Crown councillors define, organize and bring forward to the presence of the monarch the issues that require his ultimate decision. Their appointment is left to monarchical discretion. In agreement with Constant and the French *doctrinaires*, who first introduced this idea, Hegel assigns responsibility to crown councillors individually for all the objective ingredients that go into decision-making. At the same time, majesty absolves the monarch of any personal responsibility.

Finally, the third moment concerns universality (§§285–6), which Hegel finds present subjectively in the prince's conscience, and objectively in the constitution and laws.[14] Only the emplacement of the prince at the apex of the state, as an absolute figure, can explain this claim to universality.[15] Beyond this, Hegel also claims that the universality of the constitution and laws is associated with the power of the prince. This may be interpreted as Hegel's affirmation of the monarchical principle and his endorsement of the prince as the subject of constituent power.[16] What concerns Hegel at this point is constitutional continuity and the stability of the institutions established by the constitution. He thinks that continuity is best guaranteed by hereditary succession. The will of the people is rejected because he sees it as inherently fragmented and subject to endless fluctuation. A monarchical constitution, with hereditary succession based on primogeniture as its central characteristic, is the most solid foundation a state can have. Hegel acknowledges that hereditary succession based on primogeniture constitutes a reversion 'to the patriarchal principle' (§286). But he believes that this ensures public freedom for it posits the monarch as 'the absolute apex of an organically developed state' (§286). Hegel views this as a reconciliation of freedom and authority. 'Public freedom in general and hereditary succession guarantee each other reciprocally' (§286).

The *Hegelsche Mitte*, interpreting Hegel from a normativist perspective (Kelsen/Hart), denies that the monarch may be conceived as the final validating authority. This cannot be the function of any human agency and must be assigned to a *Grundnorm*, to a secondary rule of recognition. The final decider can only be a constitutional rule charged with coordinating a string of separate human deciders, all of whom have partial final deciding authority in their respective particular and separate areas. A closed hierarchical order is undoubtedly visible in Hegel's *Philosophy of Right* – consider the subordinate role assigned to ministers and the bureaucracy. But, in Hobbesian fashion, Hegel's prince is subject of constituent power and as such retains, first of all, 'the power to decide, in the last analysis, all questions in the commonwealth'. Because of this he also retains 'the power to decide the most important question in the commonwealth, namely, whether or not the sovereign will remain in power' (Hampton, 1986: 104).

III

I return now to the first defining moment of princely power, namely princely power proper. The exposition in these paragraphs (§§276–82) is of key importance to my argument for it corroborates the Hobbesian quality of Hegel's conception of sovereignty. Princely power brings closure to a hierarchical system of authority. More importantly, it allows the derivation of the unity of the state from the personal authority of the prince, and not from an impersonal *Grundnorm* or rule of recognition.[17] Hegel's exposition of princely power asserts first and foremost the authority that is to be concentrated in his hands. A sovereign person, one and stationary, ensures the unity and stability of the state. Guarding political unity and stability is what political authority is all about. This is the great truth promoted by absolutism, a truth Hegel is prepared to defend against forerunners of liberalism like Montesquieu, who attacked the absolutist state by introducing a separation of its powers. In the eyes of Hegel this could only weaken the unity and stability of the state, and explains why he brings up Montesquieu in his exposition on princely power.

Princely power proper is 'the moment of ultimate decision as the self-determination to which everything else reverts' (§275) This, Hegel writes, constitutes the 'distinguishing principle of the power of the prince as such' and for this reason he feels it deserves to be dealt with first.[18] Starting his presentation with the rule of the prince, and not the rule of law, is indicative of the paramount importance he attributes to the monarch as a representative person, a *persona repraesentativa*.[19] The stable rule of one concrete person is the ideal representation of political unity and stability. Hegel's conception of princely power is defined by the Hobbesian notion of sovereign representation (or *Repräsentation*) as opposed to delegate representation (or *Vertretung*), by which sovereignty is delegated or mandated by a people whose identity is assumed from the beginning. Hegel, concerned with securing both the unity of the political order and an unmitigated social pluralism, seeks to reconcile sovereign and delegate representation. He ascribes sovereign representation to the prince. Delegate representation, on the other hand, is taken into consideration when he discusses the Assembly of Estates.

The following are the three moments of the sovereign will's derivation, summarized in §280 as the 'transition from the concept of pure self-determination to the immediacy of being, and hence to the natural realm'.[20]

(a) Hegel first affirms that the powers of the state are not 'self-sufficient and fixed . . . but are ultimately rooted in the unity of the state' (§278). This strong defence of the unity of the state goes hand in hand with an affirmation of what he refers to as the 'ideality of its moments'. By this he means that the powers of the state cannot be understood as separate and independent entities. What he has in mind here is Montesquieu's doctrine of the separation of powers, which he interprets as a liberal attempt to weaken the authority of the state. He equates Montesquieu's view to the feudal conception of monarchy, which he vehemently opposes. Hegel privileges the *thèse royaliste* championed by absolutists like Abbé Dubos and the Marquis d'Argenson over Count Boulainvilliers's *thèse nobiliaire*.[21] The outcome is a vigorous affirmation of the notion of sovereignty. Feudalism gave its monarchs a sovereignty limited to the domain of external affairs, 'but internally, neither the monarch himself nor the state was sovereign' (§278; see Heller, 1921: 106–7). Hegel views feudalism as a situation where the pluralism of civil society far outweighed the monism of the state. But feudal pluralism was organized corporatively and not exposed therefore to the dissolvent forces of modernity. The acceleration of the pluralistic tendencies at the onset of modernity required a reinforcement of monism. Sovereignty was necessary to solidify the unity of public authority and ensure its stability. Sovereignty, according to Hegel, defines the idealism of the state. Idealism, in this context, has in view an 'animal organism', the parts of which are not really parts but members, that is, 'members or organic moments, whose isolation and separate existence (*Für-sich-Bestehen*) constitute disease' (§278).

In order to dispel misinterpretations that may arise from his conception of sovereignty as the substantial unity or 'ideality' of the state's particular powers, Hegel distinguishes sovereignty from despotism.[22] 'Ideality' implies that the particular state powers 'are not independent or self-sufficient in their ends and modes of operation' (§278). If this, in turn, were to imply that the separation of powers is cancelled, one would be faced with despotism, the rule of 'mere power and empty arbitrariness'. Despotism, more precisely defined, is 'the condition of lawlessness in general, in which the particular will as such, whether of a monarch of the people (ochlocracy), counts as law (or rather replaces law)' (§278). Hegel rejects this implication, maintaining that 'sovereignty is to be found specifically under lawful and constitutional conditions as the moment of ideality of the particular spheres and functions' (§278). But, then, it appears that the notion of ideality constitutes both the problem and the solution he brings to it. Is Hegel arguing in circles?[23]

Sovereignty as ideality is the solution to what Hegel sees as the main difficulty posed by the separation of powers, namely the weakening of the unity of the state. If Hegel is to remain within the bounds of constitutionalism, he needs to assert the separation of state powers. But as a monarchist he cannot but assert that

> these spheres are not independent or self-sufficient in their ends and modes of operation, nor are they solely immersed in themselves; on the contrary, in these same ends and modes of operation, they are determined by and dependent on the *end of the whole* (to which the indeterminate expression 'the *welfare of the state*' has in general been applied). (§278)

It appears, then, that the notion of ideality allows him the flexibility needed to affirm the unity of the state without at the same time being forced to abandon constitutionalism and the rule of law. The flexibility of ideality is what allows it to 'manifest itself in two different ways'. Sovereignty as ideality acquires different meanings in times of peace and in situations of emergency (§278).[24]

Hegel acknowledges that sovereignty manifests itself most poignantly in situations of emergency. In such situations, he writes, 'idealism . . .

attains its distinct actuality' (§278).[25] In highlighting the role played by sovereignty in exceptional circumstances, Hegel confirms his authoritarian tendencies. For a deontological liberal like Constant, it is unthinkable to forfeit the rule of law when circumstances demand it. One ought not to violate the constitution in order to save it (see Campagna, 2001: 569–71). Hegel is willing to leave formal and abstract considerations behind and revert to the dictatorial authority exercised by the monarch. Legitimate functions are to be sacrificed and the single concept of sovereignty is entrusted with 'the salvation of the state' (§278).

(b) The second moment in Hegel's derivation emphasizes the individual and subjective nature of the monarch's authority. The sovereign state, he recognizes, 'has individuality'. By this he means that the state manifests itself essentially as an individual subject of sovereignty. The sovereign is an 'actual and immediate individual' (§321). In other words, the person of the monarch embodies 'the personality of the state, its certainty of itself' (§279). According to Hermann Heller, this implied a tacit acceptance of the monarchical principle (1921: 110–11). Situations of emergency bring this to light, cutting short the discussion of what is to be done and forcing the issue of a clear decision. The problem faced by Hegel is exactly how to define what constitutes an emergency. How does such a situation arise? Who is in charge of making such a determination? Who decides on the exception? All these questions are implicit in the need to bring the notion of sovereignty to existence. So far he has dealt with sovereignty as universal thought. Now he sees a need to descend from the 'universal thought' of sovereignty to what 'exists' (§279). Taking this step makes him realize that sovereignty can 'exist only as subjectivity which is certain of itself, and as the will's abstract – and to that extent ungrounded – self-determination in which the ultimate decision is vested' (§279). To make matters clearer Hegel adds: 'This absolutely decisive moment of the whole, therefore, is not individuality as such, but one individual, the *monarch*' (§279).

The transition from the formal concept of sovereignty as the idealism of the whole whereby each part becomes a member of a social organism, to its existence in the finality of the monarch's subjective decisions is presented by Hegel as following 'the immanent development of a science' (§279). Only if the sovereignty of princely power is derived in this fashion can his exposition 'deserve the name of a philosophical science' (§279). For this Hegel reaches back to the 'basic moment of personality' found in the figure of abstract right which has now developed and has become 'the personality of the state, its certainty of itself' (§279). The personality of the state has 'actuality only as a person', as the person of the prince who cuts short all debate and deliberation, and through his decision 'initiates all activity and actuality' (§279). Sovereignty boils down to the self-determination of an individual person. Hegel distances himself from those who assign sovereignty to abstract, objective instances. In this respect, his views are clearly Hobbesian.[26]

What lies behind this elevation of the monarch to the state's pinnacle of authority is Hegel's implied rejection of popular sovereignty (see Hocevar, 1968: 207–8). He does not find popular sovereignty objectionable when interpreted as expressing the external independence of a people with respect to other states; or internally, when taken as the sovereignty that corresponds to the state as an organic whole. But Hegel is opposed to a revolutionary understanding of this notion, that sets it against the 'existing' sovereignty of the monarch (§279). A people taken without its monarch lacks organic articulation and cannot constitute a state.[27] The idea that, in the absence of a monarch, a democracy or republic would be able to stand by itself is cursorily brushed off by Hegel.[28] Without a monarch there is no *populus*, but only a 'formless mass' or *vulgus*. This conception accords with the monarchical principle and contradicts revolutionary doctrine by taking the representation of state unity away from the people and transferring it to the monarch.[29] In Hegel's view, 'all actions and all actuality are initiated and implemented by a leader as the decisive unity' (§279). This happened naturally in traditional monarchies, but it also happened in traditional political formations other than monarchy – in aristocracies and, particularly, in democracies – where it was possible for an individual 'among the statesmen or generals' to rise to the apex of power 'in a contingent manner and as particular circumstances require' (§279).[30]

(c) The authority vested in these individual summits of power appears to be commissarial, and not absolute, because it responds to exceptional circumstances that arise externally. It is obvious that in such circumstances the state cannot ensure its autonomy and independence with respect to civil society. In order to arrive at decisions that are pure and unconditioned by external fate, Hegel removes the self-determination of the monarch's will from the circle of human temporality. Hobbes had postulated that it was necessary 'for the conservation of peace, that . . . there be order taken from an Artificiall Eternity of life . . . This Artificiall Eternity, is that which men call the Right of Succession' (Hobbes, 1968: 99). Hegel translates this artificial eternity into a form of natural eternity. Here we now have an individual, 'this individual', who is 'destined in an immediate and natural way, i.e. by his natural birth, to hold the dignity of the monarch' (§280).

Two moments have now become inseparably unified. Hegel first identifies the moment that represents the ultimate decision of the will, a moment in no need to provide grounds for its actions; and then he identifies the moment that represents the existence of 'this individual', whose destination is surrendered to nature. The fusion of these two moments constitutes the 'majesty of the monarch' (§281). Monarchical majesty elevates the unity of the state to a level where the revolutionary forces of particularity rampant within civil society cannot reach. In the permanence and continuity afforded by the majesty of the monarch resides the actual unity of the state,

> and it is only by virtue of its inwards and outward immediacy that this unity is saved from being dragged down into the sphere of particularity with its arbitrariness, ends, and attitudes, from the strife of factions round the throne, and from the enervation and destruction of the power of the state. (§281)

Particularity, arbitrariness and the resulting struggle of factions coincide with Hegel's conception of civil society. The feudal conception of a limited and intrinsically scattered monarchical authority cannot cope with the unleashing of modern freedom. The business classes have occupied the four corners of civil society, and the revolution in France proves that it could overrun a well-established summit of authority. In contrast, the more recent events in the France of Louis XVIII prove that a strong state, fuelled by the monarchical principle, is able to soar majestically above civil society. A revolutionary outbreak is thus averted and the orderly development of a free-market society is ensured. Monarchical majesty, an effective antidote against Hobbes's contractarianism and Kant's republicanism, safeguards the continuity and permanence of Hegel's sovereign.[31]

Hegel is aware of the difficulty raised by functionalist readings of authority which interpret majesty and similar notions as mere stratagems to induce the prosperity of civil society and the welfare of the people, or prudential considerations that seek to deny factions the finality of decision. When he upholds the rights of monarchical birth and inheritance as 'the basis of legitimacy', he strives to strengthen authority, but this ought not to be taken as a mere 'consequence' or 'made into a ground', for this relativizes and debases 'majesty to the sphere of raciocination' (§281).[32] Hegel intends to preserve, at all costs, the immediacy of monarchical authority. Just as 'the sun, moon, mountains, rivers, and all natural objects around us are' and possess the 'authority . . . of being in the first place' (§146), so too the authority of the prince simply exists without need of further proof. The *Fürst* comes first, the *princeps* is *principium*. With his monarch, Hegel links up with what Arendt calls 'the Roman pathos of foundation' (Arendt, 2000: 501). Reaffirmation of monarchical authority, expressed naturally by self-generation within a perennial royal family, manifests the 'foundation experience', the authority of *auctores*, and not the mere makers and builders, the *artifices* one finds in civil society (ibid., p. 487). Hegel wishes to oppose the foundational authority of his monarch to the constitutional creativity of the people in revolutionary France. This motivates his emphatic rejection of popular sovereignty, and particularly any thought of an elected monarch. Such a figure would accord with the abstract reasonings of Friesian 'superficiality'. Elections, insofar as they allow the expression of the subjective will of individuals, are 'of primary importance in civil society' (§281). But civil society represents the dissociation of ethical life, and its principles are by definition opposed to those of the family and the state. Hegel denounces an elective monarchy (*Wahlreich*) as the 'electoral capitulation' (*Wahlkapitulation*) put in place in Germany at least since Charles V, for this implies the surrender of the power of the state to the 'discretion of the particular will' (§281).

Does Hegel's conception of princely power correspond to the monarchical principle as defined by the French Charte of 1814 and the Congress of Vienna? Is the prince the subject of constituent power?[33] Surely Hegel is aware of what is implied by the monarchical principle as a constitutional doctrine, and how it came to be interpreted and applied in Germany. The monarchical principle, as Schmitt notes, does not refer to a form of government, but to a form of state. In virtue of the monarchical principle, the monarch assumes a *plenitudo potestatis* and may issue a constitution by royal decree in the manner of Louis XVIII.[34] This means that 'the monarch has the capacity unilaterally to make the fundamental political decisions as subject of constituent power', and that at no point need the monarch relinquish that power

(Schmitt, 1928: 52). In Germany, as opposed to England and France after 1830, monarchs retained the possibility of appealing to their own power when parliament refused to function, a faculty they retained until 1918.[35]

IV

A comparison between Hegel's conception of constitutional monarchy and Aristotle's classical republican view illustrates the thoroughly modern nature of Hegel's views. The kingly individual conceived by Aristotle was not legitimated by the institution of a fixed succession. Aristotle knew that such a man was, as Jaeger puts it, 'a gift from the Gods', rising to prominence as dictated by the occasion (1923: 122). In general, the Greeks accepted the kingly superiority of the men that saved them from occasional chaos, but saw no need to legislate on this matter. The fairly homogeneous citizenry of classical Greek polities constituted the basis for Aristotle's concrete universal. In spite of inevitable economic disparities, the release from the constrained particularity of occupation allowed by slavery guaranteed citizens an almost unlimited political participation. Aristotle wrote in the context of a republican politics of universality. Greek citizens could see with their own eyes the living polis which they all equally supported and from which they drew their sustenance. The universal was effectively embodied in experience and could be apprehended in sense-perception. Aristotle's account of universality did not present it as a mere abstract construct, but as already contained in sense-perception. 'Though the act of sense-perception is of the particular, its content is universal' (Aristotle, *Posterior Analytics* 100^a16; see Owens, 1981: 59–73). Randall, on the other hand, expressly relates Hegel's concrete universal to Aristotle's conception of universality (Randall, 1960: 43).

Constitutional monarchy, on the contrary, is seen by Hegel as the 'achievement of the modern world' (§273). Its absence in Aristotle, who distinguished between monarchy and other political formations in purely numerical terms, was due to the social homogeneity of the classical polis – 'a substantial, still undivided unity' (§273). These still 'undeveloped configurations of the State' demanded individual summits of authority to enact the 'unified deciding of a leader' (§279). Eminent individuals legitimated their decisions through oracular pronouncements, daimons and other external signs. Unaware of the 'depths of self-consciousness' they lacked the strength 'to look within their own being for that decision' (§279). In contrast, the decisions taken by Hegel's monarch lack external foundations. Allowed full enjoyment of his subjectivity and freedom, he himself has become the daimon, the oracular priest. All that is required of him is to stand in the position of a pinnacle, 'explicitly distinct from, and raised above, all that is particular and conditional' (§279).

The difference that separates classical and modern decision-making rests on changed social circumstances. When Hegel trains his eyes on modern society he does not see the occasional upheavals that affected the classical polis, but the generalized chaos of individual self-interest, now given free rein 'to satisfy its needs, accidental arbitrariness and subjective desires' (§289). The spontaneous order generated within civil society remains a mere form of universality incapable as such of transforming the purely external relations of persons (§181) into ethical relations. Civil society portrays the 'exhaustion of *Sittlichkeit*' (§181) and is to be thought of as 'the battlefield of the individual private interest of all against all' (§289). The fluctuating animus of the business classes (§308), immersed as they are in their private affairs, proves ineradicable. Civil institutions like the judicial state, the administrative state and the corporations succumb to the vortex of particularity if not subordinated to the higher regulation of the ethical state.

The competitive game played by the business classes is not a terrain apt for the rise of Aristotle's universal. In the rout simile at the end of the *Posterior Analytics*, the chaos of experience comes to a halt when 'first one man makes a stand and then another, until the original formation is restored' (100^b1–3). No such respite is allowed to the business classes. The spontaneous corporate spirit that arises amongst Aristotelian individuals is not available to them. Corporations by themselves fail to mediate between the individual and the ethical state. This precludes the possibility of ascribing a corporatist version of conservatism to Hegel. On the contrary, the enhanced role of the monarch, whose decisions are reached beyond the confines of civil society, determines the authoritarian nature of his conservatism. The monarch stays above the battlefield of civil society and the 'internecine struggle of factions that surround the throne' (§281). And this elevation is sustained by his extraordinary will. Steven Smith notes that for Hegel political activity is not something natural, as it was for Aristotle, but 'heroic or supererogatory', and that he thus 'tends to see true politics only in terms of war or moments of great national crisis' (Smith, 1986: 135). The prudence that determines the monarch's agency is determined in the last instance by his courage to face the challenge of exception. The substantial unity and homogeneity of classical societies allows decision-making without the constraints of an institution. But now that those substantial ties have been wasted and subjective freedom is unavoidably present even in the highest peak of authority, a natural institution must guard its position. The liberal personality of the monarch is protected by the conservative appeal to natural succession. The institution of a fixed succession purges constitutional monarchy of any residue of arbitrariness. As a person destined to be free, and be the point of convergence of freedom and nature, the monarch is the highest expression of *Sittlichkeit*.

The dialectical synthesis between liberalism and authoritarianism brought about by Hegel is not a juggling of abstract notions. It is sustained by the logic of things themselves, specifically by the logic of social interaction. The dynamism of freedom within civil society requires the elevation of one individual as sovereign authority within the state. The monarch, in Hegel's *Philosophy of Right*, is the concrete universal that summarizes his entire argument, and fuses both liberal and conservative strands of thought inextricably. Hegel's argument derives its entire content from 'one and the same concept – in this case the will' (§279). This concept, initially abstract, 'condenses its determination . . . and thereby acquires a concrete content'. From the principle of abstract free personality, Hegel derives the concrete 'personality of the state', which can only exist as a person, 'as the monarch' (§279). Hermann Heller rightly interprets this passage as Hegel's attempt to strike a 'balance between individual and universal interests, between freedom and authority' (Heller, 1921: 108).

In a way reminiscent of Aristotle's notion of the brave and noble man (ὁ σπουδαιος), whose superior individuality becomes the canon and measure of all things,[36] Hegel's monarch stands in a position of eminence. His subjective, even arbitrary, decisions are universal because eminent. The irreducible individuality of the monarch's self-determination represents the individuality of each member of civil society. In the case of the monarch, an institution sustains his individuality. The pure empiricism of Roman jurists, of statesmen like Pericles, is now imputed to whoever happens to have inherited the Crown.

7 • Hegel and Roman liberalism

Authority over all belongs to kings, property to private persons.
(Seneca, *De beneficiis*)

The functional separation between civil society and the state, whereby the latter becomes merely a means to the ends that the members of the former set for themselves, is the constitutional framework within which liberal principles can become operative. Only as a constitutionally separate and independent sphere can civil society legitimize its demands for limited government and the least possible political interference in its own affairs, thus securing for each of its members the freedom to develop and launch forth in every direction. Correspondingly, the ideal liberal state responds to this plea and allows its hands to be tied constitutionally in order to abstain from interfering with the affairs that properly belong to civil society. A liberal state retains the political as a domain of its own, but only because a measure of autonomy and independence allows it better to perform its function in the service of civil society. This, in its bare essentials, defines the constitutional framework worked out and adhered to by a whole tradition of liberal theorists which is said to include Hegel. It is now generally admitted that Hegel's *Philosophy of Right* is the first modern treatise on political philosophy which explicitly rests upon the separation between state and civil society, the hallmark of constitutionalism (see Riedel, 1970: 156–66).

The idea behind constitutionalism involves making the authority of the state compatible with the freedom to hold property. Liberals postulate a de-politicized civil society and assign priority to private property, whose vulnerability is remedied by the strict separation of civil society from the state. When Hegel points to Rome, he does so to illustrate the virtues and shortcomings of liberalism and its legal and economic corollaries. I do not think it is far-fetched to maintain, as does Lukács, that Hegel interprets the Roman Empire as 'the abstract forerunner of modern capitalism' (Lukács, 1975: 475; see Rotzovtzeff, 1926: 74, 159; Hayek, 1960: 166–7).[1] In contrast, Terry Pinkard thinks that 'despite its atomism, the Roman community could not have thought of itself in modern liberal terms' (1996: 148). Still, he acknowledges that the 'project of liberal individualism' finds its seeds in 'Roman stoicism and the Roman emphasis on law and property' (ibid.). And Pinkard goes further to acknowledge that the alienated form of Roman life was 'based on abstract rights and held together only by force' (ibid.: 334). Is it possible, then, to interpret Hegel's own project along the lines of Roman liberalism? And is that assertion validated by the experiences of modern liberal individualism? One should keep in mind that Hegel's interpretation of the rise of Caesarism cannot be abstracted from the conceptual framework which sustains his perception of Roman liberalism. If this is so, nothing seems to prevent understanding our contemporary Caesars by means of the same conceptual net. I believe, though, that if it can be shown that the liberal postulate, and the notion of rule of law resting on it, has the internal capacity to accommodate Roman authoritarianism, this would clarify aspects of contemporary liberalism that are generally put aside. An assessment of liberalism's authoritarian potential determines my present interest in Hegel's Roman argument.

I

Hegel's clearest statements expressing Roman ascription to liberal ideals may be found in his lectures on the philosophy of world history:

> In Rome we find henceforth this free universality, this abstract freedom, which, on the one hand, sets up an abstract state, the political as such and a power over concrete individuality, which subordinates it entirely, and, on the other hand, produces a personality in opposition to that universality – the freedom of the ego in itself . . . (Hegel, 1920: 662; see 241)[2]

The principle of personality has its debut on the Roman stage. In confrontation with the abstract universality of the state, the principle of personality defines individuals as free agents who express their relationship to the world in predominantly possessive terms. According to Hegel, whereas Greek ethical life irradiates the living immediate unity of subjectivity and substance, in Rome that universal life splits up into the atoms of numerical individuals. The poetic bonds that keep Greek citizens together dissolves and introduces prosaic self-interest. The only bonds remaining can now be arbitrary agreements which persons enter into contractually, without surrendering their hold on exclusive property. Possessiveness is to be blamed for the fall of the public citizen of classical times. A Roman proprietor is defined by inwardness (1920: 662). This inwardness (*Innerlichkeit*), this retreat into one's own self, is to blame for the demise of the republican tradition.

The emergence of the principle of personality sets the stage for the constitution of the political state as a separate, abstract sphere. In their retreat, individuals vacate all public places. The Roman state, unable to appeal to the internal dispositions of its members, can only function as an external artefact, and as such ends up exercising a 'prosaic practical domination', administered 'with soulless and heartless severity' (ibid.). This mechanical universal is determined as a formalism deprived of compassion and blind to considerations of prudence. In this consists the greatness of Rome, 'whose peculiar characteristic is stern inflexibility in the union of individuals with the state, with state laws and state commands' (ibid.: 672). With the entrenchment of private property rights, external compulsion becomes necessary. This is a radical departure from Athenian republicanism according to which the state expresses the immediate identity between particular and universal ethical life, and is not compelled to become a separate institution, 'a governing body functioning as a particular organization' (ibid.: 604). In Rome, with the emergence of autonomous civil society, a separate organization is the only way to limit and externally subdue the expansive drive of particular interests.

This summary characterization of Roman liberalism introduces Hegel's account of Roman life. This account focuses, first of all, on the particular structure of family life. The Roman family is marked by extreme harshness, for it is defined by the 'principles of severity of dependence and subordination' (ibid.: 669). Within the marriage relationship, the main role is played by the husband. Emerging from his inwardness a husband reaches out for a wife as he would reach for any other object of possession. Wives become 'part of the husband's possession *in manum conventio*' (ibid.: 670), and this is preserved in the marriage ceremony, which is 'based on a *coemptio*, in a form such as might have been adopted on the occasion of any other purchase' (ibid.). The fate of children, in this respect, is similar; their status is analogous to that of slaves. According to Hegel, the 'unethical active severity of Romans in the private sphere, necessarily finds its counterpart in the passive severity of their political bond' (ibid.: 671). This harshness on the part of the *pater familias* may be explained as compensation for the severe treatment he suffers at the hands of the state. Roman citizens experience a divided self: 'a servant on the one hand, a despot on the other' (ibid.). This harshness is projected onto the political. The Roman family is the school where citizens are trained according to the principle of severity.

Hegel, then, turns his attention to the Roman institution of the rule of law (*Rechtszustand*). The fulfilment of the principle of severity requires setting all state commands in a form of generality that abstracts from the will of the legislator. Hegel unveils the particular interests that underlie legality's universality and mechanical determinacy. He thinks that the rule of law does not exclude the manifestation of the arbitrary will of a ruler. This determines the fate of imperial Rome, where the rule of law coexists with the despotism of imperial measures and decrees. Historically, the emergence of the rule of law presupposes a situation in which law and custom are rent asunder. Greek legality, in Hegel's view, depends on instituted ethical dispositions and social habits. The constitution lacks the 'fixity' that could set it 'against particular subjectivity' (ibid.: 675). But Rome, by consolidating the rule of law, discovers a principle of right which is 'external and not related to disposition or sentiment' (ibid.). This is indeed progress, and to his merit Hegel recognizes that the rule of law can yield sterility and fixity when pursued in a one-sided fashion. The rule of law, as the purely mechanical ladder that allows ascent to the regions of true ethical fulfilment, is the foundation of freedom. Hegel illustrates that ascent with the example of art – an artist 'can indulge in free beauty' only after 'the technical aspects are acquired' (ibid.).

Finally, the liberal postulate comes into contact with religion, the heart of the polity and centre of the state. In Hegel's re-enactment of the Greek experience religion appears as civil religion. As such it is the highest manifestation of the unity of the nation securing the trust of the people. This recreation of the Greek landscape owes much to Rousseau's identification of state and civil society. With the Roman dissolution of that identity, and the concurrent push towards privatization, religion ceases to express an ethical community of aspirations and ideals. The demise of civil religion brings about the rise of a religion commensurate with the abstract state defined by the liberal postulate. How do these two distinct religious attitudes relate to citizens in Greece and Rome? Hegel gives the following account:

Romans were always concerned with the occult and secret; they believed in and searched for what lay hidden. While in Greek religion everything was open and clear, present to our senses and intuitions, not a beyond but something friendly and of this world, among Romans everything exhibited itself as mysterious and duplicate. (ibid.: 682)

A religion that stresses distance and mystery is consistent with a state of affairs defined by the liberal postulate. Civil society does not of itself offer a convenient seat for the divine. The divine can take residence only if protected under the authoritative mantle of the state. Correspondingly, the state cannot claim autonomy and independence without an appeal to the majesty that it attains by association with the divine. A barrier is raised between civil society and the state, one that civil society will not cross in spite of its own yearning for mystery. Hegel determines that the nature of true religion cannot be anything externally introduced, merely instrumental to the needs of civil society. If is not to lose the aura of mystery it inhabits, religion must be determined as internal to the state, self-activated within it. In Rome, at one point, civil society finally catches up with religion and turns it into one more prosaic manifestation of everyday life. This explains why Hegel is reluctant to consider Roman religion a true religion.

In the *Phenomenology of Spirit*, the Roman spirit is built on the ruins of the Greek ethical substance. Hegel defines it as the 'soulless community which has ceased to be the substance of individuals' (1979a: 290). The original community splits up into separate individuals, who now can claim the abstract status of personality. The abstraction that defines each person determines a 'rigid unyielding self' that resists dissolution into the ethical whole (ibid.). In its embrace of stoicism, Rome finds a philosophical expression for the renunciation of ethical actuality. Stoicism abstractly articulates the principle of the rule of law (*das Prinzip des Rechtszustandes*), the formal determinacy of legal right, and the soulless autonomy of individuals (ibid.: 291). Personal rights are not to be taken as determined by a universal social context nor on the actual condition of the individual.

Hegel conceives scepticism as stoicism's natural conclusion. The abstract stoic, taking refuge in inwardness and enjoying the security it dispenses, affirms its 'abstract independence' and dissolves the authoritative independence of things. It then embarks on a rampage that challenges the pivots of stability and authority. That part of ethical life that is shrouded in religious mystery is penetrated by scepticism's dissolvent gaze and rendered powerless. Scepticism is in tune with the self-assured animus of civil society. Hegel detects this affinity when he observes: 'Personal independence in the sphere of right is really a similar universal confusion and reciprocal dissolution . . . Like Scepticism, the formalism of right is . . . by its very nature without a peculiar content of its own' (ibid.).

Civil society is the result both of the breakdown of traditional bonds and the emergence of personal rights defined independently of content. The formalism of rights, like scepticism, dissolves a world of independently existing things, a world that does not retain a 'peculiar content of its own' and offers no resistance to the possessive drive. Stamped with abstract universality, possession becomes property regulated by the abstract rule of law. Property acquires a 'validity which is recognized and actual' (ibid.: 292). No new content has been determined objectively. Property is no more than an abstract right. In this respect property and scepticism have much in common. 'Both are the same abstract universal' (ibid.). What lies behind the empty form provided by the rule of law is a repressed content. Hegel recognizes that this content belongs to a power capable of defining and controlling property, 'to an autonomous power (*eigenen Macht*), which is something different from the formal universal, to a power which is arbitrary and capricious' (ibid.). The power possessed by this content produces a gravitational pull which compels it to concentrate in one point, in a direction opposed to empty singularity. Hegel has derived a new awesome figure from the original master–slave encounter. This new figure is the lord and master of the world (*der Herr der Welt*), whom Hegel defines as an 'absolute person, at the same time embracing within himself the whole of existence, the person for whom there exists no superior Spirit' (ibid.). It now appears that the purity and immaculate lack of interest constitutive of the rule of law has been replaced by the arbitrary personal interest of a *monas monadum*. Caesar is that 'solitary person who stands over against all the rest' (ibid.). The freedom of individuals depends on the severe rule of this new master, who wields absolute authority checked only by his arbitrary will. Individual freedom can be salvaged if surrendered and placed in the hands of Caesar. How is it that Roman liberalism, when it runs through its historical course, confronts an authoritarian destiny at the apex of its development? Could this be the *fatum* of liberalism generally?

II

The queries raised above concerned the conditions determining the emergence of Roman liberalism and the fulfilment of the separation between civil society and state. What is it that caused the dissipation of a unified Greek polis and led to the harsh *prosa* of Roman life? Under what conditions could the state become a separate, abstract entity? Hegel's answer to this query is to be found in the genealogy of the Roman polity traced in his lectures on the philosophy of world history.

Hegel makes the transition from the elementary account of Roman life to the account of its genealogy by invoking the role of religion. We saw earlier how Roman religiosity was reduced to pure formalism and purely external ritualism. Individual Romans are pious, but in Hegel's view, 'as the sacred here is nothing but a contentless form, it is exactly of such a kind that it can be held as an instrument of power' (1920: 684). In Rome, those who hold possession of the *sacra* as an instrument of power belong to one class – the patriciate. This class had successfully established a monopoly on religiosity, making it subservient to their particular ends and interests. 'The possession of sovereignty by the patricians is thereby made firm, sacred, immediate, asocial. Government and political rights receive the character of hallowed private possession' (ibid.). A social division whereby one class in society is able to set itself apart and take possession, as spoils, not only of the political state but also of the *sacra* cancels Rome's capacity to attain substantive national unity. A democratic identity of rulers and ruled gives way to an imposed social heterogeneity and hierarchy. The *sacra*, placed in the hands of an elite, contribute to the destruction of the unity of that nation by consecrating refractory inequality.

Hegel distinguishes three periods in Roman history: Kingdom, Republic and Empire. Each one of these periods embodies a particular manifestation of what uniformly characterizes the entire course of the Roman millennium, namely a generalized conflict between the political state and civil society. This conflict, in Hegel's mind, confronts the free-moving and reciprocally repellent atoms of civil society against a despotic power that has to be invoked in order to preserve and hold it together. Hegel studies each one of these periods in great detail. Only the main lines of his argumentation will be considered below:

Roman Kingdom

During the kingdom, those conflicting elements appear initially to maintain a fragile balance. The balance is gradually altered as civil society grows restless and there is a need to enhance the strength and unity of the state. Hegel assumes that, from the very start, Roman society is restless and dominated by centrifugal forces. The source of its internal instability is Rome's artificial formation. 'Rome was, from the beginning, something artificial and violent, not a spontaneous growth' (1920: 665). There is no primordial family, no principle of substantial femininity, presiding over its foundation. It starts simply as a harsh association of freebooters united by force and fraud. Hegel notes: 'a state which formed itself and still rests on force must be held together by force' (ibid.: 667). The Roman state as such bears the imprint of this origin throughout its history. The rule of the kings constitutes by no means 'an ethical or liberal' organization (ibid.), but one of coerced subordination. In the end, this harsh state will succumb to civil society, more precisely to its most powerful segment: the patriciate. Their coming to power marks the advent of the Republic, the second stage of Rome's historical development.

Roman Republic

The evolution of the Roman state, during the republic, responds with greater clarity to unresolved conflicts within civil society. According to Hegel, 'conflict arose between patricians and plebeians after the expulsion of the kings for the abolition of royalty only favoured the aristocracy, which in addition acquired royal power, while the plebs lost the protection it enjoyed under the kings' (1920: 694). The contradictory circumstances involving both the patriciate and the plebs marks the republican period. Their conflict takes on a novel characteristic as the patriciate devises new strategies for imposing their domination. If they learned any lesson at all from the deposed kings, it is the usefulness of translating state commands into abstract general rulings. In this manner, they now are able to fade behind the solemn objectivity and universality of laws while maintaining their decisive force, and remaining their principal beneficiaries. The state appears as an empty stage, belonging to nobody in particular, where only *personae*, not real persons, recite legal formulae. Legal formalism is thus consolidated as the trademark of the Roman state. According to Hegel, 'the fact that the Roman people were kept in check for so long evidences their respect for the legal order and the *sacris*' (1920: 695). The rule of law finds an ally in Roman religiosity. Both serve to conceal the real interests dominant within civil society. The success of this comprehensive utilization of legal and religious formalism does not escape Hegel's perceptive analysis. He notes that 'it was practically always the respect for formalism that restored order among plebeians, that determined their renunciation of violence and their peaceful retreat' (ibid.: 673; see Finley, 1983: 141).

Henceforth, the evolution of the republican constitution responds more to historical accident than to the express intention of legislators. As a result of a successful policy of expansion displayed in external wars and the conquest of the world, plundered wealth is amassed and Rome is covered in glory. Since these acquired riches are not the product of native industry, they are blamed by Hegel for the renewed civil dissension that ensues. The intensity and gravity of the conflict is due to the enormous distortions created by the application of dominant patterns of distribution to the partition of the booty. This fundamentally economic question becomes the determining factor in Hegel's explanation of the political failures of Rome. In proto-Marxist fashion he sees that economic conditions determine political changes.

The continuation of his argument indicates that Hegel does not give up on the effective centrality of moral ideas and internal dispositions. The merit of the republican constitution is its capacity to force a balance, however precarious, between the contradictory claims of the patriciate and the plebs. Unchecked avidity and the concurrent misery that accrues gradually impose upon those contradictory claims a disruptive format, juxtaposing 'particular interests against patriotic dispositions' (Hegel, 1920: 706). On these latter dispositions rests civic acquiescence and respect for the rule of law. If by now the safeguard provided by those universal sentiments, by the 'respect for the State' (*Sinn für den Staat*) vanishes (ibid.), what could reverse the thrust of the centrifugal pressures generated within civil society? In Hegel's stark estimation, only an extra-constitutional force could be entrusted with this task, 'for the Roman constitution could not any longer be saved by the constitution itself' (ibid.).[3] The traditional legal order has reached a dead end. With no regrets Hegel observes its demise, even if he understands that this means paving the way for the abolition of the republic and the advent of Caesar's sovereign dictatorship.

Roman Empire

The third moment in Rome's evolution is marked by imperial rule. It coincides with the rise to dictatorial power of one individual, Caesar, who becomes the truth of the traditional Roman constitution. As Hegel observes, 'the transition to imperial rule left the constitution practically unaltered. Only the popular assemblies became obsolete and disappeared' (1920: 712–13). Republican ideals have become obsolete and, through Caesar's hand, the state may again restore its traditional pre-eminence over civil society.

In republican Rome, 'sovereignty had become dependent on the people and the people had turned into the proletariat (*Pöbel*) which had to be fed from the public granaries' (ibid.: 709). For Hegel this means that 'the democratic constitution could no longer be maintained in Rome' (ibid.). When there is no longer any security in society, when, as described by Cicero, its affairs are transacted with weapons in hand, decided either by the wealth and power of the rich or by the tumultuous upheavals of the rabble (ibid.: 710; see §357), only a single will may bring about order, capturing the state and restoring security and reason. In the *Encyclopedia*, Hegel concedes that the aim of the state is to prevent the *populus* from turning into a *vulgus*, a multitude lacking any sense of justice, ethical life and rational articulation. Without the unity imposed by the state, society finds its way back into the state of nature. In such a condition, the *populus* becomes a 'power without form, savage and blind like an elemental, agitated sea' (1991b: §544).[4]

Republicanism and the ideals of self-government cannot prevail in the face of Roman liberalism. The liberal principle of atomism destroys the inner articulations of the Roman *populus*. Because of this, Caesar does not represent a historical contingency and so becomes Rome's necessity (1920: 710). Caesar saved the state because he was able to put 'an end to the empty formalism of *auctoritas*, made himself master and unified the Roman world by force' (ibid.: 712). Hegel's passion for unity now casts an admiring eye on this man: 'Caesar, veritable model of Roman expediency, who took his decisions with perspicuous intelligence and executed them with vigour, practicality and no superfluous passion, this Caesar completed what was world-historically right' (ibid.: 711). Caesar momentarily solves the problem which is to become a permanent crux for liberalism. Ideally, liberalism rests on the rule of law, on general and abstract rulings of *lex*, and not on the dictates of a particular *rex*. But the rule of law cannot sustain itself permanently in abstract suspension. By ignoring the tensions and contradictions within civil society, the rule of law inevitably becomes the accomplice of the dominant particularity which originally forged its spurious universality.

III

Hegel's lectures on the philosophy of world history end with a distressed admission. He confesses that 'after forty years of war and confusion unmeasurable', his 'old heart' is forced again to confront the rising tide of democratic demands (1920: 932). One of the legacies left behind by the French Revolution is laying monarchical legitimacy to rest, and simultaneously advancing a universal recognition of popular sovereignty. Henceforth, states may only claim the legitimacy that issues out of dictates arising from an ideal general will. And now, forty years after the Revolution in France, a dissatisfied faction further requires that this idealized will should become empirically general, that civil society, in its atomistic dispersion, should rule or at least have some participation in government. What Hegel fears is that the entanglement and collusion with democratic ideals will erode the autonomy and independence of the state defined by classical liberalism. Hegel feels justified in raising objections against the faction that sponsors a compromise with democracy:

> Not satisfied with the establishment of rational rights, with freedom of person and property, with the existence of a state organization in which one finds the circles of civil life each having its own business to carry out, and with the influence exercised over the people by the intellectual elites and with the trust they inspire, *liberalism* sets up in opposition to all this the principle of atomism, the principle of the individual will. Everything should emanate from the express power of atomic individuals and have their express sanction. Asserting this formal side of freedom . . . *they* allow no political organization to be firmly established. (ibid.: 932–3)

The 'they' refers, of course, to that dissatisfied liberal faction that seeks a compromise with democratic ideals of equality. By so doing, this faction has set itself against the classical liberal postulate that requires the establishment of a firmly independent political organization. If civil society were allowed to overrun the state in Rousseauean fashion, Hegel's prediction is that unstoppable unrest and agitation will follow. For Hegel this means that the French Revolution has not yet been put to rest. 'This collision, this *nodus*, this problem is that with which history is now occupied, and whose solution has to be worked out in the future' (ibid.: 933).

A certain dissonance may be discerned in this impassioned rejection of democratic values. In the lectures devoted to Greek history, one finds the rousing paeans elevated by Hegel in honour of Athenian democratic constitution. In his mind, democratic Athens represents the highest and finest moment of the Greek form of life. How is it that now the same democratic spirit elicits his contempt and distrust? A possible explanation is that Hegel understands modern democracy as standing in an equivocal relationship to its Greek counterpart. A brief review of Hegel's conception of Greek democracy should demonstrate that this is the case. The circumstances that surround the Greek experience turn it into a unique historical phenomenon. An overview of those circumstances shows that the exercise of democratic rule in classical Greece takes effect within the confines of one social class – the class of free citizens. The degree of political participation allowed to the citizenry is possible only because a large section of the population is permanently excluded from the polity. It follows naturally that, in articulating his case, Hegel finds that the condition of Athens is unique because it is determined by the size of the active body politic. The relatively reduced size of the assemblies allows recognized citizens regularly to come together, deliberate and decide the issues of the day, and prevents the onset of bureaucratic encumbrances. As a government not mediated by paper and red tape, Hegel defines it as a 'living democracy' (ibid.: 610), warmed by rhetoric and active, emotional participation. This facet explains Hegel's enthusiasm for the Greek experience and determines his pessimism *vis-à-vis* recent developments. He has only contempt for the democratic constitution proposed by Robespierre, by which the French nation was to be divided into 44,000 municipalities, and enfranchised between four to five million voters. A cold democracy of numbers may operate only by means of an abstract procedure, hindering its participants from directly deciding governmental issues, from becoming involved in what really concerns them. It can only turn into a despotism hidden 'under the mask of freedom and equality' (ibid.: 609).[5]

Second, Greek democracy rests on the shoulders of disenfranchised slaves. 'Slavery was the necessary condition of that beautiful democracy', recognized Hegel (ibid.: 611). If democracy presupposes identity as a requisite formal element, slavery makes it possible for Greek citizens to preserve their social and cultural homogeneity. Whatever economic disparities may divide them, the release from the constrained particularity of occupation, guarantees unrestricted access to the exercise of their political rights and assures their homogeneity.

Finally, according to Hegel, Greek democracy rests on the unreflective disposition of the people as a whole to abide by oracular decrees. That Hegel should notice this, seemingly a peripheral and unimportant trait, opens for us the very heart of Hegel's conception of democracy and liberalism. Reliance on oracular decisions amounts to the renunciation of one's subjectivity. Individuals surrender their rational self-determination to a contingency that, finding support in natural phenomena, like the flight of birds, the entrails of animals, the Socratic *daimon*, gains a semblance of objectivity and natural destination. 'It was when men had not yet plumbed the depths of self-consciousness or risen out of their undifferentiated unity of substance to their independence that they lacked strength to look within their own being for the final word' (§279). Greek citizens moving non-reflectively within the circle of tradition and ethical prejudice, support democracy based on non-liberal premises. Modern individuals, by contrast, have gained an independence which impels them to assert their subjective will. This makes it difficult to maintain stable democratic institutions. Greek democracy could flourish because it did not assume the liberal principle of subjectivity. A modern liberal state may endure if it does not surrender to democracy. A modern democracy will not survive the universalization of the principle of subjectivity. Democracy cannot be liberal, liberalism cannot be democratic.

From the Greek experience Hegel learns that democracy cannot function without the recognition of social ranks which ensure the existence of a passive alongside an active citizenry. Most importantly, he learns that, unless subjectivity is absorbed by oracular signs and omens, deliberation and the decision-making process will not yield a stable constitution. Hegel's political philosophy intends to make the lessons of the oracular style available to liberalism. In his *Philosophy of Right*, the monarch is assigned that role. Monarchs are allowed full enjoyment of their subjectivity and freedom; but they alone may dwell in liberal self-determination. As Hegel sees it, 'this ultimate self-determination . . . can fall within the sphere of human freedom only insofar as it had the position of a pinnacle, explicitly distinct from, and raised above, all that is particular and conditional, for only so is it actual in a way adequate to its concept' (§279). Hegel's formula for solving the difficulties of modern liberalism is drafted in Roman terms.[6] Rome's solution consists in the elevation of one majestic individual to the apex of all-encompassing power. In monarchies and aristocracies leaders are always already available. In democracies one has to admit that strong individualities 'rise to the top, as statesmen or generals, by chance and in accordance with the particular needs of the hour' (§279). And this happens of necessity 'since everything done and everything actual is inaugurated and brought to completion by the single decisive act of a leader' (§279). This is what Hegel learns from the Roman experience. Only individuals who, like Caesar or Napoleon, 'know how to rule' (Hegel, 1920: 930), possess the insight and strength necessary to lift the unity of the state to a height which the particularity of the forces rampant in civil society cannot reach, and thus solve the problem and put an end to all the confusion.

8 • Marx's critique of Hegel's *Philosophy of Right*: metaphysical not political

The main thing is to fight against the constitutional monarchy as a hybrid creature, full of internal contradictions and bound to be self-destroying.

(Karl Marx[1])

Does Marx interpret Hegel's *Philosophy of Right* as a speculative system of ideas, or does he take his philosophy as subservient to the historical realities of his time? In other words, is he Hegel's philosophical critic or his political critic? Shlomo Avineri thinks that Marx engages in 'a fundamental critique of Hegel's philosophical premises' (Avineri, 1968: 13).[2] This is his ultimate goal, in spite of the fact that his port of entry is a critique of Hegel's political options. He reproaches Hegel for 'seeing nineteenth century political institutions as the hidden meaning of the *essence* of the state *sub specie aeternitatis*', and, more specifically, for his 'idea of the state' which 'merely reflected modern constitutional monarchy' (Avineri, 1968: 16). It is from here that he works 'towards the roots of the Hegelian system – and not the other way round' (ibid.: 13). The main thrust of his argument, inspired by Feuerbach's transformative method, is to detect Hegel's inversion of subject and predicate, which means that individuals, the true substantive and independent entities, are taken by Hegel as mere attributes of the state, while the state is mistakenly seen as a substantive entity, with an independent life of its own. Because it does not start 'from the real subjects as the true bases of the state' (Marx, 1970: 23), Hegel's whole philosophical edifice vaporizes into logical mysticism.

Karl-Heinz Ilting implicitly agrees with Avineri's assessment, but questions the value of Marx's strategy. In his *Critique of Hegel's Philosophy of Right*, Marx errs by attributing the mistakes of Hegel's exposition to 'the inadequacy of its philosophical premises, instead of explaining them in terms of a political reaction to topical and politically relevant questions' (Ilting, 1984: 112). Feuerbach's influence is to blame for Marx's adoption of an (anti-)metaphysical, and not a political stance. Instead of examining the political implications of the Hegelian account, Marx is 'primarily concerned to follow up Hegel's alleged mysticism' (ibid.: 108). According to Ilting, the publication of

Hegel's Heidelberg and Berlin lecture notes brings to light the circumstances surrounding the publication of the *Philosophy of Right* and
allows a critical assessment of Hegel's intentions (Hegel, 1983a: 17–34).
In comparison to these lectures notes, Ilting detects, in the published
text of 1820, a 'retreat into a metaphysical-sounding usage of language'
(Ilting, 1984: 113), which is meant to conceal his retraction of the
political stance adopted in his lectures. This earlier stance is, in his
view, more in accordance with the republicanism of the Jena years.
Ilting dismisses Hegel's published text as the product of a reworking of
his position to fit the new scenario brought upon Prussia by the Carlsbad
decrees of October 1819. Eager to ascertain Feuerbach's transformative method, Marx fails to see 'what is indeed the politically decisive
defect in Hegel's development of his conception in the version of 1820'
(ibid.: 111).

I agree generally with the importance Avineri attributes to Marx's
Feuerbachian strategy. A critique of Hegel has much to gain from
an awareness of the inversion of subject and predicate visible in his
argumentation. But it seems to me that Marx micro-manages this
(anti-)metaphysical objection, carries it to unnecessary lengths and
then misses the political dimension of Hegel's metaphysics. Marx's
annoyingly detailed deconstruction of Hegel's exposition on the state
makes him lose sight of the overall design of *Sittlichkeit*, particularly
the intricate internal structure of civil society and the transition to the
state, and miss the political motivations of Hegel's speculative con-
tortions. Hegel's aim is to preserve the universal authority of the state,
elevating it beyond civil society's dysfunctional universality. He has
to demonstrate to liberal critics that he is indeed a liberal; hence his
conception of a free, possessive individualist, civil society. At the same
time, he is interested in proving to post-Congress of Vienna Prussian
authorities that he is neither a *political* liberal nor a republican demo-
crat; hence his option for a strong authoritarian monarchical state.
Hegel's point of departure is the liberal principle of individual autonomy, but he is not a political liberal. As Ilting puts it, Hegel 'does not
think that liberal principles alone are sufficient for a comprehensive
theory of the modern state' (1971: 95).

Ilting rightly criticizes Marx for ignoring the accommodation of
Hegel's political views after the Congress of Vienna and for taking his
abstract philosophical intentions too seriously. But I cannot follow
Ilting in his attempt to shift attention from Hegel's published text to
his unpublished lectures. Delving into what Marx considers to be Hegel's

mystified philosophical argumentation on the state and the monarch ought not to impede a better understanding of his evolving political intentions. Marx is not aware that Hegel first introduces the distinction between civil society and the state in his Heidelberg lectures, and that he does so in response to criticisms addressed to his *Proceedings of the Estates Assembly in the Kingdom of Wurtemberg 1815–1816*, published in 1817. He correctly sees that Hegel conceives the notion of civil society as a vestigial state of nature, designed as a habitat for free individuality. He also correctly observes Hegel's shift towards metaphysics. But he fails fully to grasp the political intentions that motivate that shift. Hegel engages Hobbes's regress argument which seeks to derive a strong state from the potentially chaotic circumstances facing civil society. He is aware of the deficiencies of Hobbes's empiricist derivation. The Hobbesian procedure gives rise to a stridently strong, yet ultimately weak authority, dependent on the consent of the people and capable of having a purely instrumental value. Onto the state of nature, as unreduced multitude, the state, as 'the positive unity (expressing itself as absolute totality) must . . . be tacked on as something other and alien'. In this consists his objection to empiricism: it makes the majesty of the state appear as the 'empty name of a formless and external harmony' (Hegel, 1975b: 65). In contrast, a metaphysical derivation of the state and princely power is meant to avoid use of regressive arguments. Resorting to metaphysics corresponds to the methodological strictures Hegel had already posited in his *Natural Law*. But then and now what guides metaphysics is a political motivation: enhancement of his authoritarian proposal.

I

In his Remark to §289 of the *Philosophy of Right*, Hegel states:

> Just as civil society is the field of conflict in which the private interest of each individual comes up against that of everyone else, so do we here encounter the conflict between private interests and particular concerns of the community, and between both of these together and the higher viewpoints and ordinances of the state.

Marx, in his *Critique of Hegel's Philosophy of Right*, readily detects the Hobbesian flavour of this passage. 'This [paragraph] is especially worth noting: 1. because of the definition of civil society as the *bellum omnium contra omnes . . .*' But Marx does not further elaborate this line of thought. He does not explicitly refer to the system of needs, the figure in Hegel's civil society argument that retains 'the remnants of the state of nature' (§200).[3] Though he interprets 'the separation of civil and political society to be a contradiction' (Marx, 1970: 76), he does not take Hegel's prince as a sovereign agent whose task, like Hobbes's sovereign, is first and foremost the prevention of the *bellum omnium contra omnes*, and the enhancement of the unity of the state. Hobbes's name is not even mentioned in Marx's *Critique*. It is surprising, then, that this work could have inspired a line of thought that aligns Hegel's argument with Hobbes. Hegel's Hobbesian critics argue that the extensive economic freedom allowed to the members of civil society naturally demands the establishment of an authoritarian state. These critics consider this to be a setback for those who seek to approximate Hegel to political liberalism and stress his commitment to constitutionalism.

The Hobbesian card has been played by both left-wing and right-wing critics of Hegelian liberalism. Lukács sees Hegel's social philosophy as a 'direct continuation' of the philosophies of Hobbes and Mandeville (Lukács, 1967: 517; see 441). And Marcuse writes: 'The authoritarian trend that appears in Hegel's political philosophy is made necessary by the antagonistic structure of civil society' (Marcuse, 1968: 202; see Colletti, 1975: 30–1).[4] Carl Schmitt, on the other hand, writes in *Der Nomos der Erde*:

> In Hegel's philosophy of the state, the state appears to be a realm of morality and objective reason that rises above the non-state sphere of civil society. According to both Hegel and Marx, this is a beastly realm of ruthless (and in this sense, free) egoism . . . In terms of intellectual history, this was an after-effect of the 16th century practice of counterposing a realm of agonal freedom and civil society to the state as the realm of objective reason. It is also an example of the many variations in which Hobbes's distinction between state of nature and civilized conditions survived . . . (2003: 99)[5]

Hegel's liberal apologists do not deny that he may share Hobbes's preference for a strong unified state. But, as Jean François Kervégan points out, Hegel misses no opportunity to 'multiply the concessions to liberal indecision' (1992: 156; see Cristi, 1998). Kervégan endeavours to offer a new liberal reading of Hegel, one which attempts to show the limitations and the distortions of Schmitt's Hobbesian reading of Hegel. The core of such misinterpretations take Hegel's distinction between civil society and the state as an unmediated antagonism (Kervégan, 1992: 234). In a Hobbesian political scenario, the state, as the *imperium rationis*, contradicts civil society, the animal kingdom of irrationality where 'the mechanisms of socialization are inherently conflictive' (ibid.: 196–7).[6] Kervégan objects to this dualist view by underscoring the reciprocal mediations with which Hegel bridges that separation. The argument that he unfolds for this purpose has two moments. First, he examines Hegel's notion of civil society and dispels attempts to approximate it to a state of nature devoid of any trace of ethical content. Second, Kervégan points out that Hegel's notion of the state is structurally open and responsive to the demands that arise from civil society. The rejection of popular sovereignty does not mean that a delegate representation from civil society has no role to play within the state.

First, the analogy drawn by critics of Hegel between the Hobbesian state of nature and Hegel's civil society demonstrates, according to Kervégan, their impatience with the role played by dialectical mediation. Civil society is not the riot of pure particularity which needs to be pacified externally by the offices of a Hobbesian sovereign. Hegelian civil society constitutes the synthesis of particular and universal aims. It is true that particularity remains its prevailing principle, so much so that only an unconscious formal universality (ibid.: 220) arises within it, bringing about a spontaneous market order that feeds on the selfish pursuits of individuals. Still, it is on this unconstrained order that Hegel bases the higher forms of universality which rise within civil society. According to Kervégan, civil society may only be conceived as internally related to the state. Particularity is its proper principle, but this principle can only be actualized by means of a superior one. This is why Hegel allows for an active presence of the state to surface within civil society and to constitute its higher levels.

Second, Hegel's rich and complex conception of civil society, the outcome of its partial politicization, anticipates Hegel's next move, namely the partial socialization of the state. The key to the extension of social concerns beyond their proper sphere lies, according to Kervégan, in the mediating function Hegel assigns to representation. Representation and sovereignty are the twin notions which he portrays as the mainstays of the modern conception of the state. After the collapse of traditional justifications of state authority, those notions were paraded by absolutism in its bid to secure political unity. Kervégan notes that in defining the sovereign as a *persona repraesentativa*, Hobbes identifies sovereignty with representation. In his political philosophy, the sovereign is deemed able to carve a united people out of a disaggregated multitude by assuming its representation (sovereign representation or *Repräsentation*). The state of nature is marked by the lack of popular identity; the people can only attain its identity when represented by the sovereign. By contrast, a monarchomachist like Althusius espoused a view of representation as delegated or mandated (*Vertretung*) by a people whose identity and communal existence was assumed from the beginning. Hegel, concerned with securing both the unity of the political order and an unmitigated social pluralism, seeks a compromise between sovereign and delegate representation. On the one hand, he finds a place for Hobbesian absolutism and ascribes sovereign representation to the prince. In no case does his liberal stand prevent an embrace of the monarchical principle. Delegate representation, on the other hand, takes place within the Assembly of Estates. Hegel, in accordance with the Prussian reformers, rejects the idea of a representative assembly generated by universal suffrage. Delegate representation takes communal interests into account, interests that are channelled organically through the traditional estates, but not through the abstract will of atomized individuals. This is sufficient proof to show, in Kervégan's view, that Hegel's state is open and responsive to the demands that arise from civil society, despite his rejection of popular sovereignty.

II

Marx's critique of Hegel's *Philosophy of Right* proves disappointing with respect to the first point raised by Kervégan. There is no attempt on his part to delve into the civil society argument developed by Hegel and bring out its untenable inner structure. The internal etatist mediations underscored by Kervégan fail to restrain particularity, and establish a unified and stable form of universality. This failed mediation clears the way for a proto-Hobbesian solution – a state so strong that it will not be overrun by the forces of particularity.

The egoistic competition and conflict discernible in Hegel's conception of civil society thwarts the operation of a market-oriented societal order. Hegelian civil society is a system of needs initially ruled by the 'principle of particularity' (§182). This principle replaces the solidaristic family, allows individuals to satisfy their contingent arbitrariness and subjective caprice (§185), and inevitably dissolves the *populus* into a multitude, a *vulgus*. Similar to Hobbes, Hegel's argument gains acceleration from social breakdown in a scenario reminiscent of a state of nature. The internal reintegration of society, brought forth by a 'form of universality' (§182), is premised on the centripetal impulse to move away from an unrestrained system of needs and towards forms of integration mediated by etatist institutions internal to civil society. But Hegel remains dissatisfied with these etatist solutions for they fail to offset the social disintegration that unfolds within the system of needs and are unable to reconstitute the *populus*.

To avoid the total collapse of civil society, Hegel introduces, as a measure of last resort, an embryonic corporatist system whose aim is the societal integration of the unruly business classes, the main embodiment of the principle of particularity and main source of social instability. But the corporations envisaged by Hegel are marked by the particularity of the business classes. They cannot be granted autonomy and must be subject to higher etatist regulation. Hegel's ethical state is in the offing. In Hobbesian fashion, this elevated political sphere must remain absolutely undisturbed by market forces if it is to preserve popular unity. Only when the state attains full autonomy may the spontaneous order within civil society be allowed to run its course without actualization of its revolutionary potential. Standing now on the firm ground provided by the state, civil society is able to snuff the revolutionary fires it ceaselessly ignites. Hegel reminds us: 'a spark that falls on gunpowder is more dangerous than if it falls on firm ground, where it can vanish without trace' (§319). The standard liberal argument seeks to isolate civil society from the state in order to protect the market from state intervention. Hegel supplements this liberal requirement by demanding the complete separation of the state from civil society to maintain the unity of the *populus*. Only the strong authority of a princely executive state, strengthened in Hobbesian fashion, may adopt a more liberal attitude.

Despite the idealistic wrappings of Hegel's systematic argument, which Marx denounced as mystical pantheism, it is surprising that he did not simultaneously expose its extra-systematic empirical underpinnings. Horstmann has shown that Hegel's separation of civil society and state was motivated by political considerations. This distinction was designed to offset criticism of the position he had taken in his *Proceedings of the Estates Assembly in the Kingdom of Wurtemberg* (Horstmann, 1997: 211). There he sided with King Frederick's decision, announced on 15 March 1815, to grant a constitution to his subjects, and, at the same time, he berated the Estates Assembly for what he denounced as their reactionary stance in resisting that constitution. The adoption of a constitution appeared to be a perfectly liberal, even a revolutionary step. This is what Hegel's liberal apologists have emphasized. What they do not acknowledge is that issuing a constitution by royal decree (*oktroi*) was in itself a reactionary scheme, for it meant grounding it on the constituent power of the monarch and not of the people (see Schmitt, 1928: 54). Promulgation of constitutions in all the states of the German Confederation was one of the recommendations of the *Bundesakte* issued by Congress of Vienna (see Boldt, 2000: 171). The foundation of these constitutions was not the will of the people. As expressions of the monarchical principle, they ought to be seen as royalist instruments. The procedure adopted by the Congress of Vienna was inspired by the French *Charte*, which, despite concessions to liberal ideals, was a royalist document that recognized the monarch as subject of *pouvoir constituant*.

In his Heidelberg lectures on *Rechtsphilosophie*, Hegel raised an issue related to the subject of *pouvoir constituant*. To the question: who makes the constitution, the people or someone else?, he responded: 'Nobody. The constitution makes itself' (Hegel, 1983a: 155). Constitutions rest on an 'eternal foundation', which he identified with the 'spirit of the people' or *Volksgeist* (ibid.: 156). In classical times, they were perceived as divine. Lawgivers like Moses and Solon were mediators between the people and the divine, which certified the divine legitimacy of their authority. In similar fashion, Hegel wrote: 'Louis XVIII gave his people an inviolable constitution, and it was as the highest authority that the king granted this constitution' (ibid.). The king may have been responsible for issuing a constitution, an authoritarian gesture, but the content was liberal, namely a 'refined *Volkgeist*', purified by revolutionary progress (ibid.).[7]

The simultaneous affirmation of liberal ideas and authoritarian principles coincides with the distinction he introduced between civil society and the state. While liberal ideals may flourish within civil society, the state embodies the authority demanded by conservatives. Hegel was aware of the tension that existed between freedom and authority. On 30 August 1815, in his final graduation address as rector of Nuremberg's *Ägidien Gymnasium*, Hegel noted how difficult it was to steer 'a midway between too much freedom permitted to children, and too much restriction on them'. But he then concluded: 'While both extremes constitute a mistake, so is the first the worst one' (1970b: 374; see Pinkard, 2000: 305). On 8 June 1815, the *Volkgeist* placed its authoritative signature on the German federal constitution finally decreed by the Congress of Vienna; later on in August, the philosopher of freedom took notice.

III

Marx's critique is also disappointing with respect to the second issue raised by Kervégan, namely the mediating function he attributes to representation. Marx rejects Hegel's monarchical state and demands a constitution opposed to monarchy, a democratic constitution with the people as the real subject of sovereignty. Implicit in his adherence to democracy is a concern for identity, not representation. If representation were to be taken into account, Marx would reject sovereign representation (*Repräsentation*) in favour of delegate representation (*Vertretung*). But, influenced by Feuerbach, he is more interested in debunking Hegel's logical mysticism, and does not discuss two closely connected constitutional issues at the core of Hobbesian readings of Hegel – affirmation of the monarchical principle and rejection of the division of powers. Adherence to the monarchical principle explains his rejection of the division of powers – division of powers and monarchical principle are *ratio legis* incompatible. Though Marx takes notice of Hegel's reference to the monarchical principle in §304, he does not appear to grasp its constitutional implications. The proof is that he uses it merely to counterpose the power of the prince (empirical singularity) to civil society (empirical universality), and does not advance beyond this observation (see Marx, 1970: 85).

Marx is right in judging the Assembly of Estates as contrary to democratic representation. Hegel conceives the Estates as a mediating organ, standing between the government at large (princely power and executive) and the people as the merely empirical universality. Their mediating function is superadded to the mediation already performed by the executive power. The need for this is articulated by Hegel in §302, that has to do with the need to avoid that princely power appear as an 'isolated extreme', and therefore as an 'arbitrary power of domination'. This also applies to the corporations and individuals, for they too may feel isolated from government. Hegel feels compelled to stress that mediation is essential to ensure 'that individuals do not present themselves as a crowd (*Menge*) or aggregate (*Haufens*), un-organized in their opinions and volition, and do not become a massive power in opposition to the organic state' (§302). What is to be avoided at all costs is an extreme antagonistic encounter between the monarch and the people. Mediation is then the solution. Hegel describes this solution as 'one of the most important insights of logic' (§302R), and goes on to say that the extremes in an opposition lose that quality, and become organic moments, by assuming the role of a mean. Thus, when the Estates are seen as standing in extreme opposition to govern-ment at large, conceiving them as a mean dissolves opposition and an organic union is attained between them. But this surely cannot apply to either princely power or the people. Neither can be conceived as a means and their opposition remains unbridgeable. No metaphysical explanation can fill this gap. Once the monarchical principle is affirmed, the democratic principle can only be negated.

Marx is quick to see that the mediation attempted by Hegel is a failure. 'Actual extremes cannot be mediated with each other precisely because they are actual extremes. But neither are they in need of mediation because they are opposed in essence. They have nothing in common with one another; they neither need nor complement each other' (Marx, 1970: 89). Marx perceives in all this the 'fundamental dualism' of Hegel's logic. To say more than this falls into 'the critique of Hegelian logic' (ibid.). What he misses is the political dimension of the opposition Hegel attempts to mediate: the radical negation of democracy implied by affirmation of the monarchical principle. This principle conceives the monarch as *persona repraesentativa*, which ties it immediately to the politics of the *ancien régime* and identifies the state with the person of the monarch. In other words, national unity is only to be attained through the person of the monarch. Hegel's effort to affirm the absolutist notion of representation embodied by the monarchical principle, and at the same time import a weakened form of democratic representation or *Vertretung*, is destined to fail. This is the point raised by Hobbesian critics of Hegel, a point Marx does not fully develop, dazed by Feuerbach's (anti-)metaphysical critique. It is not enough to subvert Hegel's metaphysics and make him stand on his head. Aside from introducing an empirical, nominalist perspective which disempowers republican conceptions of democracy,[8] it fails to identify the Hobbesian dimensions of Hegel's purported liberal constitutionalism.

IV

Marx's (anti-)metaphysical critique of Hegel proves disappointing for not exposing the political motivations underlying Hegel's metaphysics of the state and princely power. He interprets the Hegelian array of state institutions as mystical entities, divorced from real existence, and designed to satisfy Hegel's compulsion to build abstract logical systems. The following assertion is symptomatic of the argumentative strategy adopted by Marx: 'Hegel's true interest is not the philosophy of right but logic' (Marx, 1970: 18). This strategy was laid out originally in his *Dissertation*, where he decried the attempt of those critics who dismissed the philosophical core of Hegel's views and explained them away as an accommodation to current political circumstances (1962: 70).[9] In my view, a political interpretation of Hegel's *Philosophy of Right* does not prevent, but enhances an understanding of the guiding metaphysical aim of this work, namely the rejection of Hobbes's contractualism and its attendants – nominalism and instrumental rationalism (see Colletti, 1975: 31–2; Gauthier, 1977). For this Hegel retrieves a conception of the state grounded on the laws and powers of ethical substantivity. This corresponds to the Aristotelian notion of the state as the unmoved mover, known to its citizens as 'the end which moves' them, or the 'universal which, though unmoved, has developed through its determinations into actual rationality' (§152). In Aristotle's hands, this became the keystone of a republican metaphysics, aimed at securing the public interest and anchored in a conception of the state as universal, as an end in itself and not as means of guaranteeing private ends.

A political reading also shows how Hegel betrays Aristotle's republican metaphysics by the drastic separation he draws between state and civil society, and the failure of the mediating instances he proposes. This failure explains why he is forced to invoke the offices of a Hobbesian prince. Unable to deal with the contradictions that surface within civil society, Hegel installs a Hobbesian prince as the apex and beginning of the state. This is the final guarantee needed to contain the *bellum omnium contra omnes* within the bounds of civil society. Marx understands that the state is 'not the result of the suppression' of the struggle within civil society, but is rather 'held together by this struggle' (Rotenstreich, 1965: 91). But unable to separate Hegel's inceptive republicanism and the Hobbesian animus of his prince, Marx turns his back on the state and forsakes the political.[10]

Marx's (anti-)metaphysical reading of Hegel's *Philosophy of Right* results from his disregard for Hegel's political intentions. He takes his metaphysics too seriously and so is unable to understand that Hegel's idealization of princely power is meant to compensate for the apparently strong, but ultimately weak authority held by Hobbes's leviathan state. In opposition to classical republicanism, and particularly to Aristotle's notion of a ζῷον πολιτικὸν (*De Cive* 1, 1, §2), Hobbes assigned only contractual and instrumental value to the state. Hegel rejects contractarianism, which he thinks destroys the divine element in the state and debases its 'absolute authority and majesty' (§258R). Political metaphysics is in full display when he proceeds to describe the revolutionary triumph of contract:

> Consequently, when these abstractions were invested with power, they afforded the tremendous spectacle, for the first time we know of in human history, of the overthrow of all existing and given conditions within an actual major state and the revision of its constitution from first principles and purely in terms of thought . . . [S]ince these were only abstractions divorced from the Idea, they turned the attempt into the most horrible and drastic event. (§258R)

Unfortunately, the first four pages of Marx's manuscript were lost, and with them his commentary on this paragraph. The extant manuscript begins with a quotation of §261 of the *Philosophy of Right*:

> In relation to the spheres of civil law (*Privatrecht*) and private welfare, the spheres of the family and civil society, the state is, on the one hand, an external necessity and the higher power to whose nature their laws and interests are subordinate and on which they depend. But on the other hand, it is their immanent end, and its strength consists in the unity of its universal and ultimate end with the particular interests of individuals; in the fact that they have duties towards the state to the same extent as they also have rights.

Marx detects in this paragraph an 'unresolved antinomy: on the one hand external necessity, on the other hand immanent end' (1970: 6).

But he is not aware of the dialectical import of this antinomy, and how it serves Hegel in his aim to transcend the purely external, and thus politically ineffective etatist figures that arise within civil society. The judicial and administrative states, utilitarian mainstays within civil society, prove themselves unable to demand absolute moral obligations. This is the intrinsic weakness of Hobbes's otherwise over-powering leviathan. To this end Hegel postulates an internal state, one that evokes moral allegiance on the part of individuals. But, most importantly, Hegel rejects an empirical derivation of the state which only recognizes its instrumental value. The state postulated by Hegel is, in contrast, 'the higher power' able to place civil society, or 'external state' (§183), under its rule. The state is the intrinsic end of civil society and not a means subordinate to its wishes.

Ilting correctly identifies the republican temperament of this conception, an echo of the republican ideals of Hegel's youth, which he sees embodied in democratic Athens and the Roman republic (Ilting, 1984: 96). Ilting also rightly notes how Hegel, in his Remark to §261, inverts what he maintains in the main body of this paragraph, where he states: individuals 'have duties towards the state to the same extent as they have also rights'. This absolute identity of rights and duties defines his republicanism. But in his Remark to §261, which he adds after the promulgation of the Carlsbad decrees in 1820, Hegel betrays the ideals of his youth.

> That absolute identity of duty and right [referred to above] occurs here only as an equivalent identity in content, in that the determination of the content is itself wholly universal; that is, there is a single principle for both duty and right, namely the personal freedom of human beings . . . – But in the internal development of the concrete Idea, its moments become differentiated, and their determinacy becomes at the same time a different content: in the family, the rights of the son are not the same in content as the son's duties towards his father, and the rights of the citizen are not the same in content as the citizen's duties towards the prince (*Fürst*) and the executive (*Regierung*).

The republican identity of rights and duties, that is, citizens' duties to the state that are grounded on their rights, falls out of joint. According to Hegel, individual rights and duties do not coincide and are no longer simultaneously grounded on 'the personal freedom of human beings'. In a metaphysical inversion, presented by Hegel as the 'internal development of the concrete Idea', citizenship duties to prince and government gain the upper hand, so that the individual 'in fulfilling his duties as a citizen, . . . gains protection for his person and property, consideration for his particular welfare, satisfaction of his substantial essence, and the consciousness and self-awareness of being a member of the whole' (§261R). Only after the metaphysical priority of princely power and the government are recognized may the judicial and administrative instrumental states of civil society attain political viability.

The next paragraph expedites the metaphysical exercise planned by Hegel as his parting of ways with Hobbesian utilitarianism:

> The actual Idea is the spirit which divides itself into the two ideal spheres of its concept – the family and civil society – as its finite mode, and thereby emerges from its ideality to become infinite and actual spirit for itself. In so doing, it allocates the material of its finite actuality, i.e. individuals as a mass, to these two spheres, and in such a way that, in each individual case, this allocation appears to be mediated by circumstances, by the individual's arbitrary will and personal choice of vocation. (§262)

Marx's commentary reads as follows: 'in this passage the logical, pantheistic mysticism appears very clearly'. And he proceeds to apply Feuerbach's transformative method:

> The Idea is given the status of a subject, and the actual relationship of family and civil society to the state is conceived to be its inner imaginary activity. Family and civil society are the presuppositions of the state; but they are the really active things; but in speculative philosophy it is reversed. (Marx, 1970: 7–8)

Satisfied with exposing the metaphysical nature of Hegel's argument, Marx abstains from laying out its political implications. He is content to note that here 'the conditions are established as the conditioned, the determining as the determined, the producing as the product'; and observes that the 'entire mystery of the *Philosophy of Right* and of Hegelian philosophy in general is contained in these paragraphs' (p. 9; compare Ilting, 1984: 105–6). But Marx does not perceive that Hegel postulates the metaphysical priority of the state as a way of strengthening its authority. While this accords with Aristotelian republicanism, Hegel takes a further step – he uses republican metaphysics to conceal his rejection of political republicanism. This is shown by the surreptitious emergence of the prince and the executive in §261 quoted above.

Marx is not fully aware of the special role assigned by Hegel to the prince. In the main section of §273, Hegel says that the prince, as an 'individual unity', is the 'apex and beginning of the whole'. This is a crucial step in Hegel's argument for it confirms his acceptance of the monarchical principle and what it implied (see Ilting, 1983: 185–92). Unaccountably, Marx decides not discuss the issues involved here and promises to 'return to this division after examining the particulars of its explanation' (1970: 19). But he never does, which prevents him from fully understanding Hegel's debt to Hobbes in relation to the power of the monarch. Furthermore, Marx does not discuss the long and substantive Remarks added by Hegel to §272 and §273, foregoing the opportunity critically to bring out the Hobbesian background that sustains Hegel's acceptance of the monarchical principle.

Marx seems to be unaware of the full measure of authority and power that Hegel concentrates in the hands of the prince. When Hegel raises the issue of the states of emergency (either internal or external), he appeals to 'the simple concept of sovereignty' and the sacrifice 'of [the] particular authorities whose powers are valid at other times', on order to bring about the 'salvation of the state'. He recognizes that in these occasions 'ideality comes into its proper reality' (§278). Marx's comments show a complete lack of understanding of what Hegel has in mind when he writes:

> Accordingly, sovereignty, the ideality of the state, exists merely as internal necessity, as idea. And Hegel is satisfied with that because it is a question merely of the idea. Sovereignty thus exists on the one hand only as unconscious blind substance. We will become equally well acquainted with its other actuality. (Marx, 1970: 23)

What Hegel postulates in §278 is that the unity of the state attains its highest fulfilment when situations of exception require that all power and authority revert to the prince. He, of course, assigns to the prince the task of deciding on the exception.[11] Marx thoroughly misses here, and again in his commentary to §279, the Hobbesian gist of Hegel's remark. In chapter 42 of the *Leviathan*, Hobbes writes: 'For Subjection, Command, Right, and Power are accidents, not of Powers, but of Persons' (1968: 601). In agreement with Hobbes, Hegel thinks that the unity of the state is attained and defined by the figure of a concrete and singular person, the prince as an absolutist *persona repraesentiva*.

Marx's commentary shows how distant he is from grasping the sense of what Hegel stipulates. Marx writes:

> Precisely because Hegel starts from the predicates of universal determination instead of from the real *Ens* (*hypokeimenon*, subject), and because there must be a bearer of this determination, the mystical idea becomes this bearer. This is the dualism: Hegel does not consider the universal to be the actual essence of the actual, finite thing, i.e. of the existing determinate thing, nor the real *Ens* to be the true subject of the infinite.

First, Marx appears to be unaware that Hegel here reverses the flow of his dialectical procedure and begins with the moment of singularity, namely with the figure of the prince. His point of departure is not constituted by predicates of universal determination, as Marx claims. Second, for Hegel the prince is not only the apex of the whole, but also its beginning – an open affirmation of the monarchical principle on his part. Third, there is nothing mystical in Hegel's reasoning, no predicate that turns into a subject, or subject that turns into a predicate. The monarch is the real *Ens*, the *hypokeimenon*, and Hegel simply postulates his priority.

Marx is aware that Hegel's civil society is the Hobbesian *bellum omnium contra omnes*, but he thoroughly misses the real proportions of Hegel's monarch. He writes his *Critique* in 1843, thirteen years after the July Revolution, by which time France was no longer a constitutional monarchy, as defined by the Charte of 1814, and had in effect become a parliamentary monarchy.[12] Marx acknowledged the changed circumstances: 'During the Restoration the Chamber of Peers was a reminiscence (*Reminiszenz*), while the Chamber of Peers resulting from the July Revolution is an actual creature of constitutional monarchy' (1970: 114). Just as the Restoration Senate was now just a reminiscence, so the monarch of the French Charte of 1814 was also just that in 1843.[13] But Marx should have known that in Germany, a Hegelian monarch, animated by the monarchical principle as defined by the Congress of Vienna's *Schlußakte*, was very much centre stage. In fact, the *monarchisches Prinzip* was abrogated in Germany only in 1918, and came back to life in 1933, under the guise of the *Führerprinzip*. Ilting is right when he points out that, in his eagerness to ascertain Feuerbach's transformative method, Marx leaves unexamined a politically decisive issue. But he is wrong in thinking that Hegel's republican credentials can be saved by putting his metaphysics aside. Hegel's metaphysical turn is not an optional extra, but the pillar needed to sustain the unmediated separation of the state and in this way secure its autonomy. Making peace with Aristotle proves to be a convenient political move.

Conclusion

Je conçait la république; je conçait la monarchie absolue; mais je ne conçais pas la monarchie constitutionnelle; c'est le gouvernement du mensonge, de la fraude, de la corruption.

(Nicholas I of Russia[1])

I

On 3 April 1814, with France occupied by foreign forces, the Senate dethroned a defeated Napoleon. The void left by his fall would be filled by the returning Bourbons, an event that made 1814 'one of the most extraordinary years in the history of France' (Mansel, 1981: 170). At the time, the consensus was that restoring the monarchy would not mean turning back the clock to the status quo antecedent to 1789. It was possible to conceive of a monarchical regime that did not necessarily claim absolute sovereignty and approximate, in this respect, the monarchical system defined by the constitution of 3 September 1791 (Rosanvallon, 1994: 18–19). This document manifested perhaps the most fundamental political change brought about by the Revolution – the transfer of the representation of state unity from the monarch to the national assembly (Prélot, 1984: 313–14). This change was inspired by Sieyès's conception according to which the true subject of constituent power was no longer the monarch but the nation represented in the assembly. The constitution of 1791 was promulgated on that basis.[2] This matched the desire of the main players in this constitutional drama who aimed at the substitution of monarchical absolutism by a mixed form of government 'monarchical only in name' (ibid.: 317). Faithful to Sieyès, the constitution was made to rest on the constituent power of the people delegated to their elected representatives, who did not see themselves acting as commissars or agents of the people. Rejection of the imperative mandate allowed the assembled representatives to exercise constituent power with autonomy and independence.

On 6 April 1814, the Senate, under the leadership of Talleyrand, approved the text of an Acte constitutionnel which proposed, in the spirit of 1791, a constitutional regime presided over by a monarch. The Senate defined constitutional monarchy in the following terms: 'Un monarque constitutionnel n'existe qu'en vertu de la Constitution et du pacte social' (Bagge, 1952: 161). The Senate required that Louis-Stanilas-Xavier, Louis XVI's brother, swear by and sign the Acte constitutionnel, if he was to be proclaimed king of all the French (Capefigue, 1843: 165–7).[3] When the future monarch landed triumphantly in Calais at the end of April, he had already decided that he would not accept to be addressed as Louis-Stanilas-Xavier. He was Louis XVIII, 'who had never ceased to reign' and whose claim to the throne did not stem from signing a piece of paper, but was grounded on his birth and divine grace (Capefigue, 1843: 185). He surmised that a return to absolutism was out of the question,[4] but understandably he refused to acquiesce to the framework instituted by the 1791 constitution for this had paved the way for the formation of the National Convention and the abolition of monarchy on 21 September 1792. A compromise was reached at the very outskirts of Paris. In the Declaration of Saint-Ouen, the future king promised a 'liberal constitution' which consecrated individual liberty, freedom of the press and inviolable property rights. He also proposed that a commission should meet in Paris to rectify the redaction of the Senate's Acte constitutionnel (Rosanvallon, 1994: 209–10). This compromise allowed him to enter the capital on 3 May and assume the task of governing France (Diez del Corral, 1973: 65).

The commission appointed to revise the text redacted by the Senate met for five days, from 22 to 27 May, and it became clear that the discussion was dominated by the King's four *commissaires*, particularly by Chancellor Dambray, who responded to every objection raised by members of the commission by an appeal to the 'principe monarchique' (Capefigue, 1843: 207). On 4 June, the legislative body met, convened not as a constituent assembly and purged of members not sympathetic to Louis XVIII. After a short speech by the King, Ferrand presented the Charte and introduced the monarchical principle: 'En pleine possession de ses droits héréditaires sur ce beau royaume, le roi ne veut exercer l'autorité qu'il tient de Dieu et de ses pères, qu'en posant lui-même les bornes de son pouvoir' (Rosanvallon, 1994: 248; see Jellinek, 1919: 469–72). Next, Dambray read the Charte's preamble which linked Louis XVIII to the rule of his predecessors and acknowledged that 'l'autorité tout entière résidât en France dans la personne du monarque' (Rosanvallon, 1994: 250). In virtue of the authority that came from God and his predecessors, Louis XVIII retrieved their constituent power and declared: 'Nous avons volontairement, et par le libre exercise de notre autorité royale, accordé et accordons, fait concession et octroi à nos sujets, tant pour nous que pour nos successeurs, et à toujours, de la charte constitutionelle qui suit' (ibid.: 251). The general feeling at the assembly was that the constitution was in complete harmony with the aspirations of freedom of the French, but there was also consternation at the way Ferrand and the Charte's preamble had asserted Louis XVIII's authority.[5] This dual reaction would accompany constitutional monarchy throughout its lifetime in France and Germany, and would also determine Hegel's initial enthusiasm and ultimate disillusionment with respect to this experiment.[6]

The circumstances surrounding the birth of the Charte gave rise to partisan division and dissatisfaction with the constitution itself. Royalists, on the one hand, were unhappy because the Charte introduced *constitutional* monarchy, which they saw as tying the hands of the monarch and shattering their *ancien régime* prerogatives. As defined by the French Senate, on the occasion of Napoleon's dethronement, constitutional monarchy was legitimated by a pre-existing constitution and a social pact. The Charte, therefore, must have evoked in royalists memories of the constitution of 1791. Liberals, on the other hand, were unhappy because the Charte introduced constitutional *monarchy*. A constitution issued by royal decree was the result of a crypto-absolutist 'coup d'État' (Capefigue, 1843: 207) that effectively robbed the people of its sovereignty. In their case, the Charte did not evoke memories of the constitution of 1791. Ambiguity would haunt constitutional monarchy from its very inception. Limits were set to royal power, but those limits were self-imposed and based on an authority that did not reside in the people represented by legislative bodies.

According to Carl Schmitt, the French Charte was 'issued by decree (*oktroyiert*) on the basis of the monarchical principle, namely the constituent power of the monarch' (1928: 53). This meant that Louis XVIII could claim the same divine authority affirmed by his absolutist predecessors. Not the liberal content, but the generation of the Charte, was patently authoritarian and counter-revolutionary: the unity of the state was no longer based on the people organized as a nation, but on the person of an authoritarian monarch.

II

In the contest between royalist and liberal interpretations of the Charte, Hegel sides with the *doctrinaires*, liberal royalists who hail the civil liberties acknowledged by the Charte, but also favour Louis XVIII's assertion of the monarchical principle.[7] As Hegel grows closer to the views espoused by Royer-Collard and Guizot, he distances himself from Constant and political liberalism. He opts for constitutional *royalism*, and is, at the same time, definitely opposed to the *constitutional* royalism delineated by the constitution of 1791.[8] Constitutional monarchy, as defined by the constitution, presupposed that the unity of the people was conjointly represented by the king and a legislative assembly. The Charte avoids this predicament. Hegel and Schmitt stand in agreement on this point. In the Heidelberg lectures of *Rechtsphilosophie*, Hegel finds all French constitutions prior to Napoleon and Louis XVIII defective. Those constitutions lacked 'the subjective unity, the apex, which came necessarily into being in the form of [Napoleon's] imperial power and then [with Louis XVIII's] royal power' (Hegel, 1995: 237).[9] With respect to the constitution of 1791 we read in his 1817 lectures on *Rechtsphilosophie*:

> In France, where the king was only involved in negative fashion in the universal power, being able to do no more than veto the proposals of the legislative body, the apex was too weak, and a state of tension became unavoidable the more the legislative body considered itself justified in its proposals that were rejected. In this mutual independence of the powers these two powers stood over against one another, and unity could only be decided by means of conflict. (1995: 238)

Later on, in 1830, in his lectures on world history, he will have substantively the same thing to say about the constitution of 1791:

> The first French constitution . . . was the constitutionalization (*Konstituierung*) of monarchy. At the apex of the state stood the monarch and the executive power was entrusted with him and his ministers. In contrast, the legislative power was put in charge of a law-making chamber. But this constitution was from the start internally contradictory, because the whole administrative power was placed in the hands of the legislative: the budget, war and peace, recruitment of military forces resided in the legislative chamber . . . Everything was ruled by law . . .

Government was transferred to the chamber, as in England to Parliament. (1920: 929)

The constitutionalization of the French monarchy was an unavoidable revolutionary outcome, but the way this was attained in 1791 was contrary to Hegel's own understanding of constitutional monarchy.[10] What went wrong in 1791 was a structural design that drastically separated the executive and legislative powers, without providing for coordinating or mediating instances. The constitution also allowed the legislative to perform key executive tasks and stripped the monarch of the mediating role retained by the British Crown. As a result, Louis XVI, armed with a treacherous veto power, lost prestige and set himself on a collision course with the legislative. The abolition of monarchy in 1792 was the natural death of this constitution.

Hegel's enthusiasm for Louis XVIII's Charte is unbridled. He sees in it a 'beacon' built upon the form of permanence (1995: 241). The king bestows a constitution on his people and this ought to be seen as an 'act of authority', though its content is the *Volkgeist*. His enthusiasm is in tune with political developments in southern German states which followed the French Restoration model. The constitutions of Bavaria, Baden and Wurtemberg are founded on the monarchical principle, and they recognize representative institutions. Though strictly circumscribed, the power of their parliaments includes approval of legislation, supervision of the budget and control over the ministry. But when Hegel arrives in Berlin on 29 September 1818, he finds a political scene that diverges from what he had seen in southern Germany. In Prussia, Hardenberg's efforts to enact the constitution promised by King Frederick William III on May 1815 encounter Metternich's stiff opposition. His ambition is to halt the spread of German constitutionalism. In a memorandum sent to Frederick William in November 1818, Metternich writes: 'A central representation through representatives of the *Volk* will be the dissolution of Prussia . . . because such an innovation cannot be introduced into a great state without a revolution or without leading to a revolution' (Sheehan, 1989: 423).

The assassination of Kotzebue on 23 March 1819 seems for a while to make a constitution for Prussia impossible. But on 11 August of that same year, Hardenberg presents to the King his final constitutional proposal. 'In sharp contrast with the improvised constitutions of the south, he desired to establish parliamentary rights upon the broad foundation of self-government in the commune, the circle and the province' (Treitschke, 1917: 255). Hardenberg's reform policies intend to uproot the last vestiges of feudalism and complete the liberalization of Prussia. But these reforms had to take place under the auspices of the sovereign monarch. 'The chancellor insisted upon the firm maintenance of the monarchical principle' (ibid.: 256). In the end, Metternich and the Prussian feudalist opposition will win the day. Article 57 of the Congress of Vienna's *Schlußakte* is the final nail in the coffin of Hardenberg's constitutional plans. 'By the time of Hardenberg's death in 1822 the Prussian constitutional movement had come to a halt' (Sheehan, 1989: 424).[11]

Hegel coincides with the policies espoused by Prussian reformers like Hardenberg, Humboldt and Altenstein. But this does not mean that he can escape being categorized as an authoritarian thinker. Baron von Stein once observed that Hardenberg was a man of 'liberal phrases and despotic realities' (Treitschke, 1917: 255). Though reactionaries and reformers clash on the issue of constitutionalism and representation, they all share the classical conception of royal sovereignty proclaimed by the monarchical principle. All agree that only the monarch can represent the unity of the state (see Kervégan, 1992: 275). In Prussia, constitutional monarchy is understood as monarchical rather than constitutional.

Despite changed political circumstances, Hegel retains his espousal of constitutional monarchy in his *Philosophy of Right*. For him, the monarchical principle has not been initially advanced by the Carlsbad decrees and the *Schlußakte*, but inaugurated earlier by the Charte, which he continues to see as constitutional monarchy's prototype. Both in France and in southern German states, the monarchical principle has been diluted in practice and coupled with crypto-democratic forms of representation. Benjamin Constant, who favours popular sovereignty, appears as one of the Charte's chief apologists. This is reason enough for Metternich and the Prussian absolutist reaction to distance themselves from the Charte and reject the notion of constitutional monarchy. They fear that constitutionalism will open the doors to democracy and revolution. With the publication of his book, Hegel thinks he can sell Prussian authorities a model of constitutional monarchy that is truly monarchical in that it clearly affirms the monarchical principle and conjoins it with a form of representation impregnable to democracy.[12] He reaffirms the counter-revolutionary view that the monarchical principle charges the prince, and not the people, with the role of representing the unity and the will of the state.

Besides, democracy cannot be said to tinge his conception of the legislative power. Members of the first section of the Assembly of the Estates he sketches are entitled by birth (§307), and members of the second section are entitled to their deputation 'at the request of the power of the prince' (§308).

At this point, Hegel has only praise for Louis XVIII's Charte. Only later, in 1830, will his enthusiasm subside. He will then blame the Charte for having perpetuated a 'fifteen year farce' (1920: 932; see Fleischmann, 1986: 89), and express the view that the French 'were lying to each other when they expressed their love and devotion towards the monarchy' (ibid.). The blame he will place squarely on the shoulders of French liberalism for espousing the 'principle of atomism', according to which 'everything should emanate from the express power of atomic individuals and have their express sanction' (ibid.: 933). Hegel defines as liberal what is in effect a democratic demand, namely assertion of popular sovereignty and express popular consent. Thus, French democratic dispositions and lack of devotion towards the monarchy have pushed the Charte into the same predicament that wrecked the constitution of 1791. In Hegel's view, political liberalism is to blame for having compromised the effectiveness of the monarchical principle and is conducive to an affirmation of popular sovereignty. Contrary to Ilting (Hegel, 1973: 108), Hegel thinks the monarchical principle is compatible with the modern theory of subjective rights.

In his *Philosophy of Right*, Hegel supports the liberal conception that postulates the priority of subjective rights and the right of private property. But he does not extend these principles, constitutive of liberal civil society, to the political sphere. The unity of the state should be represented only by the monarch, and not by the people understood as a multitude of dispersed individuals. In Hegel's view, 'the term "the people" denotes a particular category of members of the state; it refers to that category of citizens who do not know their own will' (§301R). The people lack the capacity to know what reason wills, and only the highest officials within the state 'necessarily have a more profound and comprehensive insight into the nature of the state's institutions and needs' (§301R). Hegel is aware that by affirming the monarchical principle he faces the risk of re-enacting the politics of the *ancien régime*, leaving the prince and his advisers in extreme isolation, detached from a popular base that has lost its traditional social articulations. This explains the pains he takes in devising mediating functions which he entrusts to the executive and legislative powers of the state. Mediation guarantees that princely power does not appear 'as an arbitrary power of domination' (§302). It also guarantees that 'individuals do not present themselves as a crowd or aggregate, unorganized in their opinions and volitions, and do not become a massive power in opposition to the organic state' (§302).[13] If these mediating institutions were to acknowledge and serve the monarchical principle, they would cease to function democratically.

In his Remark to §302, Hegel explains the mediating role he attributes to the Assembly of Estates. What interests him most is that this mediating function ought not to be interpreted as an opposition to the government. If opposition were to develop, it should be treated as 'mere semblance'. Were it to cease to be merely superficial, and take on a 'substantial character', the state would become 'close to destruction' (§302). Present in Hegel's mind are the very real problems that beset the constitution of 1791: an unmediated antagonism between the powers of the state which ultimately led to its demise. In his mind that constitution embodied that most fundamental revolutionary change by which representation of the unity of the state is wrested away from the monarch and assumed by the people. Against this, Hegel thrusts forward the authority embodied by the monarchical principle – 'without its monarch and that articulation of the whole which is necessarily and immediately associated with monarchy, the people is a formless mass' (§279R) This explains why Hegel describes the role of the Assembly of Estates as 'purely accessory' with respect to the business of the state (§314). This does not mean that they are dispensable. Through the publicity of its proceedings 'the moment of universal knowledge' attains its extension (§314). And Hegel attributes to this publicity 'great educational value' (§315A; see Schmitt, 1923: 59).[14] Parliamentarianism of this sort does not meddle with the business of government and does not constitute a real opposition. It is compatible with the monarchical principle so long as democracy is not taken seriously, something that political liberalism cannot be trusted to do.

At the core of Hegel's clash with Rousseauean and Kantian republicanism is his view that politics is not the people's business. Citizenship, in Kantian terms, 'involves a reciprocal relationship between authority and freedom. Freedom implies the possibility of coercion but it is a coercion that we respect as emanating from our own wills' (Williams, 2003: 130). The fractured reality of Hegel's free-wheeling civil society requires an already constituted authority to hold it in check. By espousing the monarchical principle, Hegel eradicates the possibility of a self-governing people. This is consistent with the Hobbesian belief that politics should be wrested away from the civil society and left in the hands of a separate state. Majesty elevates the monarch to a height which cannot be touched by the competitive struggle raging within market society. Only then can Hegel be assured that the spark that ignites modern revolutions will not fall on a powder keg, but on solid ground, 'where it disappears without trace' (§319R). Members of civil society are not granted the rights of active citizenship, but this is for their own interest. Under the protective mantle of a conservative state, liberal market society blooms within its own borders. Hegel's aim is the protection and safeguarding of civil society and its most unruly element – the business classes. It is in the best interest of civil society that he unseats the republican conception which introduces the chapter on the state in the *Philosophy of Right* (§§257–69). Not doing so 'would call into question the monarchical principle of the restoration state' (Ilting, 1984: 99).

It does not escape Hegel's attention that this defence of monarchy may appear to relativize its authority. If one adduces the benefits that accrue to civil society as the reason for denying it the possibility of self-government, the centre of gravity shifts from the state to society. Judged from the point of view of empiricist natural law this is not totally inconsistent with revolutionary democratic theory. The claim that hereditary monarchical power guarantees peaceful competition within civil society invests a monarch with a purely commissarial role. To avoid this ambiguity, and the difficulties that attend Hobbesian contractualism (see Hampton, 1986: 189–207), Hegel consistently rejects popular sovereignty and the idea of a social pact, but does not retrieve medieval conceptions of legitimacy. While he acknowledges that grounding the monarch's right in divine authority is closer to the truth, for 'it conveys the unconditional aspect' of the right of the monarch, he does not pursue this idea and buries it under a cloud of theological scepticism – there are 'misunderstandings connected with this idea' (§279R). His solution lies in an appeal to the bare notion of majesty. Majesty cannot be mediated or deduced through clever reasoning; its truth is immediate and lacks any foundation (§281). The dignity of the monarch, whose 'very concept . . . is that it is not deduced from something else but [is] entirely self-originating' (§279R), is defined by this groundlessness.[15] This immediacy, that requires no further legitimation, is the foundation of the state. The monarch, with his 'I will', resolves and 'initiates all activity and actuality' (§279R). Above and beyond the constitutional *Rechtsstaat* one finds the bare fact of the will that decides its existence. The *Hegelsche Mitte* consistently ignores the decisionist component in Hegel's conception of constitutional monarchy and is blinded by its normativist aspects. If *lex* is allowed to play a prominent role, this is only because an authoritarian *rex* lends it support.[16]

The authoritarian monarch, in whose hands Hegel concentrates political power, is needed to secure the free initiative of individuals. Hegel clearly perceives that the social disruption brought about by the agency of the business classes within market society, particularly after that free agency is legitimated by his own defence of property as an absolute real right, cannot be addressed either by the mild centralization represented by the *Polizei*, or by an administration of justice. Perry Anderson has elucidated the modern conjunction of an absolutist state and a conception of private property defined absolutely as a *ius in rem*. As he puts it, 'the age in which "absolutist" public authority was imposed was also simultaneously the age in which "absolute" private property was progressively consolidated' (Anderson, 1974: 429).[17]

Like Spinoza, Hegel conceives individuals simultaneously as sovereign subjects of freedom and as dutiful subjects of an authoritarian state.[18] In this consists the reciprocal relationship he envisages between civil society and the state, the *complexio oppositorum* of freedom and authority discerned by Schmitt. 'In Hegel's political and legal philosophy, the state is the unifying ethical power that stands above the centrifugal clash of selfish interests within civil society. The state is the highest ethical authority . . . to which individuals submit in order to gain true freedom' (Schmitt, 1926: 98–9). To be viable, civil society's exorbitant freedom requires authoritative supervision and leadership. Counter-revolutionary France and Germany deployed the monarchical principle in order to strengthen the political authority of the state and cancel the rule of pure constitutional law. Hegel approves of this historical development. If what the *Hegelsche Mitte* wants to maintain is that Hegel is a liberal in the sense that he does not envision a despotic regime bent on tyrannizing society, I stand in full agreement. His endeavour aims at the protection and safeguard of civil society and its most mercurial component – the business classes. In *The English Reform Bill*, Hegel criticizes the myopic vision of English society for allowing the monarchical principle to be irretrievably diluted. In the *Philosophy of Right*, his awareness that laissez-faire policies lead to pauperization fuels his fear that republican ideologues may turn the poor into a revolutionary rabble.[19] For this reason he remains deeply diffident of democracy and the rule of constitutional law. Like the French *doctrinaires*, Hegel dethrones popular sovereignty and concentrates political authority in the person of an absolutist monarch.

Notes

Introduction

1 In 1929, Dewey recognized that 'the relation of individuality to collectivity, freedom to law, liberty to authority, is and always has been a central issue in social and political thinking' (Dewey, 1929b: 174).

2 By relating the antinomy of freedom and authority to the old question of the One and the Many, and, as Dewey does, to the question of stability and change, one should escape the charge that this is a platitude without philosophical import.

3 In 'Construction and criticism', an autobiographical essay, Dewey wrote: 'I should never think of ignoring, much less denying, what an astute critic occasionally refers to as a novel discovery – that acquaintance with Hegel has left a permanent deposit in my thinking. The form, the schematism, of his system now seems to me artificial to the last degree. But in the content of his ideas there is often extraordinary depth' (Dewey, 1929a: 154; compare with Ryan, 1995: 61).

4 Franz Neumann takes a similar approach. He sees Hegel engaged in an effort to solve the 'problem of a synthesis of liberty and sovereignty, of the rights of men and the state' (1986: 171).

5 This cleft between Germany's economic and political conditions is reflected in the views of Prince von Hardenberg, the Prussian reformist chancellor, who was close to 'the traditions of eighteenth-century enlightened absolutism' (Sheehan, 1989: 304). Hardenberg's political views could be encapsulated by the formula he used in his *Rigaer Denkschrift* of 1807 – 'Democratic principles in a monarchical government.' According to Sheehan, this formula meant 'freedom for individuals in the economic and social realm – and virtually unlimited power for the state in the conduct of public affairs' (ibid.: 305). While visiting Prussia in 1820, Thomas Hodgskin reported: 'The monarch set trade free from the fetters of ancient custom, and he pinioned it with his own . . . By the abolition of all ancient regulations, the sovereign increased his own power and influence very much' (ibid.: 437).

6 When it comes to dealing with emergency situations, it seems that some liberals have no qualms in joining forces with conservatives and rush to subordinate individual liberty to the demands of authority. Hegel is no different than Locke, who was ready to grant the executive the power of prerogative, namely a discretionary power to act 'for the public good,

without prescription of the law, and sometimes even against it' (Locke, 1980: 84; compare with Campagna, 2001). This, in spite of the fact that he stringently defended the rule of law, which binds the sovereign to govern by 'established, *standing laws*' and not by 'extemporary decrees' (Locke, 1980: 68). On those occasions when the common good demands it, when the welfare of the people is in serious jeopardy, then the executive may impose its prerogative, and proceed to do 'public good without a rule' (ibid.: 87). Locke was not at all intimidated by the difficulty in responding to the question *quis judicabit*. Who can the people turn to in order to judge when prerogative is made good use of? His response was terse: since 'there can be no judge on earth' the people have no other recourse left than an 'appeal to heaven' (ibid.: 87). On matters of self-preservation there ultimately was no better judge than the one whose survival is in peril. Life was the higher value and all others were subordinate. Locke's liberalism opted for a utilitarian solution. Similarly, M. J. Petry thinks that 'like Hegel, James Mill was convinced that a powerful constitutional monarchy was essential to the effective and efficient administration of a country' (1984: 152).

[7] In the *Philosophy of Right* he sees confusion in England's administration of law which he blames on the indeterminacy of unwritten law. He sees progress in the determinacy offered by legal codes (§211). Inevitably law retains a moment of indeterminacy, and in hard cases it is important 'that some kind of determination and decision should be reached, no matter how this is done' (§214). The contingency and indeterminacy of *lex* makes *rex* necessary.

[8] Hobbes's direct acquaintance with the upheavals of 1640 and the demands of revolutionary freedom made him more receptive to stronger calls for authority. This is something Hegel readily acknowledged in his *Lectures on the History of Philosophy*: 'Hobbes found in the events of that time, in the English Revolution, an occasion for reflecting on the principles of state and law, and in fact he succeeded in making his way to quite original conceptions' (Hegel, 1986: 225).

[9] In book 2 of the *Republic*, the rise of the state coincided with class stratification. Hegel must have been struck by Plato's characterization of the inhabitants of the luxurious city as possessive individuals who 'surrendered themselves to the infinite (ἄπειρον) appropriation of wealth and overstepped the boundaries of necessity' (373d). Plato also noted that this possessive animus required territorial expansion, leading ultimately to inter-state wars. He then charged a separate class, the guardians, with the protection of this luxurious society. This meant that he could match the productive class, responsible for the fluctuations of a freely expanding market society, with a protective class that guaranteed the unity and stability of an authoritative state.

[10] The proper function of the monarchical principle is best understood in terms of Bruce Ackerman's dualist constitutional conception (see Ackerman,

1993: 6–7). Ackerman discerns two kinds of political decisions: some involve higher lawmaking and concern issues of grand institutional design; others involve normal lawmaking and correspond to ordinary governmental decisions of daily occurrence. Only the former need to invoke the constituent power of the people (democracy) or of the monarch (monarchical principle) and occur rarely and under special circumstances. According to Hegel, not the people, but the monarch is the 'apex and beginning of the whole' (§273) and initiates 'all activity and actuality' (§279R). In that capacity, Hegel's monarch must be regarded as the subject of constituent power.

11 The monarchical principle does not refer to a form of government, but to a form of state (Schmitt, 1928: 289). In virtue of this principle, a monarch like Louis XVIII could issue a constitution by royal decree without requiring the consent of the people. This means, as Carl Schmitt sees it, that 'the monarch had the capacity unilaterally to make the fundamental political decisions as subject of constituent power', and that at no point did the monarch relinquish that power (1928: 52). As opposed to France after 1830, in Germany the monarchical principle was not abolished until 1918. As a result, German monarchs retained the possibility of appealing to their own power when parliament refused to function. Based on the constitutional views advanced by Max von Seydel, Schmitt admits that 'in Germany, in cases of serious conflict, namely those that concerned sovereignty and constituent power, the constitutional monarch could appeal to his own state power. The monarch continued to be the subject of constituent power, of a power that could not be circumscribed constitutionally' (1928: 55). This means that German constitutional monarchs were not 'neutral', but 'higher' third parties.

12 Wood believes that Hegel is 'fundamentally a theorist of the modern constitutional state', and asserts that 'this was always the position of the Hegelian "centre", including Hegel's own students and most direct nineteenth-century followers. This more sympathetic tradition in Hegel scholarship has reasserted itself decisively since the middle of this century' (Hegel, 1991a: p. ix; see Ottmann, 1977).

13 Conservative or authoritarian liberalism acquired political relevance in Restoration France with thinkers like Royer-Collard and Guizot (see Bagge, 1952: 159–60). Claudio Cesa has noticed the affinities between these *doctrinaires* and Hegel (1979: p. xxviii; compare with Fleischmann, 1986: 89). In private communication (dated 1 September 1979), Cesa wrote: 'Penso anch'io che quello di Hegel sia stato un liberalismo conservatore o dottrinario (anzi, penso che ci siano delle vicinanze non irrilevanti tra Hegel e i *doctrinaires* francesi suoi contemporanei, come Royer-Collard, o il primo Guizot; del resto, al riguardo, c'è una esplicita testimonianza di Victor Cousin)' ['I think that Hegel was a doctrinaire or conservative liberal (and I also think that there are relevant similarities between Hegel

and the contemporary French *doctrinaires* like Royer-Collard, or the early Guizot; there is an explicit testimony of Victor Cousin in this respect)'].

[14] Hegel's attempt to reconcile freedom and authority is noted by Seyla Benhabib (1984: 174–7; see Hocevar, 1968: 5; Burns, 2002: 179). This peculiar association of freedom and authority is not a Hegelian trademark. Krieger views it as a common German phenomenon, one that 'has been traced back to Luther and up to Hitler' (1957: p. ix). Similarly, Claudio Cesa notes that for Hegel 'the inevitable broadening of the sphere of freedom requires not a weakening but a strengthening of state authority' (Cesa, 1982: 205; see Cesa, 1976: 165). For a contrasting view, see Allen Patten (1999: 63–73).

[15] According to Richard Tuck, it is not at all clear that a 'liberal political theory' can be said to follow a strong affirmation of individual rights. He argues, instead, that 'most strong rights theories have in fact been explicitly authoritarian rather than liberal' (Tuck, 1979: 3)

[16] This tradition stretches back to Eduard Gans, who wrote, in his 1833 preface to volume 7 of the *Sämtliche Werke*, that Hegel's notion of freedom was not only the 'fundamental element' but also the 'only stuff' the *Philosophy of Right* was made of (Hegel, 1964a: 7).

[17] According to Rosenkranz (1844: 2), Hegel's acquaintance with Constant's writings dates back to his Berne years. Lasson indicates that Hegel 'gave attention to Constant until the end of his life, and owes to him a good part of his monarchical liberalism' (Lasson, 1920: p. xi).

[18] Similarly, Paul Franco writes that 'human freedom is the first, last, and in many respects *only* theme of Hegel's political philosophy' (1999: p. x).

[19] As Jean-François Kervégan puts it, Hegel's political philosophy may be defined as a 'philosophie de propiétaire' (Hegel, 2003: 155).

[20] A relationship between Hegel and contemporary free-market liberals like Hayek has been suggested by Carl Friedrich (1955: 512).

[21] Kervégan has accurately observed the close association that Carl Schmitt establishes between Hegel and Hobbes throughout his entire work (Kervégan, 1992: 192, note 2). In certain respects, 'Hegel demeure, plus encore que Marx, redevable a Hobbes de la structure fondamentale de sa pensée politique' (ibid.: 197).

[22] In doing so Hegel stood in agreement with Friedrich Gentz. In 1819, during the Carlsbad Conference, Gentz argued against implementing representative assemblies in Germany for this would introduce the 'false idea of popular sovereignty' (Huber, 1975: 643; see Stolleis, 2001: 43; Korioth, 1998: 44).

1 The *Hegelsche Mitte* and Hegel's monarch

1 See Bagge, 1952: 100.
2 The monarchical principle was inaugurated by Louis XVIII in the Charte
   constitutionelle of 4 June 1814. The formula 'monarchical principle' was
   not mentioned in the Charte, but was used during deliberations within the
   constitutional commission by Dambray, one of its members (Meisner,
   1913: 46). The monarchical principle was thereafter sanctioned and
   reinforced by article 57 of the Congress of Vienna's *Schlußakte* (15 May
   1820). According to Treitschke, article 57 became 'the principal article of
   the new German constitutional law'. In this manner, 'the "monarchical
   principle", which in Carlsbad . . . had secured general recognition, was
   formally recognized as the rule for all German territorial constitutions.
   Article 57 specified: "The entire state-authority must be centred (*muß
   vereinigt bleiben*) in the supreme head of the state . . ." ' (Treitschke, 1917:
   325; see Kaufmann, 1906: 37–8; Stolleis, 2001: 62). In Hermann Heller's
   view, Hegel draped the monarchical principle in a 'constitutional garb' and
   in this guise it then became dogma for Prussian and German jurisprudence
   (Heller, 1921: 111).
3 Hocevar characterizes Ritter's thesis as an 'inadmissible simplification'
   (Hocevar, 1968: 5). Similarly, H. S. Harris calls it a 'dangerously ambi-
   guous oversimplification' (1977: 12). In Hans Boldt's view, the mature
   Hegel felt sceptical and repulsed by the constitutional proposals advanced
   by the French Revolution (Boldt, 2000: 208).
4 For a recent comprehensive account of Ilting's achievement and the extensive
   discussion it has stimulated over the years, see Kervégan, 2003: 15–18.
5 According to Laurence Dickey, in Hegel's opinion 'the organization of civil
   society actually encourages individuals to put their private lives before
   the public good. At best, this arrangement creates depoliticized individuals who hold high personal standards of *Moralität* and are indus-
   trious, frugal, and honest. At worst, the organization of civil society
   produces a mental outlook that is conducive to what scholars from Carl
   Schmitt to C. B. Macpherson have called "possessive individualism" '
   (Hegel, 1999: p. xxix).
6 Ilting's interpretation of Hegel is significantly influenced by Carl Schmitt.
   In a personal letter to Schmitt, dated 6 March 1965, he acknowledged that
   debt 'Hochverehrter, lieber Herr Schmitt: Ihre Äusserung zu meinem
   Hegel-Essay erfüllt mich mit grossem Stolz, und ich fühle mich von Ihnen
   vollkommen verstanden. Im Grunde ist der ganze Essay ein Versuch, auf
   Fragen zu antworten, die Sie mir vor ungefähr 10 Jahren gestellt haben'
   ['Dear most honourable Mr Schmitt: your comment on my essay on Hegel
   fills me with great pride. I feel that you have thoroughly understood me. In
   essence, this whole essay is an attempt to respond to questions that you
   posed to me approximately ten years ago'] (letter to Schmitt, 4 July 1973;

held at the Carl Schmitt Nachlass, NordRhein-Wesfalen Staatshauptarchiv, Düsseldorf).

7 Dudley Knowles discerns the coexistence of authoritarian and liberal aspects within the *Philosophy of Right* (Knowles, 2002: 9–10). In this regard, he acknowledges that Hegel's account of the powers of the monarch in paragraph §279 may sustain two different readings (2002: 329–30). A 'hard reading' takes into account the monarch's power of ultimate decision by which he 'cuts short the weighing of arguments and counter-arguments . . . and resolves them by its "I will", thereby initiating all activity and actuality' (§279R). A 'soft reading' points to his assertion that the monarch 'has no more to do than to sign his name' (§279A), and is only required 'to say "yes" and dot the "i" ' (§280A). This latter reading is magnified by the *Hegelsche Mitte* interpreters. Knowles, in contrast, allows both readings to run parallel. My own view is that the role of Hegel's monarch is defined by the monarchical principle and can therefore only sustain a 'hard reading'. Much cannot be made about the monarch being required only to say 'yes'; nothing prevents him from saying 'no'.

8 Cousin reported on his conversations with Hegel in late 1817: 'En politique, M. Hegel est le seul homme d'Allemagne avec lequel je me suis toujours bien entendu . . . [I]l ne cessait de m'interroger sur les choses et les hommes de cette grande époque' ('With respect to politics, Mr Hegel is the only person in Germany with whom I have always agreed . . . He never ceased to ask me about events and men of that great epoch') (Cousin, 1866: 616).

9 Hocevar (1968: 207) observes that the 1814 Charte is the only modern constitution that Hegel makes reference to.

10 According to Carl Schmitt, the Charte was based on the monarchical principle, and therefore recognized the monarch as the subject of constituent power. In his view, 'as a consequence of the monarchical principle the king, by virtue of the plenitude of his power, *enacted* a constitution. This meant that the monarch, by unilateral action, took the fundamental political decision that defined the constitution as such. The monarch was able to do this as the subject of constituent power and without giving up that power' (Schmitt, 1928: 52). He did not share Constant's view of the monarch as a neutral third. Schmitt saw it as a higher third, not within but above the constitution (Schmitt, 1931: 132). Whether Schmitt's interpretation of Constant is the right one is another matter. Constant maintained that the fact that Louis XVIII decreed the Charte by *oktroi* meant that he was above it and could revoke it at his pleasure. But that now in 1815, under the strictures of the Acte Additionnel, Napoleon was hostage to the sovereignty of the people. 'Louis XVIII octroyant une Charte de sa seule autorité pouvait la révoquer par le même droit. Maintenant, rien ne se pourra faire que par les trois pouvoirs réunis' (Constant, 1978: 166). Constant clearly enunciates the difference between the monarchical principle, namely

recognition of the monarch as the subject of constituent power, and the principle of popular sovereignty.

[11] Capefigue (1843: 207) reports that Dambray, Louis XVIII's Chancellor, used the expression '*principe monarchique*' during the conferences that debated the text of the Charte between 22 and 27 May 1814.

[12] In Erich Kaufmann's view, the Bourbon restoration provided the ideal conditions 'for giving birth to the monarchical principle, which emphasized legitimacy, the original non-limitation of the monarch and its connection with absolute monarchy and its apex, which it set against popular or national sovereignty' (1906: 42). Kaufmann's attempt to oppose Stahl's espousal of the monarchical principle to Hegel's alleged constitutionalism is rejected by Heller as an 'implausible enterprise' (Heller, 1921: 110, n. 23).

[13] While royalists thought that the king should not have alienated his royal authority and accepted constitutional rule, liberals criticized a constitution whose origin was imperfect inasmuch as it was not based on a compact entered by the king and the people (see Capefigue, 1843: 217–18).

[14] Like Ilting, Kervégan assimilates Hegel's prince to Constant's view of a 'pouvoir monarchique "neutre et intermédiaire" ' (Kervégan, 1992: 267).

[15] Constant published his *Réflexions sur les constitution et les garanties* on 24 May 1814, before the promulgation of Louis XVIII's Charte. Here he made public, for the first time, the distinction between royal power and executive power, which is adopted by the Charte and subsequently by Hegel. He conceived the royal power as a neutral power which is supposed to mediate between the executive, legislative, and judiciary powers. In this manner, 'le pouvoir royale est . . . le pouvoir judiciaire des autres pouvoirs' (Constant, 1982: 181). A year later, in his *Principle of Politics*, he restated this doctrine: 'Constitutional monarchy offers us that neutral power so indispensable for all regular liberty. In a free country the king is a being apart . . . having no other interest than the maintenance of order and liberty' (1988: 186). In his view, the monarch 'floats . . . above human anxieties'. Inhabiting 'an inviolable sphere of security, majesty (and) impartiality' the monarch allows the conflicts of civil society to rage unchecked, 'provided they do not exceed certain limits, and which as soon as some danger becomes evident, terminates it by legal constitutional means, without any trace of arbitrariness' (ibid.: 187).

[16] Schmitt rightly observed that Constant's conception of a 'neutral third' power, a *pouvoir neutre et intermédiaire*, needs to be distinguished from the absolutist view of a 'higher third', who is not a protector of the constitution but a sovereign head of state (Schmitt, 1931: 132–3). Schmitt also thought that Hegel, together with Lorenz von Stein and national economists like Schmoller and Knapp, assumed that the state as a whole was a sovereign 'higher third', and not a 'neutral third' (Schmitt, 1929: 112).

[17] Their motivation for strengthening the authority of the King was more political than doctrinal, as they saw the need to neutralize the power of the

ultra-royalists who controlled the Chambre introuvable and who desired a monarch who reigned but did not govern. The debate pitted ultra-royalists Vitrolles and Chateaubriand against Royer-Collard and Villemain (Prélot, 1984: 400–2). Paradoxically, the *doctrinaire* liberals, and not the conservative ultra-royalists, affirmed the authority of a strong monarch as the best guarantee to safeguard freedom (Ilting, 1983: 190–1).

[18] Cousin again writes: '[Hegel] était donc sincèrement constitutionnel et ouvertement déclaré pour la cause que soutenait et représentait en France M. Royer-Collard' (Cousin, 1866: 616–17).

[19] Use of the formula 'constitutional monarchy' in §273 of his *Philosophy of Right* is a clear indication that Hegel was in the thick of contemporary German constitutional politics. With respect to the formula itself, as Ernst Rudolf Huber sees it, it remains an open question whether constitutional monarchy was a free-standing political form, or a simple formula of compromise, that could be interpreted as crypto-absolutism garnished with liberal flavouring, as a way to retain the *summa potestas* in the hands of a monarchical figure in an epoch of transition (Huber, 1970: 3–4). A similar view is offered by Otto Hintze, for whom Hegel's constitutional monarchy is merely a 'metamorphosis of the old enlightened absolutism' (Hintze quoted in Heller, 1921: 114).

[20] This view coincides with Hans Boldt's decision to privilege the published text of the *Philosophy of Right*: '[B]ei ihr handelt es sich um den vom Autor autorisierten und der Mitwelt zunächst bekannt gewordene Text, um den sich die späteren Ausseinandersetzungen rankten' (2000: 167).

2 Freedom and authority: *complexio oppositorum*

[1] Quoted in Kissinger, 1954: 1029. Henry Kissinger comments (1024): 'Metternich did not have a solution of his own to the query regarding the nature of freedom, because he thought it inseparable from the notion of authority'.

[2] In his *Lectures on the Philosophy of World History*, Hegel defines freedom as being with oneself without reference or dependence on an other. '. . . to be with one self (*Bei-sich-selbst-sein*). This is freedom, for when I am dependent I am related to an other (*ein Anderes*) that I am not; I cannot exist without something external. I am free when I am with myself (*bei mir selbt bin*)' (Hegel, 1970c: 30; see Hegel, 1980: 48) This often-quoted definition of Hegelian freedom corresponds to merely subjective freedom, not to concrete or absolute freedom.

[3] Hegel indicates that these two moments are prefigured in the philosophies of Fichte and Kant (§6). The first proposition in Fichte's *Wissenschaftslehre*

postulates that 'the self simply posits in an original way its own being'. The point of departure is a free subject. The second proposition, 'a non-self is simply opposed to the self', postulates that self needs an 'other', an obstacle, to challenge its subjective freedom. For consciousness to arise the self must encounter some resistence; or a reflecting surface which functions as a sounding board. As the self's 'other' this second proposition does not denote freedom but the determination of an external authority.

4 In similar fashion, the ethical point of view results from the synthesis or union of subjective or formal conscience and true conscience (§137). Conscience as purely subjective knowledge, or formal conscience, lacks objective content. In the Addition to §136, Hegel describes it as 'that deepest inner solitude within oneself in which all externals and all limitation have disappeared', a description that matches his conception of subjective freedom. True conscience, he continues in paragraph §137, is 'the disposition to will what is good in and for itself'. Its content corresponds to the authority of fixed and objective duties. Hegel then adds: 'The objective system of these principles and duties, and the union of subjective knowledge with this system, are present only when the point of view of ethics has been reached.'

5 Williams points in the same direction when he writes that substantive freedom 'refers to and includes ethical powers, duties, rights, and institutions (family, laws and customs) that unify individuals and govern their lives' (1997: 264). In this way, concrete or substantive freedom involves the determining authority of ethical institutions.

3 The epistemology of freedom and authority

1 Hegel was aware that the constitutions of Bavaria, Baden and Wurtemberg recognized fundamental rights of individuals in the form of civil rights: personal freedom, the right to private property, freedom of the press and religious freedom (see Boldt, 2000: 169).

2 *Encyclopaedia*, §145, describes subjective freedom as freedom in form (*formelle Freiheit*).

3 A metaphysics of freedom and authority is briefly sketched in the addition to §158 of the *Encyclopaedia* where Hegel examines the notion of reciprocity. Abstract freedom and abstract necessity are external to each other. Abstract freedom, as pure internality, implies the renunciation of all what we immediately are and have. Abstract necessity, in turn, manifests itself as pure externality. Necessity and freedom are alien to each other. But the process of necessity reveals its internal aspect. It appears then that freedom and necessity are not alien to each other, but moments of a whole. Each of

them, in its relation with the other, remains with itself (*auf das andere bei sich selbst ist*). 'In this way necessity is transfigured into freedom – not the freedom that consists in abstract negation, but freedom concrete and positive. From which we may learn what a mistake it is to regard freedom and necessity as mutually exclusive.' The illustration given by Hegel shows that what is at issue here is the reconciliation of freedom and authority. To criminals punishment might appear to be a restriction of their freedom. But punishment is not an alien power or authority (*fremde Gewalt*), but a manifestation (*Manifestation*) of their own activity. If criminals serving their sentences 'recognize' this, they will reconcile their internal freedom with external authority, and comport themselves as free individuals.

4 Hegel's epistemology is a restatement, at this point, of what he maintained in §7 of the *Philosophy of Right*, where concrete freedom was defined as the 'I' who is 'with itself (*bei sich*) in its limitation, in this other'. Epistemological and practical issues are interlaced because, according to Hegel, the will is a form of thought.

5 See Aristotle, *De Anima* 3. 4. 429^{b}30–430^{a}1.

6 See Tocqueville's description of French revolutionaries in *The Old Regime and the French Revolution*: 'Our revolutionaries had the same fondness for broad generalizations, cut-and-dried legislative systems, and a pedantic symmetry; the same contempt for hard fact; the same taste for reshaping institutions on novel, ingenious, original lines; the same desire to reconstruct the entire constitution according to the rules of logic and a preconceived system instead of rectifying its faulty parts' (Tocqueville, 1955: 147). Like Royer-Collard and Guizot, his fellow *doctrinaire* liberals, Tocqueville admired Burke's distaste for constructivism and prefabricated systems (see Bagge, 1952: 100).

7 The articulation of the forward-moving synthetic moment with the backward-moving analytical moment in Hegel's argument is compared to a *Springprozession*, a carnival dance that moves to and fro (Ottmann, 1982: 383–4).

8 See Kant's account of the matter. An analytic or regressive procedure, according to Kant, 'signifies only that we start from what is sought, as if it were given, and ascend to the only conditions under which it is possible' (1975: 23, n. 4). And in Kant's *Fragments* one reads: 'Rousseau proceeds synthetically and begins with natural man; I proceed analytically and begin with civilized man' (quoted in Cassirer, 1965: 22).

9 In Hegel's view, Montesquieu avoided the one-sidedness of both idealism and empiricism for he 'did not merely deduce individual institutions and laws from so-called reason, nor merely abstract them from experience to raise them thereafter to a universal . . . (but) comprehended both the higher relationships of constitutional law and the lower specifications of civil relationships down to wills, marriage laws, etc., entirely from the character of the (national) whole and its individuality' (Hegel, 1975b: 128).

10 According to Kant, our understanding goes 'from the analytical universal (of concepts) to the particular (of the given empirical intuition)' (Kant, 2000: 276). But one can also think of another understanding, an *intellectus archetypus*, which would proceed 'from the synthetically universal (of the intuition of a whole as such) to the particular, i.e. from the whole to the parts' (ibid.). Our understanding is forced to consider isolated parts first, and from there it can recreate a whole in a composite manner. To an intuitive understanding, on the contrary, it would be possible to grasp the whole in itself immediately, and from it proceed to view the parts as issuing from that original unity.

11 In his 1819–20 lectures on *Rechtsphilosophie*, Hegel states: 'The *Sittliche* has no duties' (Hegel, 1983a: 127).

12 In Hobbes's words, 'a son cannot be understood to be at anytime in the state of nature' (1991: 117; see Hobbes, 1998: 29, where the translation appears to be incorrect).

4 Property and recognition

1 Ilting grudgingly acknowledges that Hegel allows for 'an isolated individual to become a proprietor' (1982: 233; see Williams, 1997: 139–40; Ryan, 1984: 185; Hüning, 2002: 250, n. 41). Earlier, Marx had come to the same conclusion (1980: 581–2, n. 26; see Piontkwoski, 1960: 114). My argument (see Cristi, 1978) coincides with that of Margaret Jane Radin: 'because Hegel believes the rights he describes . . . concern only the Kantian "abstract personality", he treats them as both logically and developmentally prior to any relationship arising from the person's interaction with others in society. Subsequent sections of the book introduce other, more particular property relationships that arise from the nature of groups . . . rather than from individual autonomy alone' (Radin, 1993: 46). Later on, Radin recanted: 'Because I focused on what he said about property in his section on "Abstract Right", it was open for readers to think I misunderstood Hegel as holding that the property relationship is something unmediated between the person and the object, rather than always a matter of social mediation. Neither Kant nor Hegel . . . thought property . . . to be anything but socially mediate' (ibid.: 7–8).

2 Like Hobbes, Hegel reinforces the sovereignty of the state, but he does not subscribe to his conception of property. Hobbes required a strong state to dismantle the customary rights held by feudal tenants and cottagers. For this reason, Macpherson points out, he defined property as 'the right to exclude all others *except the sovereign*' (Macpherson, 1985: 143; see Macpherson, 1962: 95–6). In 1820, with primary capital accumulation well established in Europe, Hegel saw the need for a strong monarchical state to protect property from the redistributive exactions of a democratic sovereign.

³ Hans Kelsen characterizes property as the paradigmatic subjective right. In the French edition of his *Reine Rechtslehre*, he extends this view to Hegel: 'la philosophie du droit de Hegel . . . voit dans le droit subjectif, qu'elle identifie avec la propriété, la réalisation extérieur de la liberté' (1953: 98; see Stillman, 1980: 105).

⁴ To clarify this issue Kelsen quotes from Heinrich Dernburg's *Pandekten* (Kelsen, 1934: 41). Dernburg writes: 'Subjective rights existed historically long before any explicit state order was formed. These rights were grounded on the personality of the individual and in the respect they were able to gain for their persons and their property . . . It is, therefore, unhistorical and an incorrect conception to view subjective rights as emanating from objective law. The legal order guarantees and shapes subjective rights, but is not their creator' (Dernburg, 1894: 88). Like other nineteenth-century German *Pandects* theorists, Dernburg seeks to legitimize a radical individualist conception of property by an appeal to Roman law (Rittstieg, 1975: 207–8).

⁵ In the 1953 French version of the *Reine Rechtslehre*, Kelsen comments on §46 of the *Philosophy of Right* – Hegel's notion of subjective right 'n'est donc qu'une idéologie destinée à soutenir un système politique fondé sur le principe de la propriété privée' (Kelsen, 1953: 99).

⁶ This distinction corresponds to the one drawn in Roman law between *iura in rem* and *iura ad personam*. It also corresponds to Hart's distinction between general and special rights (Hart, 1989: 77–90; see Cristi, 1994) and to the one proposed more recently by Laura Underkuffler between 'property as things' and 'property as rights' (2003: 11–12).

⁷ Kelsen attributes an explicit ideological character to the notion of real rights. 'Parallel to the dualism of subjective right and objective law, one finds the distinction between personal rights and real rights, that is, the relation between persons, and the relation between a person and a thing. The latter is *par excellence* the relationship defined by property . . . This relationship is determined by the exclusive power of a person over a thing, a description that distinguishes it fundamentally from obligations based on personal relations. This important civil law distinction has an explicit ideological character. In spite of the reiterated objection that the legal power of a person over a thing consists in nothing else than a specific relation to other persons, that distinction continues to be defended because its decisive socio-economic function is masked by the definition of property as a relation between a person and a thing' (Kelsen, 1934: 45).

⁸ Hegel refers to Heineccius who defined *ius in rem* as the *facultas homini in rem competens, sine respectu ad certam personam* (Heineccius, 1729: §332).

⁹ For an account of the classical distinction between possession and property, see Buckland and McNair, 1936: 58–66 and Kaser, 1956: 6–16.

¹⁰ In his *System of Ethical Life* (Hegel, 1979b), possession appears as a moment within the first potency or degree of the development of ethical

life. The first potency is defined as 'the natural ethical life as intuition' (ibid.: 103). It constitutes the realm of nature properly speaking. Possession appears as the apex of a development that progresses in the following manner – taking in possession, work, possession of the product. Possession is the synthesis of the two preceding moments; the object produced is now preserved and saved. Hegel describes this procedure as a purely natural one, devoid of juridical significance. Possession is the result of abstract individual interaction with the surrounding world. Property emerges when the second potency in the development of ethical life is attained. In the first potency individuals expressed themselves as such. In the second potency, it is universality that dominates. Accordingly, intuition is subsumed under the concept (ibid.: 116). The subject is '[not] simply determined as a possessor, but is taken up into the form of universality' (ibid.: 118). The subject becomes 'a possessor recognized as such by others' (ibid.). Hegel concludes: 'the individual is not a property owner, a rightful possessor, absolutely in and of himself . . . It is not in individuality that right (*Recht*) and property reside' (ibid.). Property, then, is not an individual right preceding recognition, but presupposes a social formation. In the *Realphilosophie*, vol. 2 (Hegel, 1967), the distinction between possession and property presupposes the distinction between a state of nature and a state of right and duty (ibid.: 205). When individuals exist within a state of nature their relation to the world is a purely possessive one and, as Hegel asserts, 'this possession is still not property'. This means that 'possession is related immediately to things, and not to a third party' (ibid.: 207). Hegel adds: 'taking possession also means the exclusion of a third party' (ibid.). Recognition allows possession to attain a juridical status. When recognition of third party takes place, this allows my possession to attain a juridical status. Possession when 'recognized by another, becomes my property' (ibid.; see Hegel, 1970a: 237).

11 In accordance with the view advanced here, Stephen Munzer (1990: 150) characterizes Hegel's theory of property in the section on Abstract Right of the *Philosophy of Right* as 'a highly individualistic, natural-rights view of property'. Property rights, he admits, are 'unfettered rights gained by occupancy' (ibid.: 150 and 82). But then, unaccountably, Munzer postulates that, in this same section, Hegelian property appears to be 'an intersubjective concept'. He notes: 'Property could not exist, Hegel seems to think, if there were only one human being in the world. For a person to have something as *his* or *her property* there must be other persons who (1) do not have it as their property and (2) can recognize that the thing belongs to someone else' (ibid.: 69).

12 Nisbet's translation reads: 'includes its ability to be recognized by others' (Hegel, 1991a: 81). My own translation accords with Kervégan's. He translates *schließ die Erkennbarkeit für andere in sich* as follows: 'inclut en soi le fait d'être connaissable par d'autres' (Hegel, 2003: 159).

[13] Patten offers a 'strongly individualistic' interpretation of Hegel's theory of property, which he supplements with his observation that 'property mediates the recognition of others' (1999: 158–9). This allows individuals 'to demonstrate their free personality to one another' (ibid.: 161). Patten also admits that the 'emphasis on property as a mediator of recognition is less prominent but not altogether absent from the published *Philosophy of Right* version of Hegel's account' and offers what Hegel writes in §51 as evidence (pp. 159–60).

[14] Hegel agrees again with Heineccius, for whom *feuda iure Romano ignota* (Heineccius, 1729: §338; see Xifaras, 2004: 77).

[15] In the *Heidelberger Enziclopaedie*, Hegel writes: 'contract, namely the arbitrary agreement between different persons with respect to an arbitrary and adventitious thing' (§440).

[16] Stillman rightly observes that Hegel's political philosophy is 'founded on property only so that it can transcend property' (1980: 108). He also notes that this transcendence is *Aufhebung*, 'property is not only overcome, it is also preserved' (ibid.).

[17] The sovereignty of the general will, Rousseau admits in *Emile*, in the passage that contains a summary of the *Social Contract*, is not allowed to expropriate individuals, except when the rights of private property are considered as common to all citizens. 'Thus the sovereign has no right to touch the property of one, or several individuals, but it may legitimately take possession of the property of all, as was done in Sparta in the time of Lycurgus' (Rousseau, 1973: 303). In this way, the right of property ceases to be an absolute right of the individual. In the *Social Contract*, it is conditioned by the requirement that 'no citizen shall ever be wealthy enough to buy another, and none poor enough to be forced to sell himself' (ibid.: 204).

[18] H. B. Acton observes that that the publication of Fichte's *Grundlage des Naturrechts* anteceded that of Kant's *Metaphysik der Sitten*. Contrary to the conventional way of writing the history of philosophy, 'in which the views of each famous philosopher are presented as a continuous whole and each philosopher is discussed after his "predecessors" and before his "successors" ', he thinks it would be misleading to consider Kant's political philosophy as an antecedent to Fichte's (Hegel, 1975b: 28).

[19] Villey, for instance, believes that Kant's theory of property is in the last analysis conducive to socialism: 'On s'imagine tirer de Kant une doctrine très affirmative de la propriété privée: Kant décrivant, approuvant l'ordre de son temps, a pris soin de marquer fortement l'antériorité à l'état de l'appropriation privée, mais aussitôt il reconnaît que cette propriété de "droit privé", de "droit naturel", n'est que "provisoire". Quand le droit deviendra péremptoire, à l'état sera reconnu un droit éminent sur tous les biens des citoyens, et ce principe peut nous conduire tout aussi bien au socialisme' (Villey, 1962: 60, n. 1). A different view is expressed by Richard Saage (1973: 39).

[20] Hegel's notion of property is not regulated by the principle of equality (§49). Therefore not much should be made of his assertion in §46 that 'those determinations which concern private property may have to be subordinated to higher spheres of right, such as a community or the state'. This has nothing to do with the limited redistributive functions attributed later in his argument to the *Polizei*. Those higher spheres of right can rule only when common ownership has been instituted. But common ownership *per se* cannot belong to the sphere of abstract right, which is purely individual right. It is because of this that Hegel presents common ownership as purely exceptional insofar as it is 'an inherently dissolvable community', which implies that each individual's private share may always be reclaimed.

5 Liberal civil society

[1] Manfred Riedel states that this distinction appears for the first time in his *Philosophy of Right*. Hegel occasionally employs the term 'civil society' in his early writings, but does not distinguish it systematically from the political state (Riedel, 1970: 154, n. 3; see Horstmann, 1997; Kervégan, 2003: 58–9).

[2] The 'civil society argument' fosters societal, as opposed to etatist forms of integration. The former has been imputed to Central and Eastern European intellectuals (Walzer, 1992), whose dissidence is interpreted as having contributed to creating the new democracies. Their aim was to rebuild the autonomous societal networks (unions, churches, neighbourhoods, political parties) dismantled by Soviet etatism.

[3] Kervégan rightly observes that 'civil society is not, according to Hegel, a state of nature'. He thinks that a principle of formal universality is inherent to civil society and everyone is equally pulled into market competition. In addition, the universality of institutions like the *Polizei* and the administration of justice is evidence that a more substantive universality is also constitutive of civil society. Kervégan concludes: 'civil society, because it cannot be confused with the system of needs, cannot be identified with a pure state of nature' (Hegel, 2003: 292, n. 2). My point is that Hegel identifies only the system of needs with a state of nature situation. The purely formal universality of that system does not solve but aggravates the tensions inherent in the system of needs. Likewise in Hobbes, where the universal insecurity that affects everyone in the state of nature is the postulate required to set the war of all against all in motion (see Macpherson, 1962: 74–81). The substantive role played by the universalist institutions introduced later in the argument are etatist solutions whose ultimate failure requires the establishment of Hegel's ethical state.

⁴ Riedel limits the societal moment of civil society to the system of needs. In the *Polizei*, which Hegel includes within civil society, Riedel recognizes etatist functions (Riedel, 1970: 161).

⁵ I borrow from Carl Schmitt this distinction between four specific forms of state: *Juridiktionsstaat, Regierungsstaat, Gesetzgebungsstaat, Verwaltungsstaat* (Schmitt, 1931).

⁶ 'The market economy, functioning as it is supposed to, generates the problem, that is, the disintegration' (Williams, 1997: 259).

⁷ By contrast, Williams identifies the external state with a system of needs and distinguishes it from the *Polizei*, which he calls 'public authority' (1997: 227–8).

⁸ Avineri mistakenly interprets this passage to refer to members of civil society (1987: 218). But in §187, Hegel describes the 'transition to the infinitely subjective substantiality of ethical life', i.e. to the ethical state. If the passage in question is read in this light, it must refer to members of the ethical state.

⁹ 'Die bürgerliche Gesellschaft ist also wesentlich ein Zwecksystem zum Nutzen den Einzelnen, das aber ganz beherrscht ist von der Spannung zwischen den zentrifugalen Prinzip der Besonderheit und den zentripetalen Prinzip des Allgemeinen' (Kraus, 1931: 14).

¹⁰ A fear of social revolution haunts the collective conscience of post-revolutionary Europeans at this historical juncture. This passage from Constant's *Principles de Politics* is representative of this attitude: 'Notice that the necessary aim of those without property is to obtain some: all the means which you grant them are sure to be used for this purpose. If, to the freedom to use their talents and industry, which you owe them, you add political rights, which you do not owe them, these rights, in the hands of the greatest number, will inevitably serve to encroach upon property.'

¹¹ Following Schmitt, Kervégan draws an analogy between Hegel's civil society and a state of nature. He notices that Hegel gives a different location to the state of nature. Instead of conceiving it in Hobbesian fashion as a moment prior and external to the political order, he makes it appear as an 'interstice of irrationality' within the state. At the same time, Kervégan thinks that an interpretation of Hegel's civil society that reduced it to a competitive market society constitutes a 'profound distortion' (1992: 220). True, universality is not absent from civil society, but one ought to recognize the different modality of its presence – within the system of needs universality is related to independent particular aims in a blind and unconscious manner. The analogy with the state of nature applies only to the system of needs. I have criticized Kervégan's interpretation in Cristi, 1998: 100–1.

¹² In his 1818–19 lectures on *Rechtsphilosophie*, Hegel refers concretely to London, where the highest luxury he sees accompanied by horrendous misery and despondency (1973: 599).

13 Avineri notices Hegel's failure to integrate workers into civil society. 'Both in the *Realphilosophie* and the *Philosophy of Right*, the worker remains for Hegel in civil society but not of civil society' (Avineri, 1971: 118).

14 English-speaking Hegelian scholars have translated *Stand* as 'class'. Plant has done so without reservations (Plant, 1973). Avineri and Taylor indicate that 'estate' is a better translation, but continue to refer to the different *Stände* as 'classes'. Avineri indicates that 'for Hegel, classes always remain estates in the sense that they represent a legitimized differentiation. Each estate stands for a different mode of consciousness' (1972: 105). He acknowledges that Hegel also uses the term *Klasse* but restricts its reference to the working class (1972: 96, n. 40). Avineri does not consider §245 and §253 of the *Philosophy of Right* where Hegel uses *Klasse* to refer to the business class. Taylor acknowledges Hegel's preference for the older term 'estate' and believes that 'it is better to follow him here since these groups are not just differentiated by their relation to the means of production, but by their life-style' (1975: 433).

15 According to Smith, Hegel 'was perhaps the first to recognize and describe the burgher as bourgeois . . . and turn it into the defining principle of a new form of civilization' (1995: 349).

16 This is a theme frequently sounded by conservative thinkers. 'The manufacturing classes require more regulation, superintendence and restraint than the other classes of society, and it is natural that the powers of government should increase in the same proportion as those classes' (Tocqueville, 1974: 370).

17 This is another theme evoked by conservative thinkers. 'La propriété industrielle . . . met dans [la] vie moins de regularité; elle est plus factice et moins immuable que la propriété foncière. Les operations dont elle se compose consistent souvent en transactions fortuites' [Industrial property . . . gives life less regularity; it is more artificial and less stable than landed property. The operations that it gives rise to consists for the most part of contingent transactions] (Constant, 1957: 1150).

18 'I possess something, own property, which I occupied when it was without an owner. This property must now be recognized and legalized (*gesetz*) as mine. Hence, in civil society formalities arise in connexion with property, boundary stones are erected as a symbol for others to recognize, mortgage and property registers are established' (Hegel, 1973: 658–9).

19 Hegel's *Polizei* must be understood in the context of German cameralism, an eighteenth-century theory of public administration that sought to centralize and formalize bureaucratic tasks within the absolute state. According to Pinkard, cameralism 'was very much tied into the leading ideas of the German Enlightenment and its related concepts of "enlightened absolutism" and the state as a "machine" ' (Pinkard, 2000: 178; see Neocleous, 1998). The cameralists were influenced by Frederick II's mechanistic conception of government. Johann von Justi, his faithful disciple, wrote: 'A

well-constituted state must perfectly resemble a machine where all wheels and gears fit each other with utmost precision; and the ruler must be the engineer, the first driving spring or the soul . . . that sets everything in motion' (quoted in Mayr, 1989: 111; see Krieger, 1975: 50). In the *German Constitution*, Hegel criticized the view of the state that conceived it as "a machine with a single spring which imparts movement to all the rest of the infinite wheelwork" (Hegel, 1964b: 161). This is the reason why Hegel confines the *Polizei* within the sphere of civil society. Since the ethical state is modelled on an organicist conception, this is another reason for separating the state from civil society.

20 Hegel re-enacts the failure of the civilized legal system devised by the rich for the protection of property in Rousseau's *Discourse on the Origin of Inequality*.

21 Steven Smith marks the mediating role of corporations in Hegel's political philosophy. They allow him successfully 'to find a middle course between Hobbes and Robespierre, between the market place and citizen virtue' (Smith, 1986: 137). By contrast, Charles Larmore notices Hegel's only 'fleeting reference' to corporations and his 'neglect of intermediate associations'. Hegel's conception of civil society, accordingly, 'comprises only egoistic behaviour', leading in the end to 'social atomism' (Larmore, 1987: 105). Similarly, Levin and Williams believe that in Hegel's corporations 'particularity has not been overcome but merely elevated' (1987: 111).

22 These intermediate associations were hailed by Burke: 'To be attached to the subdivision, to love the little platoon we belong to in society, is the first principle (the germ as it were) of public affection' (Burke, 1969: 135).

23 'The first blow fell on November 2, 1810. On that day the Prussian government promulgated a decree effectively destroying the coercive powers of artisan organizations . . . The law of September 7, 1811, reduced the competence of police authorities in the regulation of economic affairs and deprived artisan corporations of the last vestiges of power' (Hamerow, 1958: 24–5).

6 Hegel's constitutional monarchy: monarchical rather than constitutional

1 'In 1814, the royal prerogative took its stand above and beyond the Constitution' (Tocqueville, 1974: 420).

2 In his introduction to the edition of Hegel's 1817/18 lectures of *Rechtsphilosophie*, Ilting notes that Constant was the first to use the expression 'constitutional monarchy' (Hegel, 1983b: 20–8 and 339, n. 282; compare Giusti, 1987: 318–21). Constant first introduced the notion of constitutional monarchy in his *Réflexions sur les constitutions et les garanties*,

published on 24 May 1814, prior to the enactment of Louis XVIII's Charte promulgated 4 June 1814.

3   Bernard Yack writes: 'The power of the constitutional monarch is, to use Benjamin Constant's term, the *"pouvoir neutre"* ' (1980: 715). Ilting reaches a similar conclusion (Ilting, 1983: 191). In contrast, Ulrich Thiele thinks that Hegel's monarch 'is not in harmony with the office of a merely balancing *pouvoir neutre et intermédiaire*' (2002: 162).

4   Pelczynski, a commentator with affinities to the *Hegelsche Mitte*, detects the ambiguity of this notion. He acknowledges that Hegel 'seems to arrive at a doctrine of monarchical absolutism', but backs away from that conclusion, stating that this contradicts Hegel's belief that 'the rational form of the modern state is a constitutional monarchy' (1971: 231). The ambiguity manifested by that notion may be due to its transitional nature: 'The kind of monarchy Hegel has in mind is one that is moving away from the absolutist and authoritarian tradition towards that of a limited form of constitutional monarchy' (Avineri, 1972: 185). For Brandt, Hegel's use of that term 'is not a testimony of liberal tendencies, but an indication of a not yet ingrained linguistic convention' (1968: 158, n. 140; see Hocevar, 1973: 98–9). And Franco notices 'an air of unreality' in Hegel's constitutional outlook: 'In its announcement that constitutional monarchy is the achievement towards which the modern world has been developing, it seems to belong to a world quite remote from the democratic one that we currently inhabit' (1999: 306).

5   'Comme ceux qui avoient part aux affaires n'avoient point de vertu . . . le gouvernement changeoit sans cesse' [Since those that participated possessed no virtue at all . . . the government changed without end] (Montesquieu, 1951: 252). While Montesquieu attributes lack of virtue to citizens at large, Hegel confines this to their leaders.

6   Paul Franco correctly observes that 'Hegel is very concerned to elaborate a realistic constitutional scheme in which reliance on virtue is reduced to a minimum and the actualization of the right order is guaranteed' (1999: 312).

7   Montesquieu, in his *De l'esprit de lois* (11, 6), leaves the executive power in the hands of a monarch 'parce que cette partie du gouvernement, qui a presque toujours besoin d'une action momentanée, est mieux administrée par un que par plusieurs' [because that part of government, which is almost always in need of immediate action is better administered by some than by many] (1951: 401–2).

8   Constant advanced this new function in his *Principles of Politics*, by introducing the idea of constitutional monarchy and the distinction between 'responsible authority' and 'authority invested with inviolability'. This distinction justified the separation of executive and princely power (Constant, 1988: 184; see Boldt, 2000: 173–4). The executive power is the active power of ministers who are not merely blind and passive agents. In Constant's view, though ministerial power emanates from the monarch, the

ministers themselves are responsible towards the nation. The *pouvoir royal*, by contrast, is a neutral and intermediate inviolable power. The monarch is answerable to nobody. 'He is a being apart at the summit of the pyramid' (1988: 189).

⁹ In his Heidelberg lectures on *Rechtsphilosophie*, Hegel confirms his prevention with respect to democracy: 'But with every monarchy it is a necessity that the highest point, the ruler, should not depend on the choice (*Willkür*) of the people' (1995: 83). Ilting interprets this passage as evidence that Hegel embraced the monarchical principle, but because he mistakenly equates Hegel's notion of princely power with Constant's *pouvoir neutre*, he thinks that that principle remains 'alien and only externally adjoined' to his theory of the state (Hegel, 1983a: 334).

¹⁰ Of Hegel one could say what Marx said of Napoleon: 'Napoleon possessed an understanding of the essence of the modern State, which has as its basis the untrammeled development of civil society, the free movement of private interests, etc. He decided to recognize and protect that basis. He was no mystical terrorist. But Napoleon also perceived the State as an end in itself and civil life as a treasurer and as subordinate to the State, without a will of its own' (Marx, 1975b: 123; see Lukács, 1967: 468). The same may be said of Hobbes. Jean Hampton, for example, defends Hobbes from the charge of totalitarianism. 'It is his [Hobbes's] view that concentration of power in the hands of one person will bring about benevolent rather than tyrannic rule . . .; he never advocates a regime that would terrorize and radically constrain its citizens' (Hampton, 1986: 104–5).

¹¹ According to Schmitt, 'dictatorship . . . is essentially the elimination (*Aufhebung*) of the separation of powers, i.e. elimination of the constitution' (1923: 52; see Schmitt, 1921: 148–9).

¹² If one were to think in terms of Bolingbroke's dictum – 'there must be an absolute, unlimited and uncontroulable power lodged somewhere in every government' (1965: 18) – it is obvious that Hegel has found what Bolingbroke was pointing to.

¹³ According to Prélot, 'the political order of the ancien regime was essentially grounded on the identification of the state and the person of the monarch'. In contrast, the political order generated by the Revolution identifies the state with the nation (Prélot, 1984: 318–19). To say, as Ritter does, that Hegel is essentially a philosopher of the Revolution is highly misleading.

¹⁴ This extraordinary attribution of universality to an individual has affinities with Aristotle's conception of the universality associated to priority in the *Metaphysics* E1, 1026ᵃ30–1: καθόλου οὕτως ὅτι πρώτη.

¹⁵ Steinberger acknowledges Hegel's choice of an absolute monarch and suggests that there is 'nothing in Hegel's absolutism for a modern liberal to fear. The king, insofar as he fulfills the requirements of his role, will indeed be fully responsive to the needs and judgements of the people' (1988: 227).

¹⁶ In §273 Hegel states that the constitution 'should not be regarded as

something made, even if it does have an origin in time'. Given that for Hegel the term 'constitution' is polysemous (Planty-Bonjour, 1986: 16; see Siep, 2004: 270), he must be thinking here of 'absolute' as opposed to 'positive' constitution. Only the positive constitution is both 'made' and has an origin in time (Schmitt, 1928: 3–11; see Cristi, 2000: 1752–4). Only if Hegel is thinking of an 'absolute' constitution, understood as an already existing state, as the 'reality of the nation' (Planty-Bonjour), can he say that we should be prevented from thinking 'that no constitution as yet exists, so that an atomistic aggregate of individuals is present' (§273). An atomistic aggregate of individuals corresponds to a state of nature situation where we do not find an existing state or constitution in place. Furthermore, since, as Wood notes, Hegel maintains a 'general advocacy of written, codified laws' (Hegel, 1991a: 462), and considers Louis XVIII's Charte as a model constitution, the use of the notion of constituent power does not seem untimely. Otherwise Hegel would appear to espouse constitutional monarchy without an existing constitution (Boldt, 2000: 180).

[17] Jean Hampton makes a similar case with respect to Hobbes (Hampton, 1986: 98–105).

[18] Hegel discerned three moments in the development of that notion – universality, particularity and individuality – but, unaccountably, he reversed that order when he continued to develop it (see Reyburn, 1967: 240–4 and Ilting, 1971: 106).

[19] 'The king is a truly representative individual, in the medieval sense, he bodies forth the moment of subjective free decision' (Taylor, 1975: 441).

[20] Here Hegel explicitly emphasizes the speculative nature of this process and related it to the derivation of the will which I examined in Chapter 2.

[21] According to Franz Neumann, these two French schools of historical thought were locked in a bitter struggle. The *thèse royaliste* 'saw the salvation of France in a strong monarchy, annihilating the intermediate powers and basing itself on the bourgeoisie'. By contrast, the *thèse nobiliaire* sought 'the recognition of autonomous powers of the nobility and the corporations which were to limit the sovereignty of the king and to act as the guardians of the fundamental laws of France and the rights of the citizens' (Neumann, 1957: 109). Because Montesquieu 'followed closely Boulainvillers' and thus sided with the nobility (p. 111), Hegel is justified in characterizing his views as feudalist. This also confirms his own perception that absolute monarchy favoured the progressive point of view of the bourgeoisie. According to Mathiez, Dubos intended to consolidate the union between the king and the bourgeoisie, which justifies defining his position as the *thèse royaliste et bourgeoise*. From the point of view of the bourgeoisie 'il fallait un roi fort pour refouler les nouvelles prétentions de la féodalité' (Mathiez, 1930: 99).

[22] Similarly, Kant distinguished between monarchy and autocracy: 'The expression "monarchic" instead of "autocratic" does not properly cover the concept here intended, for a monarch is one who has the highest power,

while the autocrat or absolute ruler is one who has all the power; the latter is the sovereign, whereas the former merely represents him' (Kant, 1991: 161).

[23] Meisner observes the same tension in art. 57 of the Congress of Vienna's Final Act (15 May 1820). He believes that to attribute the unification of the entire power of the state to one head of state is a 'contradiction in itself' (Meisner, 1913: 47).

[24] While Hegel was writing the *Philosophy of Right* in 1819–20, the accompanying political situation seemed to go from bad to worse in his eyes. The assassination of Kotzebue in March 1819 marked a turn towards authoritarianism in Prussia. In February 1820, the assassination of the Duc de Berry, the heir to the throne, marked a turn towards authoritarianism in French politics. This event had profound effect in Germany. 'In February occurred the murder of the Duc de Berry . . .; the edifice of legitimacy was crumbling everywhere, and the Bundestag dolorously agreed with Count Reinhard, who reported the assassination which had taken place in Paris, when he said: "Such an occurrence will cause the whole civilized Europe to mourn". Immediately afterwards, a sinister conspiracy was discovered in London, the disturbance spread all over Spain, and involved Portugal as well. The revolution once more raised its head in every corner of the world' (Treitschke, 1917: 323). Hegel's state of mind corresponds to that Pierre-François de Serre, the only *doctrinaire* to retain a ministry under the government of the Duc de Richelieu in 1820. Pressed by his *doctrinaire* friends to resign his post he replied: 'There are times when it is necessary to sacrifice freedom in the interest of order' (Diez del Corral, 1973: 210).

[25] The prominence attained by sovereignty, when associated with exceptional situations, has affinities with Hobbesian sovereigns who wield Alexander's sword in order to leave no legal knots untied (see Hobbes, 1968: 322). One is also reminded of Schmitt when he wrote 'Souverän ist, wer über den Ausnahmezustand entscheidet' ('Sovereign is he who decides on the exception') (1922: 11; see Ilting, 1983: 199).

[26] Hobbes, in his dispute with Cardinal Bellarmine's *De Summo Pontifice*, observed that 'Subjection, Command, Right and Power are accidents not of Powers but of Persons' (Hobbes, 1968: 315). The neo-absolutist Carl Schmitt takes Hobbes to be the classical representative of 'decisionism' (1922: 45). The Hobbesian formula *auctoritas, non veritas, facit legem* has a certain kinship with Plato's observation that 'the best thing is that the man who is wise and kingly, and not the laws, should rule' (*Statesman* 294). The young Hegel celebrates this assertion (Hegel, 1975b: 96).

[27] Hermann Heller interprets this passage as Hegel's failed attempt to reconcile Rousseau's popular sovereignty with the monarchical principle. As Heller acknowledges, popular sovereignty understood internally 'absolutely precludes the monarchical principle' (1927: 70–1).

[28] 'Hegel's rejects the doctrine of popular sovereignty as incompatible with the monarchical principle' (Brandt, 1968: 155, n. 127).

29 'In practical politics, the monarchical principle was supposed to be the firm point which would definitely secure the overcoming of the revolution' (Jellinek, 1919: 472, 526).

30 It is difficult not to read in this a reference to Napoleon. Hegel's high estimation for the Napoleonic conception of the state is well-documented (see Pinkard, 2000: 456, 515). This contrasts with Constant who admired the English system of government and thought that Napoleon was an abominable despot. Nonetheless, Constant was able to collaborate closely with him in 1815 during the One Hundred Days.

31 Like Hobbes, Kant condemns revolution but, under the influence of Rousseau, supports popular sovereignty (see Williams, 2003: 30–9). Hegel rejects the contractarianism assumed by all these authors for it 'implies the whim or freedom (*das Belieben, die Willkür*) of individuals to choose whether to enter [into the contract] or not. The national spirit (*Volkgeist*), however, is something necessary, and has merely to be known; and this knowledge cannot be the affair of the whole people, but only of the best educated, of the wise' (1995: 240). Hegel rejects contractarianism because it opens the revolutionary floodgates. Louis XVIII, the new Theseus, has now given a constitution and is endowed with the divine authority once claimed by Moses and Solon. 'The princely authority in general was viewed as something divine, but the constitution must be so regarded' (ibid.: 241).

32 The plausibility of this argument has been noted by Yack (1980), Levin and Williams (1987) and Tunick (1991). But only Levin and Williams and Tunick take seriously Hegel's explicit rejection of consequentialist arguments, which survive in his exposition as mere 'icing on the cake' (Tunick, 1991: 489), while seeking to develop his deontological conception of monarchy. Tunick believes he can preserve Hegel's conceptual derivation of hereditary monarchy, dispensing with any metaphysical (or foundationalist) progression. Based mainly on the notes stemming from the lectures that Hegel gave after the publication of the *Philosophy of Right*, Tunick assumes that the monarch is thoroughly dependent on his ministers and limits himself merely to dotting the i's. In his view, 'the monarch does not make laws or the constitution, they are prior' (ibid.: 489–90). This view, which coincides with that assumed by the *Hegelsche Mitte*, induces Tunick to ignore Hegel's allegiance to the monarchical principle (§304), which recognizes the prince as the subject of constituent power. While the monarch does not make or posit a Schmittian 'absolute' constitution, Hegel celebrates Louis XVIII for positing the 1814 Charte.

33 Siep rightly distinguishes between constitution as the already existing 'historical development of an understanding of right and law within a people' and constitution as the positive codification of this historical constitution (2004: 272). This distinction coincides with the one drawn above between absolute and positive constitutions. But Siep wrongly concludes that '*who* it is that finds, declares, and realizes these [historical] formulations

is then a secondary matter'. For Hegel, it is essential that the *who* be a monarch and not the people, and for this reason he affirms the monarchical principle. 'Acceptance through the people', as Siep puts it (ibid.), is not an option for Hegel.

[34] In the *Wurtemberg Estates*, Hegel clearly enunciates the monarchical principle when he writes: 'There surely cannot be a greater secular spectacle on earth than that of a monarch's adding to the *Staatsgewalt*, which *ab initio* is entirely in his hands, another foundation, indeed *the* foundation, by bringing his people into it as an essentially effective ingredient' (Hegel, 1964b: 251).

[35] The monarchical principle still defined Germany's 1871 constitution. According to Max von Seydel: 'The monarch continued to be the subject of constituent power, of a power that could not be circumscribed constitutionally. The monarch retained a power that could not be limited' (quoted in Schmitt, 1928: 55).

[36] Aristotle, *Nicomachean Ethics* 1113^{a}32 (see Aubenque, 1962: 45–6).

7 Hegel and Roman liberalism

[1] A view similar to Hegel's is maintained by John Neville Figgis: 'It was the Roman pagan conception of absolute property that triumphed at the close of the Middle Ages. This idea, which is the foundation of modern capitalism, led at the same time to further attempts to depress the peasants into slavery. It has been fraught with a thousand evils, from which even now the world is slowly and with many struggles trying to recover. The "reception", as it is called, of the Roman Law in 1495 in Germany may be taken as the date when the Middle Ages came to an end and the Roman idea of property had conquered the West' (Figgis, 1921: 99).

[2] Hegel's lectures on the philosophy of world history were originally edited by Eduard Gans in 1837 and then re-edited by Karl Hegel in 1840. But only Georg Lasson's edition in 1917 (Hegel, 1920), has presented the surviving notes in their entirety, without adding or leaving out parts of the manuscripts, and has tried to preserve Hegel's diction (see Hoffmeister, 1975: 221–6).

[3] Juan Donoso Cortés stands on similar ground when he declares: 'Cuando la legalidad basta, la legalidad, cuando no basta, la dictadura' (1970: 306; see Schmitt, 1922: 69–84; Löwith, 1953: 271–3).

[4] In *On the Citizen*, Hobbes distinguishes between a people (*populus*) and a crowd (*multitudo*). He characterizes the people as 'a single entity with a single will' (Hobbes, 1998: 137). A crowd, on the contrary, cannot be said to have 'one will given by nature, but that each man has his own will. And therefore one must not attribute to it a single action (*una actio*) of any kind' (ibid.: 76).

⁵ Hegel may hold an over-idealized picture of Athenian direct democracy. In Athens, the institution that most clearly allows the direct participation of citizens is the *ekklesia*. But within this institution participation varies. M. H. Hansen divides citizens into three groups. First, there are those citizens who choose not to attend the meetings of the *ekklesia*, and thus abstain from participating effectively in political affairs. Then, there are those who attend meetings and serve as *nomothetai*, but who merely listen to deliberations and cast votes. Finally, there is that active minority of citizens who bring forth motions and debate them (Hansen, 1993: 267–8). If one considers other political institutions, like the Council of the 500 and the Areopagus, it appears that Athenian democracy is much closer to a representative regime than to direct democratic rule (see Larsen, 1966: 4).

⁶ For an interesting approximation of modern and Roman circumstances see George Heiman (1971: 117–20).

8 Marx's critique of the *Philosophy of Right*: metaphysical not political

¹ Letter to Ruge, 5 March 1842 (Avineri, 1968: 9)

² 'The most immediately striking thing about the essay is that the first part of it (from the beginning down to at least the comments on paragraph 274) is much more a criticism of Hegel's dialectical logic than a direct criticism of his ideas on the state' (Colletti, 1975: 18–19).

³ In a letter to Engels (18 June 1862), Marx again chooses to refer the Hobbesian state of nature to the *Phenomenology* instead of relating it to Hegel's civil society argument in the *Philosophy of Right*. Marx notes that Darwin 'has discerned anew among beasts and plants his English society with its division of labour, competition, elucidation of new markets, "discoveries" and the Malthusian "struggle of existence". It is Hobbes *bellum omnia contra omnes*, and it reminds me of Hegel's *Phenomenology*, wherein civil society figures as a "spiritual animal kingdom", while in Darwin the animal kingdom figures as civil society' (Marx, 1979: 157).

⁴ What Hegel writes in his *1803–4 Lectures* confirms this view: 'Need and labour, when raised to this universality, form for itself in a great people a prodigious system of communality and mutual interdependence, an in itself self-moving life of what is dead, which in its movement fluctuates hither and yonder in a blind and elementary way, and like a wild beast calls for strong permanent control and curbing' (Hegel, 1975a: 324). Marcuse comments: 'Hegel's early political philosophy is reminiscent of the origins of political theory in modern society. Hobbes also founded his Leviathan state upon the otherwise unconquerable chaos, the *bellum omnium contra omnes*, of individualistic society' (1968: 79–80).

5 The Carl Schmitt Nachlass (Nord-Rhein Westfalen Hauptstaatsarchiv, Düsseldorf) holds an article by Robert Heiss on Marx's critique of Hegel's political philosophy (Heiss, n.d.). Heiss begins his exposition with a quotation of Marx's comment on Hegel's Remark to §289 of the *Philosophy of Right*. Schmitt has written 'Hobbes' besides Marx's comment.

6 'The state is an empire of reason (this formula came first from Hobbes and not from Hegel), an *imperium rationis* (*De Cive* 10, 1), which transforms civil war into peaceful civil coexistence' (Schmitt, 1963: 121; see Kervégan, 1992: 191).

7 On 22 May 1815, Frederick William III, the King of Prussia, promised a constitution that would include representative institutions. Later on, under pressure from aristocratic factions and the events that followed the murder of Kotzebue in 1819, his constitutional project was shelved. Its fate was definitely sealed with the Congress of Vienna *Schlussakte*. It is difficult to assess Hegel's position with respect to the demise of reform in Prussia. After all, he has only praise for the Charte, the constitution 'made' by Louis XVIII, which accords with his denial that the legislative was subject of *pouvoir constituant* (§298).

8 Marx's (anti-)metaphysical critique of Hegel has been interpreted as determined by individualism and nominalism (see Berki, 1971: 208 and 213). This, of course, matches Feuerbach's own nominalism and naturalist point of view. At the same time, Marx stresses the social constitution of individuals and agrees with Aristotle that the human being is a *zoon politikon*. Evidence of Marx's effort to solve this tension, and its impact on the notion of civil society, is his Tenth Thesis on Feuerbach (see Rotenstreich, 1965: 86–91).

9 'Thus for Marx the conservative and apologetic character of Hegel's philosophy is not to be explained by factors outside his thought (his personal compromises with authority, etc) as the Young Hegelians had tried to explain it. It springs from the internal logic of his philosophy' (Colletti, 1975: 22).

10 Hobbes combined a critique of Aristotelian social holism with a powerful challenge to the republican tradition of thinking (see Pettit, 1993: 166; 1997: 38–9; Williams, 2003: 34).

11 In Schmitt's personal copy of Hegel's *Philosophy of Right*, this last section of Hegel's Remark to §278 bears the following side notations – *Diktatur* and *dezision* (Nachlass Carl Schmitt, NordRhein-Wesfalen Hauptstaatsarchiv, Düsseldorf).

12 Huber offers a more discerning view: 'At the time of the Bourbon restoration, French monarchy was crypto-absolutist reaction; at the time of the Orleanist bourgeois monarchy, it was a façade for a system of bourgeois parliamentarism' (1970: 6).

13 I agree with Fleischmann when he states: 'Les principaux antagonistes de Hegel comme Marx ou Haym le jugeaient d'une manière tout à fait a-

historique, à la lumière des idées et idéologies politiques qui existaient à leur époque mais pas encore du vivant du philosophe' [Hegel's principal antagonists, like Marx or Haym, judged him in a completely a-historical fashion, through political ideas and ideologies that existed at their own epoch, but not while the philosopher was alive] (1986: 69). Colletti makes the same point when he writes: 'Marx does not take [Hegel] to be the theorist of the post-1815 Restoration. He is seen, rather, as the theorist of the modern representative state' (Colletti, 1975: 29).

Conclusion

[1] Quoted in Boldt, 1975: 55.

[2] It was inappropriate for Louis XVI to claim that his signature on the document, and his formal pledge to protect it, meant that he was the subject of constituent power. His signature was affixed on 14 September 1791, at a point when the constitution had been promulgated by the assembly ten days earlier (Prélot, 1984: 315–16).

[3] According to Prélot, for Louis XVI to be proclaimed in 1791 'roi des Français' and not 'roi de France et de Navarre' meant the nationalization of monarchy (Prélot, 1984: 310). Louis XVIII, with an eye on the constitution of 1791, demands the latter title and the Charte complies with his demand.

[4] Absolutism may have been out of the question, but not monarchy. According to Mansel, early nineteenth-century France 'was a profoundly, passionately and *logically* monarchical country . . . From the point of view of the Frenchmen of 1814, the anti-authoritarianism of 1787–92 and the "democratic" Republicanism of 1792–1800 had been absurd aberrations' (1981: 171–2). At the same time, constitutionalism was, as Louis XVIII himself recognized, 'l'Esprit de notre siècle' (ibid.: 179).

[5] Capefigue observes: 'Le fin de ce discours excita encore un sourd mécontentement . . . Le preámbule fut mal accueilli. Le roi n'y parlait que de la divine providence comme de la cause active de la restauration. Pas de voeux de la France et des actes du sénat' [The end of this speech stimulated a muffled discontent . . . The preamble was not well received. In it the king referred to divine providence as the active cause of the Restoration. No vows given by France on Senate proceedings] (Capefigue, 1843: 209–10; see Mansel, 1981: 170–88).

[6] Only in hindsight may one say, as Leon Duguit does, that 'the preamble of the Charter of 1814 affirmed the permanence of the monarchical principle and divine right; but that was a platonic concession to the wishes of Louis XVIII and it deceived no one; 1830 was the re-statement of national sovereignty' (1921: 15–16).

[7] A French *doctrinaire*, Victor Cousin, had a very clear picture of Hegel's political options. 'Il était profondément liberal sans être le moins du monde

républicaine. Ainsi que moi, il regardait la république comme ayant peut-être été necessaire pour jeter bas l'ancienne société, mais incapable de servir a l'établissement de la nouvelle' [He was profoundly liberal without being at all a republican. Like me, he saw the republic as in all likelihood necessary to bring down the old society, but incapable of establishing a new one] (Cousin, 1866: 616–17; compare D'Hondt, 1968: 138; Gulyga, 1980: 256).

8   What was at issue here (namely, who represented the people, the legislative assembly or the monarch) entailed the feasibility of the monarchical principle. In Schmitt's view, 'when an assembly, as the representative of the people as a whole, defies the monarch, the monarchical principle receives a blow. This principle assumes that the king is the sole and exclusive representative of political unity of the people' (1928: 211).

9   In this, Planty-Bonjour rightly points out, Hegel stands in direct opposition to Sièyes, the father of modern constitutionalism. 'L'intention de Hegel . . . est d'établir une constitution en laquelle l'autorité ne réside pas dans le parlement mais dans le Prince . . . Il pense donc à une constitution qui donne a pouvoir exécutif une autorité suffisante pour contrebalancer les tendances libertaires que le protestantisme avait faire naître' (1986: 31 and 34).

10 Kervégan notes that, in his Remark to §272, Hegel probably alludes to the difficulties that followed adoption of the 1791 constitution (Hegel, 2003: 366).

11 Hardenberg's plans suffered a definitive setback in March 1821 when Benjamin Constant praised a German essay that anticipated the triumph of constitutionalism in Prussia and mistakenly attributed it to someone in Hardenberg's entourage. Constant presented Hardenberg as the 'standard bearer of parliamentarianism, of the ideas of the Revolution' (Treitschke, 1917: 568). Indignant, the Chancellor immediately 'had a protest published in the French newspapers', but the 'cackle of malicious tongues did not cease' (ibid.). Constant's political views were well-known, and not welcome, in Prussian official circles. Hegel, who was in all likelihood aware of Constant's disrepute, cannot be said to have modelled his book on his principles, for he would have exposed himself to needless attack on that score.

12 In a dedication to Hardenberg written in October 1820, shortly after the publication of the book, Hegel expressed his hope that his philosophical treatise 'give immediate support to the Government's beneficent intentions' (1984: 459).

13 In the *Encyclopedia*, the state is said to aim at disallowing the people from becoming a mere aggregate, *vulgus* as opposed to *populus*. As a Hobbesian *multitudo* the people is an 'unformed, wild and blind power, similar to that of an agitated elemental sea' (1991b: §544R).

14 Brandt defines this mediating function tersely: the Estates 'convey information upwards and propaganda downwards' (1968: 156).

15 This passage induces Claudio Cesa to suggest a comparison with Carl

Schmitt's discussion of Hobbesian decisionism in his *Political Theology* (Schmitt, 1922: 44–6; see Cesa, 1982: 201, n. 66).

16 Bourgeois, Cesa and Kervégan offer similar interpretations. Bourgeois asserts that the prince's power of decision is 'l'alpha et l'omega de la vie de l'Etat hegelien' (1979: 116). Even if one were to accept that his decision is purely formal, its defining feature is not its material content, but the formalism that determines 'sa valeur politique absolue' (p. 117). Bourgeois admits that the prince's absolute power is circumscribed within the framework of a constitutional monarchy and suggests this tantalizing formula: 'le pouvoir de prince hegélien est le pouvoir absolu d'un monarque non absolu' (1979: 129). Cesa agrees with Bourgeois's assessment and uses it as starting point for his own argument (1982: 185–6). More recently, Kervégan again reaffirms Bourgeois position when he writes: 'Le prince de 1820 est un monarque constitutionnel, et, si son pouvoir de décision ultime est absolu, c'est le pouvoir d'un monarque non absolu' (Kervégan, 2003: 19). What is missing here is a clear understanding of what is implied by Hegel's acceptance of the monarchical principle. Affirmation of this principle allows the monarch to stand above the constitution and to claim sovereignty as inherent to his person. Kervégan notices that Hegel's attribution of sovereignty to the monarch in §282 is a 'rare occurrence', but does not consider that Hegel's reference to 'constitutional monarchy' in §273 is also a rare occurrence.

17 In a similar vein Macpherson writes: 'The more nearly a society approximates a possessive market society . . . the more necessary a single centralized sovereign power becomes' (Macpherson, 1962: 95).

18 In his *Political Treatise*, Spinoza writes: 'the more a man is guided by reason, that is, the more he is free, the more constantly he will keep the laws of the commonwealth, and execute the commands of the supreme authority, whose subject he is' (1908: 303; see Krieger, 1975: 4).

19 Bentham's sanguine view that 'the poor have more to gain by maintaining the institution of property than by destroying it' (Macpherson, 1977: 37) is foreign to Hegel.

References

Works by Hegel

1920   *Vorlesungen über die Philosophie der Weltgeschichte*, ed. Georg Lasson, Leipzig: Felix Meiner Verlag.

1923   *Schriften zur Politik und Rechtsphilosophie*, in *Sämtliche Werke*, vol. 7, ed. G. Lasson, Leipzig: Felix. Meiner Verlag.

1964a   *Grundlinien der Philosophie des Rechts*, with a preface by Eduard Gans, *Sämtliche Werke*, vol. 7, Stuttgart-Bad Canstatt: Friedrich Frommann Verlag.

1964b   *Hegel's Political Writings*, trans. T. M. Knox, with an introductory essay by Z. A. Pelczynski, Oxford: Clarendon Press.

1967   *Jenaer Realphilosophie*, ed. Johannes Hoffmeister, Hamburg: Felix Meiner.

1970a   'Rechtsphilosophie für die Unterklasse', *Werke*, vol. 4, ed. Eva Moldenhauer and Karl Markus Michel, Frankfurt: Suhrkamp.

1970b   'Rede zum Schuljahrabschluß am 30. August 1815', *Werke*, vol. 4, ed. Eva Moldenhauer and Karl Markus Michel, Frankfurt: Suhrkamp, pp. 368–76.

1970c   *Vorlesungen über die Philosophie der Geschichte*, *Werke*, vol. 12, ed. Eva Moldenhauer and Karl Markus Michel, Frankfurt: Suhrkamp.

1971   *Frühe Schriften*, *Werke*, vol. 1, ed. Eva Moldenhauer and Karl Markus Michel, Frankfurt: Suhrkamp.

1973   *Vorlesungen über Rechtsphilosophie 1818–1831*, ed. K. H. Ilting, vol. 1, Stuttgart-Bad Canstatt: Fromann-Holzboog.

1974a   'Differenz des Fichteschen und Schellingschen Systems der Philosophie', in *Werke*, vol. 2, *Jenaer Schriften (1801–07)*, ed. Eva Moldenhauer and Karl Markus Michel, Frankfurt: Suhrkamp.

1974b   *Vorlesungen über Rechtsphilosophie 1818–1831*, ed. K. H. Ilting, vol. 4, Stuttgart-Bad Canstatt: Fromann-Holzboog.

1975a   *Gesammelte Werke*, vol. 6, ed. Klaus Düsing and Heinz Kimmerle, Hamburg: Meiner Verlag.

1975b   *Natural Law*, trans. T. M. Knox, with an Introduction by H. B. Acton, University of Pennsylvania Press.

1979a   *Phenomenology of Spirit*, trans. A. V. Miller, Oxford: Oxford University Press.

1979b   *System of Ethical Life (1802/3)*, ed. H. S. Harris and T. M. Knox, Albany: State University of New York.

1980   *Lectures on the Philosophy of World History*, trans. H. B. Nisbet, Cambridge: Cambridge University Press.

1983a   G. W. F. Hegel. *Die Philosophie des Rechts. Die Mitschriften Wannemmann (Heidelberg 1817/18) und Homeyer (Berlin 1818/19)*, ed. Karl-Heinz Ilting, Stuttgart: Klett-Cotta.

1983b   *Hegels Philosophie des Rechts: Die Vorlesungen von 1819/1820 in einer Nachschrift*, ed. Dieter Henrich, Frankfurt: Suhrkamp.

1984   *Hegel: The Letters*, trans. Clark Butler and Christiane Seiler, with commentary by Clark Butler, Bloomington: Indiana University Press.

1986   *Vorlesungen über die Geschichte der Philosophie III*, ed. Eva Moldenhauer and Karl Markus Michel, Frankfurt: Suhrkamp.

1989   *Hegel's Science of Logic*, trans. A. V. Miller, Atlantic Highlands, NJ: Humanities Press.

1991a   *Elements of the Philosophy of Right*, ed. Allen W. Wood and trans. H. B. Nisbet, Cambridge: Cambridge University Press.

1991b   *The Encyclopedia Logic*, trans. T. F. Geraets, W. A. Suchting, and H. S. Harris, Indianapolis: Hackett.

1995   *Lectures on Natural Right and Political Science: The First Philosophy of Right (Heidelberg 1817/1818)*, transcribed by Peter Wannenmann, trans. J. Michael Stewart and Peter C. Hodgson, Berkeley: University of California Press.

1999   *Political Writings*, eds Laurence Dickey and H. B. Nisbet, trans. H. B. Nisbet, Cambridge: Cambridge University Press.

2003   *Principes de la philosophie du droit*, Text intégral, accompagné d'annotations manuscrites et d'extraits des cours de Hegel, présenté, révisé, traduit et annoté par Jean-François Kervégan, Paris: Presses Universitaires de France.

Secondary Sources

Ackerman, Bruce (1993). *We the People: I. Foundations*, Cambridge: Harvard University Press.

Anderson, Perry (1974). *Lineages of the Absolutist State*, London: New Left Books.

Arato, Andrew (1991). 'A reconstruction of Hegel's theory of civil society', in D. Cornell, M. Rosenfeld and D. G. Carlson (eds), *Hegel and Legal Theory*, New York and London: Routledge.

Arendt, Hannah (2000). 'What is authority?', in *The Portable Hannah Arendt*, ed. with an introduction by Peter Baehr, London: Penguin Books.

Aubenque, Pierre (1962). *La Prudence chez Aristote*, Paris: Presses Universitaires de France.

Avineri, Shlomo (1967). Review of *Hegel's Political Writings*, ed. Z. A. Pelczynski, *Hegel-Studien*, vol. 4, p. 260.

—— (1968). *The Social and Political Thought of Karl Marx*, Cambridge: Cambridge University Press.

—— (1971). 'Labor, alienation and social classes in Hegel's *Realphilosophie*', *Philosophy and Public Affairs*, vol. I, pp. 96–119.

—— (1972). *Hegel's Theory of the Modern State*, Cambridge: Cambridge University Press, pp. 257–61.

—— (1987). 'The paradox of civil society in the structure of Hegel's view on *Sittlichkeit*', *Hegel-Jahrbuch*, pp. 216–25.

Bagge, Dominique (1952). *Les idées politiques en France sous la Restauration*, Paris: Presses Universitaires de France.

Benhabib, Seyla (1984). 'Obligation, contract and exchange: on the significance of Hegel's abstract right', in *The State and Civil Society: Studies in Hegel's Political Philosophy*, ed. Z. A. Pelczynski, Cambridge: Cambridge University Press, pp. 159–77.

Berki, R. N. (1971). 'Perspectives in the Marxian critique of Hegel's political philosophy', in *Hegel's Political Philosophy: Problems and Perspectives*, ed. Z. A. Pelczynski, Cambridge: Cambridge University Press, pp. 199–219.

Bobbio, Norberto (1981). *Studi hegeliani*, Turin: Giulio Einaudi.

Böckenförde, Ernst-Wolfgang (1991). 'The German type of constitutional monarchy in the nineteenth century', in E.-W. Böckenförde, *State, Society and Liberty: Studies in Political Theory and Constitutional Law*, tr. J. A. Underwood, New York: Berg.

Boldt, Hans (1975). *Deutsche Staatslehre im Vormärz*, Düsseldorf: Droste Verlag.

—— (2000). 'Hegel und die konstitutionelle Monarchie: Bemerkungen zu Hegels Konzeption aus verfassungsgeschichtlicher Sicht', in Elisabeth Weiser-Lohmann and Dietmar Köhler (eds), *Verfassung und Revolution: Hegels Verfassungskonzeption und die Revolutionen der Neuzeit*, Hamburg: Felix Meiner.

Bolingbroke (1965). *The Idea of a Patriot King*, ed. Sydney Jackman, Indianapolis: Bobbs-Merrill.

Bourgeois, Bernard (1979). 'Le Prince Hegelien', in Guy Planty-Bonjour (ed.), *Hegel et la Philosophie du Droit*, Paris: Presses Universitaires de France.

Brandt, Hartwig (1968). *Landständische Repräsentation im deutschen Vormärz: Politisches Denken im Einflußfeld des monarchischen Prinzips*, Luchterland: Neuwied and Berlin.

Buckland W. W. and A. D. McNair (1936). *Roman Law and Common Law: A Comparison in Outline*, Cambridge: Cambridge University Press.

Burke, Edmund (1969). *Reflections on the Revolution in France*, Harmondsworth: Penguin Books.

Burns, Anthony (2002). 'Hegel (1770–1831)', in Alistair Edwards and Jules Townshend (eds), *Interpreting Modern Political Philosophy: From Machiavelli to Marx*, Houndmills: Palgrave Macmillan.

Campagna, Norbert (2001). 'Prärogative und Rechtstaat: das Problem der Notstandsgewalt bein John Locke und Benjamin Constant', *Der Staat*, vol. 40, pp. 553–79.

Capefigue, J. B. R. (1843). *Histoire de la Restauration: des causes qui on amené la chute de la branche aînée des Bourbons*, Brussels: Wouter, Raspoet & C. Imprimeurs.

Cassirer, Ernst (1965). *Rousseau, Kant and Goethe*, New York: Harper & Row.

Cesa, Claudio (1976). *Hegel Filosofo Politico*, Naples: Guida Editori.

—— (1979). *Il pensiero politico di Hegel: Guida storica e critica*, Rome: Laterza.

—— (1982). 'Entscheidung und Schicksal: die fürstliche Gewalt', in Dieter Henrich and Rolf-Peter Horstmann (eds), *Hegels Philosophie des Rechts. Die Theorie der Rechtsformen und ihre Logik*, Stuttgart: Klett-Cotta.

Chateaubriand, François-René (1987). *De l'Ancien Régime au Nouveau Monde: Écrits politiques*, ed. Jean-Paul Clément, Paris: Éditions Hachette.

Cohen, Morris (1933). *Law and the Social Order*, New York: Harcourt, Brace & Co.

Colletti, Lucio (1975). 'Introduction', *Karl Marx: Early Writings*, tr. Rodney Livingstone and Gregor Benton, New York: Vintage.

Constant, Benjamin (1957). 'Principes de Politique', *Œuvres*, Paris: Gallimard.

—— (1978). *Recueil d'articles 1795–1817*, introduction, notes and commenty by Éphraïm Harpaz, Geneva: Droz.

—— (1982). *Réflexions sur les constitutions et les garanties*, in *Cours de politique constitutionelle*, ed. E. Laboulaye, Geneva: Slatkine.

—— (1988). *Principles of Politics Applicable to All Representative Governments*, in *Political Writings*, ed. Biancamaria Fontana, Cambridge: Cambridge University Press.

Cousin, Victor (1866). 'Souvenirs d'Allemagne', *Revue des Deux Mondes*, vol. 64, pp. 606–19.

Cristi, Renato (1978). 'Hegel on possession and property', *Canadian Journal of Political and Social Theory*, vol. 2, pp. 111–24.

—— (1994). 'Waldron on special rights *in Rem*', *Dialogue*, vol. 33, pp. 183–9.

—— (1998). *Carl Schmitt and Authoritarian Liberalism: Strong State, Free Economy*, Cardiff: University of Wales Press.

—— (2000). 'The metaphysics of constituent power: Carl Schmitt and the genesis of Chile's 1980 constitution', *Cardozo Law Review*, vol. 21, pp. 1749–75.

Cristi, Renato, and Pablo Ruiz-Tagle (2004). 'Hvad er Konstitutionalisme?', *Tidsskriftet Politik*, vol. 7, pp. 6–15.

Dernburg, Heinrich (1894). *Pandekten*, vol. I, 4th edn, Berlin: Verlag von H. W. Müller.

Dewey, John (1915). *German Philosophy and Politics*, in *The Middle Works, 1899–1924*, vol. 8, ed. Jo Ann Boydston, Carbondale and Edwardsville, IL: Southern Illinois University Press, 1979, pp. 135–204.

—— (1929a). 'Construction and criticism', in *The Later Works, 1925–1953*, vol. 5 (1929–30), ed. Jo Ann Boydston, Carbondale and Edwardsville, IL: Southern Illinois University Press, 1984, pp. 125–60.

—— (1929b). 'Philosophy', in *The Later Works, 1925–1953*, vol. 5 (1929–30), ed. Jo Ann Boydston, Carbondale and Edwardsville, IL: Southern Illinois University Press, 1984, pp. 161–77.

—— (1935). *Liberalism and Social Action*, in *The Later Works, 1925–1953*, vol. 11 (1935–7), ed. Jo Ann Boydston, Carbondale and Edwardsville, IL: Southern Illinois University Press, 1987, pp. 1–65.

—— (1936). 'Authority and social change', in *The Later Works, 1925–1953*, vol. 11 (1935–7), ed. Jo Ann Boydston, Carbondale and Edwardsville, IL: Southern Illinois University Press, 1987, pp. 130–45.

D'Hondt, Jacques (1968). *Hegel en son temps: Berlin 1818–1831*, Paris: Éditions Sociales.

Diez del Corral, Luis (1973). *El Liberalismo Doctrinario*, Madrid: Instituto de Estudios Públicos.

Donoso Cortés, Juan (1970). 'Discurso sobre la dictadura', *Obras Completas*, vol. 2, Madrid: Biblioteca de Autores Cristianos.

Duguit, Leon (1921). *Law in the Modern State*, tr. Frida and Harold Laski, London: George Allen & Unwin.

Fichte, Johann (1845). *Grundlage des Naturrechts*, in *Sämmtliche Werke III*, Berlin: Veit & Comp.

Figgis, John Neville (1921). *The Political Aspects of Saint Augustine's City of God*, London: Longmans.

Finley, M. I. (1983). *Politics in the Ancient World*, Cambridge: Cambridge University Press.

Fleischmann, Eugène (1986). 'Hegel et la Restauration en France', in Hans-Christian Lucas and Otto Pöggeler (eds), *Hegels Rechtsphilosophie im Zusammengang der europäische Verfassungsgeschichte*, Stuttgart-Bad Canstatt: Frommann-Holzboog, pp. 69–92.

Forbes, Duncan (1975). *Hume's Philosophical Politics*, Cambridge: Cambridge University Press.

Franco, Paul (1999). *Hegel's Philosophy of Freedom*, New Haven and London: Yale University Press.

Friedrich, Carl J. (1955). 'The political thought of neo-liberalism', *American Political Science Review*, vol. 49, pp. 509–25.

Gauthier, David (1977). 'The social contract as ideology', *Philosophy and Public Affairs*, vol. 6, pp. 130–64.

Giusti, Miguel (1987). 'La diferencia entre sociedad y estado como rasgo esencial de la modernidad', *Revista Latinoamericana de Filosofia*, vol. 13, pp. 318–21.

Goethe, Johann Wolfgang (1967). *Goethes Briefe*, vol. 4, Hamburg: Christian Wegner Verlag.

Goldsmith, M. M. (1980). 'Hobbes's "Mortall God": is there a fallacy in Hobbes's theory of representation?', *History of Political Thought*, vol. 1, pp. 33–50.

Gulyga, Arseny (1980). *George Wilhelm Friedrich Hegel*, Leipzig: Verlag Philipp Reclam.

Hamerow, Theodore S. (1958). *Restoration, Revolution and Reaction: Economic and Politics in Germany 1815–1871*, Princeton: Princeton University Press.

Hampton, Jean (1986). *Hobbes and the Social Contract Tradition*, Cambridge: Cambridge University Press.

Hansen, Mogens Herman (1993). *The Athenian Democracy in the Age of Demosthenes*, Oxford: Blackwell.

Harris, Henry S. (1977). 'Hegel and the French Revolution', *Clio*, vol. 7, pp. 5–18.

Hart, H. L. A. (1989). 'Are there any natural rights?', in Jeremy Waldron (ed.), *Theories of Right*, Oxford: Oxford University Press.

Hayek, Friedrich A. (1960). *The Constitution of Liberty*, South Bend: Gateway.

—— (1973). *Law, Legislation and Liberty*, vol. 1, *Rules and Order*, Chicago: University of Chicago Press.

Haym, Rudolf (1857). *Hegel und seine Zeit*, Berlin: Verlag von Rudolph Gaertner.

Heiman, George (1971). 'The sources and significance of Hegel's corporate doctrine', in Z. A. Pelczynski (ed.), *Hegel's Political Philosophy: Problems and Perspectives*, Cambridge: Cambridge University Press, pp. 111–35.

Heineccius (1729). *Elementa Juris Civilis*, Leipzig: Beer.

Heiss, Robert (n.d.) 'Hegel und Marx', *Aus dem Symposion*, Freiburg: Karl Alber Verlag.

Heller, Hermann (1921). *Hegel und der Nationale Machtstaatsgedanke in Deutschland: Ein Beitrag zur Politischen Geistesgeschichte*, Aalen: Otto Zeller Verlagsbuchhandlung, 1963.

—— (1927). *Die Souveränität: Ein Beitrag zur Theorie des Staats- und Völkerrechts*, Berlin and Leipzig: Walter de Gruyter.

Hobbes, Thomas (1968). *Leviathan*, ed. C. B. Macpherson, Harmondsworth: Penguin Books.

—— (1969). *The Elements of Law: Natural and Politic*, with an introduction by M. M. Goldsmith, London: Frank Cass & Co.

—— (1991). *Man and Citizen (De Homine and De Cive)*, ed. with an introduction by Bernard Gert, Indianapolis: Hackett.

—— (1998). *On the Citizen*, ed. Richard Tuck and Michael Silverthorne, Cambridge: Cambridge University Press.

Hocevar, Rolf K. (1968). *Stände und Repräsentation beim jungen Hegel: Ein Beitrag zu seiner Staats-und Gesellschaftslehre sowie zur Theorie der Repräsentation*, Munich: C. H. Beck.

—— (1973). *Hegel und die Preußische Staat: Ein Kommentar zur Rechtsphilosophie von 1821*, Munich: Wilhelm Goldmann Verlag.

Hoffmeister, Johannes (1975). 'Preface', in Hegel, *Lectures on the Philosophy of World History. Introduction: Reason in History*, Cambridge: Cambridge University Press.

Holmes, Stephen (1984). *Benjamin Constant and the Making of Modern*

Liberalism, New Haven and London: Yale University Press.

Horstmann, Rolf-Peter (1974). 'Ist Hegels *Rechtsphilosophie* das Produkt der politischen Anpassung eines Liberalen?', *Hegel-Studien*, vol. 9, pp. 241–52.

—— (1997). 'Hegels Theorie der bürgerlichen Gesellschaft', in Ludwig Siep (ed.), *G. W. F. Hegel Grundlinien der Philosophie des Rechts*, Berlin: Akademie Verlag, pp. 193–216.

—— (2004). 'The role of civil society in Hegel's political philosophy', in Robert Pippin and Ottfried Höffe (eds), *Hegel on Ethics and Politics*, tr. Nicholas Walker, Cambridge: Cambridge University Press, pp. 208–38.

Huber, Ernst Rudolf (1970). *Deutsche Verfassungsgeschichte seit 1789*, 2nd edn, vol. 3, Stuttgart: Verlag W. Kohlhammer.

—— (1975). *Deutsche Verfassungsgeschichte seit 1789*, 2nd edn, vol. 1, Stuttgart: Verlag W. Kohlhammer.

—— (1978). *Dokumente zur Deutschen Verfassungsgeschichte*, vol. 1, Stuttgart: Verlag W. Kohlhammer.

Hume, David (1977). *An Inquiry Concerning Human Understanding*, Indianapolis: Hackett.

—— (1894). *Essays: Literary, Moral and* Political, London: George Routledge.

—— (1803). *The History of England*, vol. 7, London: Wallis.

Hüning, Dieter (2002). 'Die "Härte des abstracten Rechts": Person und Eigentum in Hegels *Rechtsphilosophie*', in Dieter Hüning, Gideon Stiening, and Ulrich Vogel (eds), *Societas Rationis: Festschrift für Burkhard Tuschling zum 65. Geburtstag*, Berlin: Duncker & Humblot.

Hyppolite, Jean (1968). *Introduction à la philosophie de l'histoire de Hegel*, Paris: Marcel Rivière.

Ilting, Karl-Heinz (1971). 'The structure of Hegel's *Philosophy of Right*', in Z. A. Pelczynski (ed.), *Hegel's Political Philosophy: Problems and Perspectives*, Cambridge: Cambridge University Press, pp. 90–110.

—— (1975). 'Zur Dialektik in der "Rechtsphilosophie" ', *Hegel Jahrbuch*, pp. 38–44.

—— (1977). 'Hegels Begriff des Staates und die Kritik des jungen Marx', *Rivista di Filosofia*, 7–9, pp. 116–45.

—— (1982). 'Rechtsphilosophie als Phänomenologie des Bewußtseins der Freiheit', in Dieter Henrich and Rolf-Peter Horstmann (eds), *Hegels Philosophie des Rechts. Die Theorie der Rechtsformen und ihre Logik*, Stuttgart: Klett-Cotta, pp. 225–54.

—— (1983). 'Zur Genese der Hegels "Rechtsphilosophie" ', *Philosophische Rundschau*, vol. 30, pp. 161–209.

—— (1984). 'Hegel's concept of the state and Marx's early critique', in Z. A. Pelczynski (ed.), *The State and Civil Society: Studies in Hegel's Political Philosophy*, Cambridge: Cambridge University Press, pp. 93–113.

Inwood, Michael (1983). *Hegel*, London: Routledge & Kegan Paul.

Jaeger, Werner (1923). *Aristotle*, Berlin: Weidmannsche Buchhandlung.

Jellinek, Georg (1919). *Allgemeine Staatslehre*, Berlin: Verlag von Julius Springer.

Kant, Immanuel (1966). *Metaphysik der Sitten*, Hamburg: Meiner.

—— (1975). *Prolegomena to Any Future Metaphysics*, with an introduction by Lewis White Beck, Indianapolis: Bobbs-Merrill.

—— (1991). *Political Writings*, ed. Hans Reiss, Cambridge: Cambridge University Press.

—— (2000). *Critique of the Power of Judgement*, ed. Paul Guyer, tr. Paul Guyer and Eric Mathews, Cambridge: Cambridge University Press.

Kaser, Max (1956). *Eigentum und Besitz im alteren römischen Recht*, Cologne and Graz: Böhlau Verlag.

Kaufmann, Erich (1906). *Studien zur Staatslehre des monarchischen Prinzipes*, Leipzig: Oscar Brandstetter.

Kelsen, Hans (1934). *Reine Rechtslehre: Einleitung in die Rechtswissenschaftliche Problematik*, Leipzig and Vienna, Franz Deuticke.

—— (1953). *Théorie pure du droit: Introduction à la science du droit*, trans. from the German by Henri Thévenaz, Neuchâtel: Éditions de La Baconnière.

Kervégan, Jean-François (1992). *Hegel, Carl Schmitt: Le politique entre spéculation et positivité*, Paris: Presses Universitaires de France.

—— (2003). 'L'institution de la liberté', in G. W. F. Hegel, *Principes de la philosophie du droit*, Text intégral, accompagné d'annotations manuscrites et d'extraits des cours de Hegel, présenté, révisé, traduit et annoté par Jean-François Kervégan, Paris: Presses Universitaires de France, pp. 1–86.

Kissinger, Henry A. (1954). 'The conservative dilemma: reflections on the political thought of Metternich', *American Political Science Review*, vol. 48, pp. 1017–30.

Knowles, Dudley (2002). *Hegel and the Philosophy of Right*, London: Routledge.

Knox, T. M. (1970). 'Hegel and Prussianism', in Walter Kaufmann (ed.), *Hegel's Political Philosophy*, New York: Atherton.

Korioth, Stefan (1998). ' "Monarchisches Prinzip" und Gewaltenteilung – Unvereinbar? Zur Wirkungsgeschichte der Gewaltenteilunglehre Montesquieus im deutschen Fruehkonstitutionalismus', *Der Staat*, vol. 37, pp. 27–56.

Kraus, J. B. (1931). 'Wirtschaft und Gesellschaft bei Hegel', *Archiv für Rechts- und Wirtschaftsphilosophie*, vol. 25, pp. 9–31.

Krieger, Leonard (1957). *The German Idea of Freedom*, Boston: Beacon Press.

—— (1975). *An Essay on the Theory of Enlightened Despotism*, Chicago and London: University of Chicago Press.

Kroner, Richard (1921). *Von Kant bis Hegel I*, Tübingen: J. C. B. Mohr [Paul Siebeck].

Landau, Peter (1973). 'Hegels Begründung des Vertragrechts', in Manfred Riedel (ed.), *Materialien zu Hegels Rechtsphilosophie*, Frankfurt: Suhrkamp.

Larmore, Charles (1987). *Patterns of Moral Complexity*, Cambridge: Cambridge University Press.

Larsen, J. A. O. (1966). *Representative Government in Greek and Roman History*, Berkeley: University of California Press.

Lasson, Georg (1920). 'Einleitung des Herausgebers', in *Hegel: Schriften zur Politik und Rechtsphilosophie*, Leipzig: Felix Meiner.

Levin, Michael, and Howard Williams (1987). 'Inherited power and popular representation: a tension in Hegel's political theory', *Political Studies*, vol. 25, pp. 105–15.

Locke, John (1980). *Second Treatise of Government*, ed. C. B. Macpherson, Indianapolis: Hackett.

Löwith, Karl (1953). *Von Hegel zu Nietzsche: Der revolutionäre Bruch im Denken des neunzehnten Jahrhunderts*, Stuttgart: W. Kohlhammer.

Lukács, Georg (1967). *Der Junge Hegel: Über die Beziehungen von Dialektik und Ökonomie*, Berlin: Luchterland.

—— (1975). *The Young Hegel: Studies in the Relations between Dialectics and Economics*, London: Merlin.

Macpherson, C. B. (1962). *The Political Theory of Possessive Individualism*, Oxford: Oxford University Press.

—— (1977). *The Life and Times of Liberal Democracy*, Oxford: Oxford University Press.

—— (1985). 'Hobbes's political economy', in *The Rise and Fall of Economic Justice and Other Essays*, Oxford: Oxford University Press.

Mansel, Philip (1981). *Louis XVIII*, London: Blond & Briggs.

Marcuse, Herbert (1968). *Reason and Revolution: Hegel and the Rise of Social Theory*, Boston: Beacon Press.

Maritain, Jacques (1969). 'The concept of sovereignty', in *In Defense of Sovereignty*, ed. W. J. Stankiewicz, New York: Oxford University Press, pp. 41–64.

Marx, Karl (1962). 'Aus den Anmerkungen zur Dissertation', *Frühe Schriften*, vol. 1, ed. Hans-Joachim Lieber and Peter Furth, Darmstadt: Wissenschaftliche Buchgesellschaft, pp. 70–6.

—— (1970). *Critique of Hegel's Philosophy of Right*, tr. Annette Jolin and Joseph O'Malley, Cambridge: Cambridge University Press.

—— (1975a). 'Critique of Hegel's doctrine of the state', in *Early Writings*, R. Livingstone and G. Benton, New York: Vintage Books.

—— (1975b). *The Holy Family*, in *Collected Works*, vol. 4, New York: International Publishers.

—— (1979). *The Letters of Karl Marx*, selected and with explanatory notes and introduction by Saul K. Padover, Englewood Cliffs, NJ: Prentice-Hall.

—— (1980). *Das Kapital: Kritik del politischen Ökonomie*, vol. 3, *Der Gesamtprozeß der kapitalitischen Produktion*, Frankfurt, Ullstein Verlag.

Mathiez, Albert (1930). 'Le place de Montesquieu dans l'histoire des doctrines politiques du XVIII siècle', *Annales historiques de la révolution française*, pp. 97–112.

Mayr, Otto (1989). *Authority, Liberty and Automatic Machinery in Early*

Modern Europe, Baltimore and London: Johns Hopkins University Press.

Meisner, Heinrich Otto (1913). *Die Lehre vom monarchischen Prinzip im Zeitalter der Restauration und des Deutschen Bundes*, Aalen: Scientia Verlag, 1995.

Mill, John Stuart (1972). *On Liberty*, in *Utilitarianism, Liberty, Representative Government*, ed. H. B. Acton, London: J. M Dent & Sons.

Miller, David (1981). *Philosophy and Ideology in Hume's Political Thought*, Oxford: Clarendon Press.

Montesquieu (1951). *De l'esprit des lois*, in *Œuvres complètes*, vol. 2, Paris: Gallimard.

Munzer, Stephen R. (1990). *A Theory of Property*, Cambridge: Cambridge University Press.

Neocleous, Mark (1998). 'Policing the system of needs: Hegel, political economy, and the police of the market', *History of European Ideas*, vol. 24, pp. 43–58.

Neuhouser, Frederick (2000). *Foundations of Hegel's Social Theory*, Cambridge, MA: Harvard University Press.

Neumann, Franz (1957). *The Democratic and the Authoritarian State: Essays in Political and Legal Theory*, Glencoe, IL: Free Press.

—— (1986). *The Rule of Law: Political Theory and the Legal System in Modern Society*, Leamington Spa: Berg Publishers.

Ottmann, Henning (1977). *Individuum und Gemeinschaft bei Hegel*, vol. 1, *Hegel im Spiegel der Interpretationen*, Berlin and New York: de Gruyter, pp. 227–43.

—— (1979). 'Hegels Rechtsphilosophie und das Problem der Akkomodation', *Zeitschrift fur Philosophische Forschung*, 33 (April–June), pp. 227

—— (1982). 'Hegelsche Logik und Rechtsphilosophie: Unzulängliche Bemerkungen zu einem ungelösten Problem', in *Hegels Philosophie des Rechts: Die Theorie der Rechtsformen und ihre Logik* Stuttgart: Klett-Cotta, pp. 382–92.

Owens, Joseph (1981). 'The universality of the sensible in the Aristotelian noetic', in *Aristotle: The Collected Papers of Joseph Owens*, ed. J. Cattan, Albany: SUNY Press, pp. 59–73.

Patten, Alan (1999). *Hegel's Idea of Freedom*, Oxford: Oxford University Press.

—— (2003). 'Hegel', in D. Boucher and P. Kelly (eds), *Political Thinkers: From Socrates to the Present*, Oxford: Oxford University Press, pp. 383–403.

Pelczynski, Z. A. (1971). 'The Hegelian conception of the state', in Z. A. Pelczynski (ed.), *Hegel's Political Philosophy: Problems and Perspectives*, Cambridge: Cambridge University Press, pp. 1–29.

—— (1984). 'The significance of Hegel's separation of the state and civil society', in Z. A. Pelczynski (ed.), *The State and Civil Society: Studies in Hegel's Political Philosophy*, Cambridge: Cambridge University Press, pp. 1–13.

Petry, M. J. (1984). 'Propaganda and analysis: the background to Hegel's article on the English Reform Bill', in Z. A. Pelczynski (ed.), *The State and Civil Society: Studies in Hegel's Political Philosophy*, Cambridge: Cambridge University Press, pp. 137–58.

Pettit, Philip (1993). *The Common Mind: An Essay on Psychology, Society and Politics*, New York and Oxford: Oxford University Press.

—— (1997). *Republicanism: A Theory of Freedom and Government*, Oxford: Clarendon Press.

Pinkard, Terry (1996). *Hegel's Phenomenology: The Sociality of Reason*, Cambridge: Cambridge University Press.

—— (2000). *Hegel: A Biography*, Cambridge: Cambridge University Press.

Pinson, Koppel (1966). *Modern Germany: Its History and Civilization*, New York: Macmillan.

Piontkowski, Andrej A. (1960). *Hegels Lehre über Staat und Recht und seine Strafrechtstheorie*, Berlin: Veb Deutscher Zentralverlag.

Plamenatz, John (1971). 'History as the realization of freedom', in Z. A. Pelczynski (ed.), *Hegel's Political Philosophy: Problems and Perspectives*, Cambridge: Cambridge University Press, pp. 30–5.

Plant, Raymond (1973). *Hegel*, London: George Allen & Unwin.

Planty-Bonjour, Guy (1986). 'Du régime reprèsentatif selon Sieyès à la monarchie constitutionelle de Hegel', in Hans-Christian Lucas and Otto Pöggeler (eds), *Hegels Rechtsphilosophie im Zusammengang der europäische Verfassungsgeschichte*, Stuttgart-Bad Canstatt: Frommann-Holzboog, pp. 13–35.

Plato (1957). *Statesman*, tr. J. B. Skemp, Indianapolis: Bobbs-Merrill.

Prélot, Marcel (1984). *Institutions politique et droit constitutionnel*, ed. Jean Boulois, Paris: Dalloz.

Radin, Margaret Jane (1993). *Reinterpreting Property*, Chicago: University of Chicago Press.

Randall, John H. (1960). *Aristotle*, New York: Columbia University Press.

Reck, Andrew (1960). 'Substance, Subject and Dialectic', *Studies in Hegel: Tulane Studies in Philosophy*, vol. 9, pp. 109–33.

Reyburn, Hugh A. (1967). *The Ethical Theory of Hegel*, Oxford: Clarendon Press.

Riedel, Manfred (1970). *Studien zu Hegels Rechtsphilosophie*, Frankfurt: Suhrkamp.

—— (1971). 'Nature and freedom in Hegel's *Philosophy of Right*', in Z. A. Pelczynski (ed.), *Hegel's Political Philosophy: Problems and Perspectives*, Cambridge: Cambridge University Press, pp. 136–50.

Ritter, Joachim (1977). 'Hegel und die Französische Revolution', in *Metaphysik und Politik*, Frankfurt: Suhrkamp.

—— (2004). 'Person and property', in Robert Pippin and Ottfried Höffe (eds), *Hegel on Ethics and Politics*, trans. Nicholas Walker, Cambridge: Cambridge University Press, pp. 101–23.

Rittstieg, Helmut (1975). *Eigentum als Verfassungsproblem: Zu Geschichte und Gegenwart des bürgerlichen Verfassungsstaates*, Darmstadt: Wissen-schaftliche Buchgesellschaft.

Rosanvallon, Pierre (1994). *La monarchie impossible: Les Chartes de 1814 et de 1830*, Paris: Fayard.

Rosenkranz, Karl (1844). *Georg Wilhelm Friedrich Hegels Leben*, Darmstadt: Wissenschaftliche Buchgesellschaft, 1963.

Rosenzweig, Franz (1920). *Hegel und der Staat*, vol. 2, *Weltepochen (1806–1831)*, Munich and Berlin: Oldenburg Verlag.

Rotenstreich, Natham (1965). *Basic Problems of Marx's Philosophy*, Indiana-polis: Bobbs-Merrill.

Rotzovtzeff, Mikhail I. (1926). *The Social and Economic History of the Roman Empire*, Oxford: Oxford University Press.

Rousseau, Jean-Jacques (1973). *The Social Contract and Discourses*, translation and introduction by G. D. H. Cole, London: Dent.

Ryan, Alan (1984). 'Hegel on work, ownership and citizenship', in Z. A. Pelczynski (ed.), *The State and Civil Society: Studies in Hegel's Political Philosophy*, Cambridge: Cambridge University Press, pp. 178–96.

—— (1995). *John Dewey and the High Tide of American Liberalism*, New York and London: Norton.

Saage, Richard (1973). *Eigentum, Staat und Gesellschaft bei Immanuel Kant*, Stuttgart: W. Kohlhammer.

Schelling, Friedrich Wilhelm Joseph (1965). *Werke*, ed. M. Schroeter, Munich: C. H. Beck.

Schmitt, Carl (1921). *Die Diktatur: Von den Anfängen des modernen Souveränitätsgedankens bis zum proletarischen Klassenkampf*, Munich and Leipzig: Duncker & Humblot, 1928.

—— (1922). *Politische Theologie: Vier Kapitel zur Lehre von der Souveranitat*, Munich and Leipzig: Duncker & Humblot, 1934.

—— (1923). *Die geistesgeschichtliche Lage des heutigen Parlamentarismus*, Berlin: Duncker & Humblot, 1961.

—— (1926). 'Absolutismus', in *Staat, Grossraum, Nomos: Arbeiten aus den Jahren 1916–1969*, ed. with an introduction by Günter Maschke, Berlin: Duncker & Humblot, 1995.

—— (1928). *Verfassungslehre*, Berlin: Duncker & Humblot, 1965.

—— (1929). 'Wesen und Werden des faschistischen Staates', *Positionen und Begriffe im Kampf mit Weimar-Genf-Versailles 1923–1939*, Berlin: Duncker & Humblot, 1988.

—— (1931). *Der Hüter der Verfassung*, Berlin: Duncker & Humblot.

—— (1963). *Der Begriff der Politischen*, Berlin: Duncker & Humblot.

—— (2003). *The* Nomos *of the Earth in the International Law of the* Ius publicum Europaeum', trans. and annoted by G. L. Ulmen, New York: Telos Press.

Scruton, Roger (1986). 'Hegel as a conservative thinker', *Salisbury Review* (July), pp. 43–9.

Sheehan, James (1989). *German History 1770–1866*, Oxford: Clarendon Press.

Siep, Ludwig (1982). 'Intersubjektivitat, Recht und Staat in Hegels *Grundlinien del Philosophie des Rechts*', in Dieter Henrich and Rolf-Peter Horstmann (eds), *Hegels Philosophie des Rechts: Die Theorie der Rechtsformen und ihre Logik*, Stuttgart: Klett-Cotta, pp. 255–76.

—— (1986). 'Hegels Theorie der Gewaltenteilung', in Hans-Christian Lucas and Otto Pöggeler (eds), *Hegels Rechtsphilosophie im Zusammengang der europäische Verfassungsgeschichte*, Stuttgart-Bad Canstatt: Frommann-Holzboog, pp. 387–420.

—— (2004). 'Constitution, fundamental rights, and social welfare in Hegel's *Philosophy of Right*', in Robert Pippin and Ottfried Höffe (eds), *Hegel on Ethics and Politics*, tr. Nicholas Walker, Cambridge: Cambridge University Press, pp. 268–90.

Smith, Steven (1986). 'Hegel's critique of liberalism', *American Political Science Review*, vol. 80, pp. 121–39.

—— (1995). 'At the crossroads: Hegel and the ethics of *bürgerliche Gesellschaft*', *Laval théologique et philosophique*, vol. 51, no. 2, pp. 345–62.

Spinoza, Benedict de (1908). *Political Treatise*, in *The Chief Works of Benedict de Spinoza*, trans. R. H. M. Elwes, London: George Bell & Sons.

Steinberger, Peter J. (1988). *Logic and Politics: Hegel's Philosophy of Right*, New Haven and London: Yale University Press.

Stillman, Peter (1980). 'Person, property and society', in Donald P. Verene (ed.), *Hegel's Social and Political Thought: The Philosophy of Objective Spirit*, Atlantic Highlands, NJ: Humanities Press.

—— (1991). 'Property, contract and ethical life in Hegel's *Philosophy of Right*', in D. Cornell, M. Rosenfeld and D. G. Carlson (eds), *Hegel and Legal Theory*, New York: Routledge.

Stolleis, Michael (2001). *Public Law in Germany: 1800–1914*, New York: Berghahn Books.

Taylor, Charles (1975). *Hegel*, Cambridge: Cambridge University Press.

Thiele, Peter (1967). *Karl August von Hardenberg, 1750–1822: Eine Biographie*, Cologne and Berlin, Grote.

Thiele, Ulrich (2002). 'Gewaltenteilung bei Sieyes und Hegel: die *Thermidor-reden* von 1795 im Vergleich mit den *Grundlinien der Philosophie des Rechts*', *Hegel-Studien*, vol. 37, pp. 139–67.

Tocqueville, Alexis de (1955). *The Old Regime and the French Revolution*, Garden City, NJ: Doubleday.

—— (1974). *Democracy in America*, vol. 2, New York: Schocken Books.

Treitschke, Heinrich von (1917). *History of Germany in the Nineteenth Century*, vol. 3, trans. Eden and Cedar Paul, New York: McBride, Nast & Co.

Tuck, Richard (1979). *Natural Rights Theories: Their Origin and Development*, Cambridge: Cambridge University Press.

Tunick, Mark (1991). 'Hegel's justification of hereditary monarchy', *History of Political Thought*, vol. 12, pp. 481–96.

—— (1992). *Hegel's Political Philosophy: Interpreting the Practice of Legal Punishment*, Princeton: Princeton University Press.

Underkuffler, Laura (2003). *The Idea of Property: Its Meaning and Power*, Oxford: Oxford University Press.

Villey, Michel (1962). 'Kant dans l'Histoire du Droit', in *La Philosophie Politique de Kant* (*Annales de Philosophie Politique*), Paris: Presses Universitaires de France.

Waldron, Jeremy (1988). *The Right to Private Property*, Oxford: Clarendon Press.

Walzer, Michael (1992). 'The civil society argument', in Chantal Mouffe (ed.), *Dimensions of Radical Democracy: Pluralism, Citizenship, Community*, London and New York: Verso.

Weil, Eric (1950). *Hegel et l'état*, Paris: Vrin.

Westphal, Kenneth (1993). 'The basis and context of Hegel's *Philosophy of Right*', in Frederick C. Beiser (ed.), *The Cambridge Companion to Hegel*, Cambridge: Cambridge University Press, pp. 234–69.

Wilks, Yvor (1969). 'A note on sovereignty', in *In Defense of Sovereignty*, ed. W. J. Stankiewicz, New York: Oxford University Press, pp. 197–205.

Williams, Howard (2003). *Kant's Critique of Hobbes: Sovereignty and Cosmopolitanism*, Cardiff: University of Wales Press.

Williams, Robert R. (1997). *Hegel's Ethics of Recognition*, Berkeley: University of California Press.

Wood, Allen (1990). *Hegel's Ethical Thought*, Cambridge: Cambridge University Press.

Xifaras, Mikhaïl (2004). 'L'individualisme possessif, spéculatif (et néanmoins romain) de Hegel: Quelques remarques sur la théorie hégélienne de la propriété', in Jean-François Kervégan and Gilles Marmasse (eds), *Hegel penseur du droit*, Paris: CNRS Éditions.

Yack, Bernard (1980). 'The rationality of Hegel's concept of monarchy', *American Political Science Review*, vol. 74, pp. 709–20.

Index

Index of *PhR* paragraphs